THE ULTIMATE COLLEGE ACCEPTANCE SYSTEM

THE ULTIMATE COLLEGE ACCEPTANCE SYSTEM

EVERYTHING YOU NEED TO KNOW TO GET INTO THE RIGHT COLLEGE FOR YOU

DANNY RUDERMAN

ST. MARTIN'S GRIFFIN ❧ NEW YORK

www.stmartins.com

Book design by Gretchen Achilles

Library of Congress Cataloging-in-Publication Data

Ruderman, Danny.
   The ultimate college acceptance system : everything you need to know to get into the right college for you / Danny Ruderman.
      p.   cm.
   ISBN-13: 978-0-312-35517-3
   ISBN-10: 0-312-35517-3
   1. College choice—United States.   2. College applications—United States.
3. Counseling in higher education—United States.   I. Title.
   LB2350.5.R836 2006
   378.1'61—dc22   2005034939

First Edition: July 2006

10 9 8 7 6 5 4 3 2 1

To my mom, for her unconditional love and support,

and to my students, who have taught me more than I have taught them

CONTENTS

TIMING IS EVERYTHING

Many students spread the application process over several months.

If you want to complete the program presented in *The Ultimate College Acceptance System* in a thirty-day stretch, here's the schedule I recommend. The times given are estimations based on how long the program has taken other students. You may spend less time or more time depending on your situation.

	CHAPTER	TIME NEEDED
Day 1: Monday	Introduction	15 minutes
Day 2: Tuesday	1	30 minutes
Day 3–5: Wednesday, Thursday, Saturday, or Sunday	2	1–3 hours
Day 6: Monday	3	30 minutes
Day 7–8: Tuesday and Wednesday	4	1–3 hours
Day 9: Thursday	5	30 minutes
Day 10: Friday or Saturday	6	30 minutes
Day 11: Saturday or Sunday	7	1–3 hours
Day 12–13: Monday and Tuesday	8	1–3 hours
Day 14: Wednesday	9	1–2 hours
Day 15–16: Thursday and Saturday or Sunday	10	1–6 hours
Day 17–18: Monday and Tuesday	11	1–4 hours
Day 19–20: Wednesday and Thursday	12	1–4 hours
Day 21–22: Saturday and Sunday	13	2–4 hours
Day 23: Monday	14	1–2 hours
Day 24: Tuesday	15	30 minutes
Day 25–26: Wednesday, Thursday, Saturday, or Sunday	16	2–5 hours
Day 27–28: Monday and Tuesday	17	30 minutes
Day 29: Wednesday	18	30 minutes
Day 30: Thursday	19	*Done!*

PART ONE
FIND THE BEST SCHOOL FOR YOU

INTRODUCTION

SO JUST WHO AM I AND WHY SHOULD YOU LISTEN TO ME?

Name: Danny Ruderman

Age: 32

High school: Fontana High School, Fontana, CA (aka "*Funtucky*")

College: Stanford U.

Height: 6'2"

Weight: 180

Number of jobs since graduating from college: 27

Current job: College admissions guru

Time spent at current job: 8 years

Cars like it: 0

Realizing you don't really care to know this stuff about me: Priceless

Summary: Okay, although it is true about the twenty-seven jobs (ranger in Yosemite, bank teller, waiter, chauffeur, and more), I have spent much of my time as a schoolteacher in both public and private schools in California. As a teacher I did things a bit differently, including teaching classes as different characters—hey, I thought most of my teachers were totally boring, and I was determined not to be one of them. After teaching, I began tutoring kids in how to do better in school and then in helping them get into college. The bottom line is, I believe college is one of the best experiences I ever had. I also believe that you *deserve* to go to a place that makes you feel this way, too. So come with me, follow me! Let's begin getting you de-stressed and confident that *you will get into college* if you really want to.

OVERALL SUMMARY AND TIMELINE

Okay, here's the deal: basically you read, write in the spaces, and get into college. Nice. Hopefully, you've listened to my sexy voice on the Resource CD and have heard an overview of what *The Ultimate College Acceptance System* is all about. In case you haven't, here's how it works.

There are nineteen chapters covering every aspect of getting into college. Some sections will take 10 to 30 minutes to read, while other sections will take 30 to 60 minutes because they require you to complete specific exercises by writing directly in the book or on separate sheets of paper—your choice. Occasionally, you will spend time away from these pages, like when you're researching schools or editing your essays.

The first part of the program (Chapters 1–6) is heavier on information and research, while the second part (Chapters 7–19) is heavier on the actual work of completing applications, essays, a resume, and so on. Because each part of the book builds on the last, I recommend you go through the *entire* book to ensure you have the best chance of getting into the right schools for you (especially if you're a junior).

What if **you already have a list of schools or are waiting for the applications to be released?** In this case, you can skip around to the sections that apply to you. However, I suggest that you take a look at each section just to see if you can learn something you didn't know before. You also need to get organized from the start, so I have discussed how to do this below.

Yeah, I hear you. You have homework and piano and football and saving the whales. I thought about that, too. So I designed this book to fit your schedule whether you are a sophomore, a junior, or—if you are like I was when I started thinking about college—a senior. As a result, if you need to, you can finish the entire college application process in thirty days. If you follow the thirty-day schedule on page xi, you'll see that much of the most time-consuming work is spaced out over a couple of days and often over weekends.

Many of you, however, will do this program over a period of six weeks to six months, depending on when you start. While many students will invest from thirty to sixty hours, you might complete it in more or less time, and that's cool, too. Just remember, I've got your back. Just about everything you need to achieve success is here in this book. Even so, I encourage you to use other resources, especially your school counselor.

Just remember, you can take control of your destiny by believing me when I tell you this:

By staying organized and having a plan of attack, you can get accepted to one or more great colleges or universities.

So ya ready? No? Too bad, because we're startin' anyway. Let's kick the horns!

GETTING ORGANIZED

You need to do two things before you can start getting organized:

1. Remember I have included samples and blank forms on a Resource CD for you, plus the MOAC (Master of All Checklists) in Chapter 7 to keep you organized.

2. Go to an office supply store and buy an organizational system. You can choose any system you like, but here's what I find works best: Get a crate or box that holds hanging files. Inside the hanging files are file folders. (The three items are usually sold separately, although some boxes come with kits that include everything.) Make sure you purchase enough file folders (at least twenty-five). Go home, put the hanging files in the box, and using those annoying little plastic tabs, make a hanging file for each school you are applying to. Then put three file folders in each of the hanging files.

- The first file folder will hold general information and research, like your visit notes, the college's viewbook, and any Internet research.

- The second file folder will hold your application materials, including your resume.

- The third file folder will hold your essay drafts (although you will eventually have to include the final draft of your essay with each school's application).

You will also need an extra hanging file to hold your financial aid stuff, including scholarship info, the PROFILE form, and the FAFSA form. Because you need to fill out the financial aid forms only once, and they get sent to schools by a processing agency, do not include them with your individual school files as they could get mixed up.

Trust me. Staying organized is half the battle of making sure you stay sane while applying to college. If you are the type who has so much junk in your room that you can't see the floor, these instructions are even more important. And I don't care if you think you can always find everything. Listen to me on this one.

CHAPTER ONE
A FIELD OF DREAMS

WHAT'S YOUR DREAM? A UNIQUE PROPOSITION

There was one class in my college that was a legend among the students. In fact, they waited in line overnight to get in. The first day, the professor announced that there would be a different kind of final at the end of the term. Instead of writing an essay or taking a test, his students were to pick something they always wanted to do and then do it. Or at least make progress on it. Each student had to make a presentation the last week of class. One guy went skydiving and videotaped it. Someone else learned to play the saxophone and played it for the class. Another student started taking flying lessons. You get the idea.

Wouldn't you love to take a class where somebody "lets" you live out one of your dreams? Well, why wait? You're not in college yet, but who cares? Write down one thing—come on, just one thing—that you have always wanted to do. It can be anything—ride a horse, meet the president, skydive, start your own company, learn to play the guitar, ride an elephant, anything!

_____

_____

_____

What do you think you would have to do to live out the dream you just wrote down? (Yeah, I know, right now many of you are thinking, "Hey, I thought this was about getting into college, not some motivational seminar.") Look, I promise you, I've got my reasons for asking you this; I would not just make you do busy work—I hated that garbage in high school. So come on, just think about it. What *actions* would you have to take to accomplish your dream? Write them down in the following lines.

_____

_____

_____

I once knew a guy who made a list of the top one hundred things he wanted to do in his lifetime. At age twenty-eight, he had finished thirty-seven of them. He scuba dived the Great Barrier Reef, earned a million dollars with his own company, bought a Ferrari, studied in a Zen monastery, climbed Mount McKinley in Alaska, and did a lot more.

Okay, you've written down one thing you want to do and some actions you would have to take to do it. Next you will write down one thing, one step, that you could do today. If you wrote, "I want to climb Mount Everest," what could you do to take a small step toward that dream? Make a phone call? Find some information on the Internet? Buy a magazine or a book? If you really want what you wrote down, it should excite you to get started.

I had a student in Los Angeles who wrote that she had always wanted to ride an elephant. She then noted that she'd have to travel to someplace like India to do it. Here's how our conversation went:

ME: Is there a way you could ride an elephant this weekend?
HER: Uh, I doubt it.
ME: Well, think about it. Is there a place around here where you could ride an elephant?
HER: Wait, there is that wild animal park in San Diego!
ME: Could you find out today if you could ride an elephant there?
HER: Yes!
ME: Would it be possible to drive down to San Diego and do it?
HER: Yes, I guess it would!

Now it turns out that the student couldn't ride an elephant in San Diego that weekend, but the zoo told her of a place in Los Angeles where she could, and guess what? She went and rode an elephant. Check one off her list of a hundred. . . .

So write down one step you could take today.

_____

_____

_____

_____

_____

Now, for the love of all things holy, take this step! Life is too short to not go after what you want.

If you took just one action everyday toward something you really wanted, guess what? Those consistent, tiny little actions would add up to produce miracles. (No joke. It works. Period.)

So, what do you think you might want to do with your life? (I realize many of you probably have no idea.) Just make a list of possibilities. Forget what you think you're *supposed* to be when you grow up, and put down what you might enjoy.

_____

_____

_____

_____

Here are six steps guaranteed to get you anything you want in life. Summarized from *Think and Grow Rich* by Napoleon Hill.

1. Listen to your heart, do what your gut tells you. Find something you are passionate about. You must have a **definite purpose**—you can't be vague. You must have a **burning desire** to get it.

2. Make an **absolute decision** to obtain your desire, no matter what it takes, as long as you do not harm anyone else in getting it.

3. Write it out as a **definite plan**. It must be expressed as **continuous actions**. In other words, you must write out exactly what you will do to achieve your desire.

4. Visualize the thing you want as if you already have it. Do this everyday until you **feel and believe** without a doubt that you will get it.

5. Close your mind to any negative and discouraging influences, including the negative comments of relatives and friends.

6. Make a **friendly pact** with one or more people to encourage you to follow through with your plan or purpose.

AND THIS APPLIES TO COLLEGE *HOW*?

Yes, the last few pages *do* have something to do with your applying to college. I'll tell you how. First, even though this book is designed around college admissions, if I want you to get into the school of your choice, I have to do the following:

- *Give you some perspective.* You might be working off ideas that you heard from family, friends, and school officials. I'm going to challenge some of these ideas so that you can find the place that best fits you. I remember what it's like to be in your shoes, and I am speaking from experience.

- *Motivate you to work on the application process*, a process during which most students procrastinate their butts off because of fear or unrealistic perceptions.

- *Get you to realize that if you want something enough, you can make it happen.* Even if the thing you want doesn't come out exactly as planned, if you put in the time and have the desire and the expectation, you will get a result even better than the one you originally hoped for. I guarantee this works for school, college admissions, and life after school.

Second, although you haven't been accepted yet, I need to introduce something important right now. You see, if I wait to only tell you this at the end, I'm sure you'll skip over it because you'll be done with your applications. I'm willing to bet that your college years will be some of the most enjoyable and rewarding years that you have had in your life thus far. One reason is that you will have so much time to do things in college. Therefore, please take advantage of it—be active, try new things, go for it. The "real world" does not quite offer the same opportunities, so:

- Go bungee jumping with your dorm buddies.

- Start your own company.

- Go up to new people and introduce yourself just for the hell of it.

- Go see plays with your dorm buddies.

- Take part in community service (and not just to fulfill a requirement).

- Play Frisbee golf at midnight.

- Volunteer in a field that might interest you.

You can take actions to fulfill your dreams—this is one of the best things about college that no one ever tells you.

I DREAM OF COLLEGE

If you could design your dream college, what would it look like? Don't think too much—just write.

_____

_____

_____

_____

_____

_____

_____

_____

_____

Now that you have some ideas about what your ideal college would look like, let's take a look at what's really out there.

CHAPTER TWO
CREATING YOUR LIST OF SCHOOLS

REALITY BITES—OR DOES IT?

Most students get information about college admissions from TV, magazines, books, friends, teachers, relatives, and small invisible aliens (wait, that's just me). Some of this stuff is helpful, but a lot of it is either wrong or specifically designed to cause fear and panic. For example, students often hear the following:

- Although the number of applicants is going up, the number of spaces each year at colleges and universities stays the same. This makes the odds tough.

- The number of applicants to selective colleges is growing and will continue to grow at a high rate for the next several years. This makes it difficult for a senior to get a space. (Example: Approximately 19,000 students applied for 2,350 "yes" spots at Stanford in 2004.)

- If all the students who had been admitted to a selective school suddenly couldn't attend, the next group of students, who had originally been rejected, would have virtually identical GPAs and test scores. This means that a lot of valedictorians are getting rejected.

What does this mean for you? It means run! Hide! Get ready to say, "You want fries with that?" Because you ain't gettin' in anywhere!
Or does it?

Now, get ready for the good news! You have to understand that colleges are essentially businesses. You know those beautiful books you get with the applications inside? They are elaborate marketing tools to try to get you to apply. (Note: I said, "apply," not "go there.")
What am I talking about? I'm saying that even though they rarely admit it, colleges and universities love things like the *U.S. News and World Report* rankings. In fact, many get upset if they are not ranked well. Although there are exceptions, schools will try to get more and more students to apply, even though this means they will have to reject more students. Why? Because a school's rejection rate makes it look more exclusive. Why can a school go in a couple of years from being ranked in the twenties on *U.S. News* list to being ranked in the top five? This change is not entirely due to its rejection rate, but do you think this school sud-

denly got that much better? That's not the important question, however. The real issue is, **Who cares what a school is ranked? What does its ranking matter if a school doesn't offer what you want?**

According to a survey taken among high school seniors, academic reputation is the number one reason why students choose a school. That's why I chose Stanford—because of its name. And while it's true that people have preconceived notions about the Harvard and Yale graduates of the world, the reality is not what you might think. Check out the following "bad-boy" stats concerning academic reputation and what it really does for you.

CHECK OUT THESE BAD-BOY STATS

- When the earnings of graduates of elite colleges were compared with those of graduates who had been accepted to elite schools but attended lesser-known schools, there was virtually no difference. One reason is this: let's say I was interviewing you for a job. You have a degree from Harvard, but are a complete dweeb. Sure, you are probably smart, but can you manage people? Are you driven? Are you trustworthy? If the answers are no for you, but are yes for a student from a lesser-known school, guess who'll get the job? (*U.S. News and World Report*)

- The best known schools don't always have the highest acceptance rates to graduate school, nor do they produce the highest number of PhDs. And while the national average acceptance rate to medical schools is around 50 percent, schools like Earlham College in Richmond, Indiana, and Knox College in Galesburg, Illinois, get almost 90 percent of those who apply to medical school. (*U.S. News and World Report*)

- In a survey of college freshman, 71.6 percent of students were attending their first choice. A total of 19.9 percent were going to their second choice. That means 90 percent of students got into their first or second choices! (*Chronicle of Higher Education*)

There are more than 2,200 colleges and universities in the United States, of which *only about 50* are exceptionally selective, meaning they accept fewer than 30 percent of those who apply. This means you can find a school that fits you, will give you a great education, and will accept you!

WHAT DO YOU REALLY WANT?

Besides the name of a school, consider the following factors when comparing smaller and larger schools.

SMALLER SCHOOLS

- Tend to offer more personalized attention.

- Often do very well at getting students into grad school, despite what people believe about the reputation of larger universities.

- Often provide more practical experience, providing students with more opportunities to do research, be the head of an organization, etc.

- Can help create a stronger bond among the students.

- Usually guarantee campus housing.

- Can have fewer rules against taking classes outside a major.

But . . .

- Can still be claustrophobic for some.

- Have stricter rules concerning class attendance.

LARGER SCHOOLS

- Offer a greater variety of classes.

- Often have more majors.

- Generally have more students.

- Offer better opportunities for a student who is talented in a certain area (sports, newspaper, etc.).

- Can have nationally known sports teams.

- Tend to have more school spirit.

- Allow students the chance to almost always meet new people—or to hide from others.

- Are often part of a city.

But . . .

- Require more individual initiative.

- Offer many classes, especially in the first two years, that are big and lecture-based.

YOUR INTEREST SHEET

Please rank the qualities that are most important to you in selecting a college. Give a 1 to the quality that is most important, a 2 to the quality that is the next most important, and so on, until you get to 13, which will be the least important quality. Use the column on the right to record any preferences you may have about a particular category.

EXAMPLE

QUALITY	RANKING	PREFERENCES
Setting	4	Must be urban

QUALITY	RANKING	PREFERENCES
Geographical location (example: West, Midwest, East Coast, South)	8	East / South
Setting (example: urban, suburban, rural)	4	urban / suburban
Size	5	medium
Climate (example: warm, outdoorsy, has four seasons)	6	cool, outdoorsy
Reputation or prestige of school	2	
Has a specific type of program (example: film, music, engineering)	1	Engineering/medical
Has an active sports program	13	
Has a sport you want to participate in	12	Golf
Has an active fraternity/sorority life	9	Delta
Has small class sizes	3	
Has diversity in terms of type of students	7	Love people [...]
Is known for having students who are serious about ideas	10	
Political climate (example: conservative, liberal, freethinking, nonconformist)	11	Liberal

HOW SELECTIVE ARE YOUR SCHOOLS?

Now you are going to learn about schools and try to find ones that fit your profile. How do you determine how selective a school is? In Table 2-1, I have provided a list of 175 schools, along with their acceptance rates and the range of SAT scores of the middle 50 percent of accepted students. I've also ranked each school as follows:

4 = exceptionally selective

3 = very selective

2 = selective

1 = less selective

Now, it's important to realize that Table 2-1 is only a starting point. A school's acceptance rates and SATs do not give the full picture as to whether you will be able to get in. In other words, many students will look at these numbers and think, "Well, I can't get in there," or "This school is a lock!" It's just not that cut-and-dry. These numbers and rankings are included so when you do find schools that interest you, you can use the data to help you put the schools into the general categories of reaches, likelies, and safeties (see page 49). However, when we discuss "CSI" (page 21), you will learn that you must also consider other factors when trying to determine your chances: for example, which states have the lowest representation at a given school, what kind of diversity a school looks for, and how your individual profile matches up with what a school wants all may give you an advantage when applying. For now, use the selectivity rankings in Table 2-1 to get an idea of what certain schools are looking for. There are, however, a few other things you need to know before you begin:

1. Table 2-1 is not a complete list. Don't feel that you have to find your schools from this table alone. Instead, think of it as a reference guide you can use to determine the selectivity of schools that may not be listed.

2. Very important! Remember, just because a school is more selective does not mean that it is better. Apply to schools that match your interests, not just to schools you have heard of.

The SAT scores listed in Table 2-1 (accurate as of 2005) reflect the students accepted to each school who are in the 25 to 75 percentile range. There is no minimum score (with the exception of some state schools). If your scores fall within a school's range, you generally match the student population they accept. However, this does not mean that if your scores aren't within the range, you shouldn't apply. Schools tend to inflate their stats, so the numbers here could be higher than the number they actually accept. SATs are only one part of the admissions process, and they are not the most important one. The scores are presented here simply to offer a basis of comparison between schools.

TABLE 2-1 SELECTIVITY RANKINGS OF SCHOOLS

PRIVATE SCHOOLS	SAT*	ACCEPTANCE RATE	RANKING
Adelphi University	V 480–580 / M 480–590	70%	1
Agnes Scott College	V 550–690 / M 530–630	66%	2
American University	V 570–670 / M 560–650	59%	1
Amherst College	V 660–770 / M 650–770	18%	4
Antioch College	optional	75%	1
Auburn University	V 510–600 / M 520–620	84%	1
Babson College	V 560–640 / M 610–680	37%	3
Bard College	optional	35%	3
Barnard College	V 650–730 / M 630–700	31%	3
Bates College	V 630–700 / M 640–710	31%	3
Baylor University	V 530–630 / M 540–645	82%	1
Bennington College	V 600–710 / M 540–640	68%	2
Boston College	V 600–690/ M 630–710	31%	3
Boston University	V 600–690 / M 620–690	52%	2
Bowdoin College	V 640–730 / M 650–710	24%	4
Brandeis University	V 620–720 / M 630–720	44%	3
Brown University	V 640–750 / M 650–750	16%	4
Bryn Mawr College	V 620–720 / M 580–680	51%	3
Bucknell University	V 600–670 / M 630–700	38%	3
California Institute of Technology	V 700–780 / M 760–800	17%	4
California Institute of the Arts	N/A	36%	3
Carleton College	V 650–750 / M 650–730	35%	3
Carnegie Mellon University	V 600–710 / M 680–770	38%	3
University of Chicago	V 650–760 / M 650–750	40%	3
Claremont McKenna College	V 650–740 / M 660–740	31%	3
Colby College	V 630–710 / M 640–710	34%	3
Colgate University	V 620–710 / M 650–720	31%	3
Colorado College	V 580–690 / M 580–670	56%	2
Columbia University	V 650–760 / M 660–750	11%	4
Connecticut College	V 603–695 / M 602–695	34%	3
Cornell University	V 620–720 / M 660–750	31%	3
Dartmouth College	V 650–750 / M 680–770	21%	4
Davidson College	V 630–720 / M 640–720	32%	3
Drew University	V 560–670 / M 540–640	72%	1

PRIVATE SCHOOLS	SAT*	ACCEPTANCE RATE	RANKING
Drexel University	V 520–620 / M 550–660	70%	1
Duke University	V 660–750 / M 670–770	25%	4
Earlham College	V 560–680 / M 520–650	77%	1
Eastman School of Music	V 500–650 / M 510–650	29%	4
Emory University	V 640–720 / M 660–740	42%	3
Franklin and Marshall College	V 570–670 / M 580–680	58%	2
Fordham University	V 530–630 / M 530–630	57%	2
George Mason University	V 490–600 / M 510–610	66%	2
George Washington University	V 590–690 / M 590–680	39%	3
Georgetown University	V 640–730 / M 650–730	23%	4
Gettysburg College	V 600–670 / M 600–670	46%	3
Goucher College	V 570–670 / M 540–640	65%	2
Grinnell College	V 610–730 / M 630–720	63%	2
Hamilton College	V 610–700 / M 630–700	33%	3
Hampshire College	V 600–700 / M 540–660	51%	2
Harvard University	V 700–790/ M 700–790	10%	4
Harvey Mudd College	V 650–750/ M 720–800	40%	3
Haverford College	V 640–730/ M 650–720	30%	3
Hoftstra University	V 510–600 / M 520–620	68%	2
College of the Holy Cross	V 580–680/ M 630–670	42%	3
Howard University	V 420–680 / M 420–680	56%	2
James Madison University	V 540–620 / M 540–630	62%	2
Johns Hopkins University	V 630–720/ M 660–750	30%	3
Kenyon College	V 620–720/ M 600–690	46%	3
Lafayette College	V 570–660/ M 610–700	36%	3
Lawrence University	V 590–690/ M 580–690	54%	2
Lehigh University	V 590–670/ M 630–710	40%	3
Lewis and Clark College	V 600–710/ M 580–670	68%	2
Macalester College	V 640–730 / M 620–700	44%	3
Marshall University	ACT 19–24	88%	1
Massachusetts Institute of Technology	V 680–760/ M 740–800	16%	4
Middlebury College	V 690–750/ M 680–740	23%	4
Mills College	V 520–660 / M 490–600	73%	1
Morehouse College	V 470–590 / M 470–590	72%	1
Mount Holyoke College	V 600–700 / M 580–670	51%	2
Mulhenberg College	V 550–650 / M 560–660	42%	3

PRIVATE SCHOOLS	SAT*	ACCEPTANCE RATE	RANKING
New York University	V 600–700/ M 610–710	32%	3
North Carolina School of the Arts	V 520–640 / M 520–620	40%	3
Northeastern University	V 510–610 / M 530–630	60%	2
Northwestern University	V 650–730/ M 660–745	33%	3
University of Notre Dame	V 620–720/ M 650–740	34%	3
Oberlin College	V 630–730/ M 610–710	36%	3
Occidental College	V 580–690/ M 590–680	44%	3
Parsons School of Design	V 450–600 / M 490–620	44%	3
University of Pennsylvania	V 650–750 / M 680–760	20%	4
Pepperdine University	V 540–640 / M 550–660	36%	3
Pitzer College	V 570–660 / M 570–670	50%	3
University of Puget Sound	V 575–685 / 570–660	71%	2
Pomona College	V 700–760/ M 690–760	21%	4
Prescott College	V 500–660 / 450–610	89%	S
Princeton University	V 680–770/ M 700–780	11%	4
Quinnipiac University	V 510–580 / M 520–610	61%	2
Reed College	V 650–750/ M 620–710	46%	3
Rennselaer Polytechnic Institute	V 580–680/ M 640–720	70%	2
Rhode Island School of Design	V 540–650 / M 550–660	35%	3
Rice University	V 660–760/ M 670–770	24%	4
University of Rochester	V 590–690/ M 620–710	49%	2
Rochester Institute of Technology	V 540–640 / M 570–670	69%	2
Rutgers University	V 530–630 / M 560–670	55%	2
Santa Clara University	V 550–650 / M 550–660	70%	2
Sarah Lawrence College	V 610–710/ M 530–650	40%	3
Scripps College	V 620–720/ M 610–690	49%	3
Skidmore College	V 580–670 / M 590–670	46%	3
Smith College	V 590–700 / M 580–670	52%	3
University of Southern California	V 610–700/ M 640–720	30%	3
Stanford University	V 660–770/ M 680–790	13%	4
Swarthmore College	V 670–770/ M 670–760	24%	4
Syracuse University	V 570–650/ M 580–670	62%	2
Temple University	V 490–590 / M 490–590	60%	2
Texas A&M University	V 520–640 / M 550–660	67%	2
Texas Christian University	V 520–620/ M 540–640	65%	2
Tufts University	V 610–710/ M 640–720	26%	4

PRIVATE SCHOOLS	SAT*	ACCEPTANCE RATE	RANKING
Tulane University	V 610–730/ M 630–690	55%	2
Union College	V 560–660/ M 590–690	44%	3
United States Air Force Academy	V 590–670 / M 620–700	15%	4
United States Coast Guard Academy	V 570–650 / M 600–680	7%	4
United States Naval Academy	V 590–680 / M 620–700	10%	4
Vanderbilt University	V 610–710/ M 640–720	40%	3
Vassar College	V 660–740/ M 640–710	29%	3
Villanova University	V 570–650/ M 600–680	53%	2
Wake Forest University	V 610–690/ M 630–700	45%	3
Washington & Lee University	V 650–720/ M 650–720	31%	3
Washington University in St. Louis	V 650–730/ M 670–750	20%	4
Wellesley College	V 620–720/ M 630–720	41%	3
Wesleyan University	V 640–740/ M 650–720	27%	4
Wheaton College	V 620–710 / M 610–700	53%	2
Whitman College	V 620–730/ M 610–700	51%	2
Williams College	V 660–760/ M 660–750	21%	4
Yale University	V 690–790/ M 690–790	11%	4

PUBLIC SCHOOLS	SAT*	ACCEPTANCE RATE	RANKING
University of Alabama	V 490–610 / M 500–610	87%	1
University of Arizona	V 490–610/ M 500–630	85%	1
Arizona State University	V 480–600 / M 490–620	88%	1
Bowling Green State University	V 450–560 / M 450–560	90%	1
California Polytechnic State University San Luis Obispo	V 520–620 / M 570–660	39%	3
California State University Fresno	V 400–530 / M 420–550	70%	1
University of California Berkeley	V 570–700/ M 620–740	24%	4
University of California Davis	V 510–630/ M 570–670	60%	2
University of California Los Angeles	V 560–690/ M 600–720	24%	4
University of California San Diego	V 550–660/ M 600–700	41%	3
University of California Santa Barbara	V 530–640/ M 550–660	50%	3
City University of New York–City College	V 400–530 / M 430–570	35%	3
Clemson University	V 550–630/ M 570–660	61%	2
College of William and Mary	V 630–730 / M 630–710	34%	3
University of Colorado	V 530–630/ M 550–650	80%	2

PUBLIC SCHOOLS	SAT*	ACCEPTANCE RATE	RANKING
Colorado State University	V 500–600 / M 510–610	79%	2
University of Connecticut	V 530–620 / M 550–640	53%	2
University of Florida	V 560–660 / M 580–680	52%	2
University of Georgia	V 560–650 / M 560–650	75%	1
University of Hawaii	V 480–580 / M 510–620	59%	1
Florida State University	V 520–620 / M 530–630	64%	2
Indiana University	V 490–600/ M 500–620	81%	1
Iowa State University	V 520–650 / M 560–680	90%	1
University of Kansas	ACT 21–27	68%	2
Kansas State University	ACT 21–26	60%	2
University of Kentucky	V 510–620 / M 510–630	81%	2
Louisiana State University	ACT 22–27	81%	1
University of Maryland	V 570–670/ M 600–700	43%	3
University of Massachusetts	V 500–620/ M 510–630	82%	2
Miami University (Ohio)	V 560–650/ M 580–670	71%	2
Michigan State University	V 490–610/ M 520–640	67%	2
University of Michigan	V 580–690/ M 620–720	53%	3
University of Minnesota	V 540–660/ M 560–680	76%	2
University of Montana	V 526–573 / M 500–571	93%	1
University of Nebraska	V 520–650/ M 520–660	76%	2
University of New Hampshire	V 500–590/ M 510–610	77%	S
New Mexico State University	ACT 18–23	81%	1
State University of New York–Binghamton	560–640 / M 590–680	45%	2
State University of New York–Purchase College	500–610 / M 480–580	33%	2
State University of New York–Stony Brook	V 510–610/ M 560–660	51%	2
University of North Carolina	V 590–690/ M 600–700	37%	2
University of Oklahoma	ACT 24–28	82%	1
University of Oregon	V 490–606/ M 500–610	84%	1
Purdue University	V 500–610/ M 530–650	79%	1
Rutgers University	V 530–630/ M 560–670	55%	2
University of Texas	V 540–660/ M 570–690	47%	2
University of Virginia	V 600–710/ M 630–720	39%	3
University of Washington	V 520–640/ M 550–670	71%	2
College of William and Mary	V 620–730 / M 630–710	35%	3
University of Wisconsin	V 550–660/ M 600–710	65%	2

Note: There are also schools that don't require tests. A partial list of these schools can be found on page 37, and a complete list can be found on the Resource CD.

INTRO TO CSI

CSI: Stands for *C*harting Your *S*trengths as an *I*ndividual. Although we will go into CSI in more detail in Chapter 4, I want to introduce the concept here. You see, putting together a general list of schools that interest you is one step. But we're going to go a step further by finding your unique strengths that match up best with what your schools are looking for.

Although schools may have similar acceptance numbers, they often have different reasons for admitting students. Remember your cousin Mikey, the one who ate his own lice? How come he got accepted to Amherst but got rejected by Pomona? Why did Greg, an above-average but not top student, get into Yale, while Stephanie, the valedictorian butt-kicker, got rejected? One reason is that each of these students matched up to the profile each school was looking for. By charting your strengths against the information provided by the schools themselves, you'll have a better idea of what your chances are of getting in.

Huh?

Okay, as an example, here are some numbers of incoming freshmen at Penn that you could use to determine what other factors might help you get admitted. You can get info like this for most schools off of websites, from college viewbooks, from your counselor, or by calling a school's admissions office.

1. Penn only accepted 20.8 percent of total applicants. However, "legacy" students (or those whose relatives went to the school) were admitted at 38 percent.

2. Penn has a decent percentage of minority students, so depending on your background, you may receive extra consideration.

3. Check out the majors. Social sciences, business/marketing, engineering, biology, and health professions are among the most popular. Therefore, if you had a real interest in an area that was not as popular, you'd want to market your strengths and your interests to help you stand out.

TIME TO START YOUR COLLEGE SEARCH

I want to make your lives a bit easier. The two best books I've found for those looking for colleges are *Fiske Guide to Colleges* and *The Insider's Guide to the Colleges*. Both give subjective insights and useful stats. I also suggest looking at *The College Finder* by Steven Antonoff, *Colleges That Change Lives* by Loren Pope, and *Arco 100 Colleges Where Average Students Can Excel* by Joe anne Adler for information about schools not found in other guidebooks.

Once you have looked through these babies, take your completed interest sheet and either talk to your counselor or go online for more options. The idea is to come up with a list of six to twelve schools to which you'll apply.

Again, remember that an exceptionally selective school is not necessarily better than a less selective one. For example, if I had wanted to major in architecture, Stanford would have been a poor choice—it doesn't offer an architecture major. So look beyond the names and numbers to find schools that will allow you to do what you want to do.

Because I often get asked for unique schools that can be difficult to find, such as performing arts schools and schools with programs for learning disabilities, I have compiled some lists (Tables 2-2 and 2-3) to give you an idea of what is available. (See Chapter 3 for more information about these schools.) I have also included lists of schools in other special categories, such as those that accept the Common Application, those that don't require standardized tests, and those that accept students with less than a B average.

After you have spent some time looking over the lists, please use the sheet on page 39 to create a first list of possibilities.

Table 2-2 is a list of performing arts schools and their specialties. Some of the schools are four-year academic schools with strong departmental programs, while others are specialty art schools that allow students to focus only on art classes, rather than on traditional academics. Please note: Although I tried to make this list comprehensive, there may be additional schools in your particular state that are not included. Another good resource is *The Performing Arts Majors College Guide* by Carole J. Everett.

TABLE 2-2 PERFORMING ARTS SCHOOLS

SCHOOL	STATE	DANCE	MUSIC	DRAMA
Academy of Vocal Arts	Pennsylvania		X	
Adelphi University	New York	X		X
University of Alabama	Alabama	X	X	X
American Conservatory Theater	California			X
American Academy of Dramatic Arts	New York			X
American Musical and Dramatic Academy	New York		X	X
Amherst College	Massachusetts	X	X	X
Arizona State University	Arizona	X	X	X
University of Arizona	Arizona	X	X	X
Bard College	New York	X	X	X
Barnard College	New York	X	X	X
Bates College	Maine	X		X
Baylor University	Texas		X	X
Bennington College	Vermont	X	X	X
Berklee College of Music	Massachusetts		X	
Boston College	Massachusetts			X
Boston Conservatory	Massachusetts	X	X	X
Boston University	Massachusetts		X	X
Bowdoin College	Maine			X
Bradford College	Massachusetts	X		X
Brown University	Rhode Island			X
Bucknell University	Pennsylvania		X	
Butler University	Indiana	X	X	X
California Institute of the Arts	California	X	X	X
California State University Fullerton	California	X	X	X
California State University Long Beach	California	X	X	X
Carnegie Mellon University	Pennsylvania		X	X
Case Western Reserve University	Ohio	X	X	X

SCHOOL	STATE	DANCE	MUSIC	DRAMA
Chapman University	California	X	X	
Chatham College	Pennsylvania	X		X
University of Chicago	Illinois		X	
Circle in the Square Theater School	New York			X
City University of New York–City College	New York	X	X	
City University of New York–Hunter College	New York	X		
Cleveland Institute of Music	Ohio		X	
College of Charleston	South Carolina	X	X	
Columbia College	Illinois	X		
Cornell University	New York	X		X
Dartmouth College	New Hampshire	X		X
Dickinson College	Pennsylvania		X	X
DePaul University	Illinois		X	X
Drew University	New Jersey			X
Duke University	North Carolina	X	X	X
Eastman School of Music	New York		X	
Emerson College	Massachusetts			X
George Mason University	Virginia	X		
Goucher College	Maryland	X		X
Grambling State University	Louisiana		X	X
University of Illinois–Urbana Champaign	Illinois	X	X	X
Hampshire College	Massachusetts	X	X	
Harvard-Radcliffe College	Massachusetts		X	
Hofstra University	New York	X		X
Indiana University	Indiana	X	X	X
Institute for Advanced Theater Training at Harvard University	Massachusetts			X
Ithaca College	New York		X	X
Joffrey II Dancers	New York	X		
Juilliard School	New York	X	X	X
University of Iowa	Iowa	X	X	X
Kansas State University	Kansas	X	X	X
University of Kansas	Kansas	X	X	X
Kenyon College	Ohio			X
Lawrence University Conservatory of Music	Wisconsin		X	X
Luther College	Iowa		X	

SCHOOL	STATE	DANCE	MUSIC	DRAMA
Manhattan School of Music	New York		X	
Massachusetts Institute of Technology	Massachusetts		X	
University of Massachusetts–Amherst	Massachusetts	X	X	X
Miami University of Ohio	Ohio		X	
University of Michigan	Michigan	X	X	X
Michigan State	Michigan	X	X	X
University of Minnesota School	Minnesota	X	X	X
Marymount Manhattan College	New York	X		X
Middlebury College	Vermont	X	X	X
Mount Holyoke College	Massachusetts	X	X	
Muhlenberg College	Pennsylvania			X
National Shakespeare Company	New York			X
New England Conservatory	Massachusetts		X	
University of New Mexico	New Mexico	X	X	X
New York University	New York	X	X	X
North Carolina School of the Arts	North Carolina	X	X	X
University of North Carolina	North Carolina			X
Northwestern University	Illinois	X	X	X
University of Notre Dame	Indiana		X	
Oberlin College and Conservatory	Ohio		X	
Ohio State University	Ohio	X	X	X
University of Oregon	Oregon	X	X	
Peabody Conservatory of Music at Johns Hopkins University	Maryland		X	
University of Pennsylvania	Pennsylvania		X	
Princeton Ballet School	New Jersey	X		
Princeton University	New Jersey	X	X	X
University of Puget Sound	Washington		X	
Rice University–Shepard School. of Music	Texas		X	
Rutgers University	New Jersey	X	X	X
Sarah Lawrence College	New York	X	X	X
Skidmore College	New York	X		X
Smith College	Massachusetts	X	X	X
University of South Carolina	South Carolina			X
Southern Methodist University	Texas	X	X	X
State University of New York–Brookport	New York	X		

SCHOOL	STATE	DANCE	MUSIC	DRAMA
State University of New York–Buffalo	New York	X	X	X
State University of New York–Potsdam	New York	X	X	
State University of New York–Purchase	New York	X	X	X
Swarthmore College	Pennsylvania		X	X
Syracuse University	New York		X	X
Temple University	Pennsylvania	X	X	X
Texas Christian University	Texas	X	X	
University of Texas	Texas	X	X	X
Tulane University School	Louisiana			X
Tufts University	Massachusetts	X		X
University of Utah	Utah	X	X	X
Vanderbilt University	Tennessee	X		
Vassar College	New York		X	X
University of Virginia	Virginia			X
Washington University in St. Louis	Missouri	X		X
University of Washington	Washington	X	X	X
University of Wisconsin–Madison	Wisconsin		X	X
Wellesley College	Massachusetts			X
West Virginia University	West Virginia		X	X
Wheaton College	Illinois		X	

The schools in Table 2-3 have specific programs for students with learning disabilities. These programs offer services such as alternative admissions procedures, tutoring, note taking, and professionals who help students learn new strategies. They often require additional fees and require participation in the program.

TABLE 2-3 SCHOOLS WITH FORMAL LEARNING DISABILITY PROGRAMS

Adelphi University	New York
American International College	Massachusetts
University of Arizona	Arizona
Barry University	Florida
Concordia College	New York
Finlandia University	Michigan
Gannon University	Pennsylvania
Hofstra University	New York
University of Indianapolis	Indiana
Louisiana College	Louisiana
Marymount Manhattan College	New York
Marshall University	West Virginia
Mitchell College	Connecticut
Monmouth University	New Jersey
Northeastern University	Massachusetts
Regis University	Colorado
Rochester Institute of Technology	New York
Schreiner College	Texas
Southern Illinois University	Illinois
Southern Vermont College	Vermont
Union College	Nebraska
Westminister College	Missouri
University of Wisconsin	Wisconsin

Table 2-4 lists schools that offer services for students with learning disabilities, but that have a less formal structure than do the schools given in Table 2-3. Services may vary among these schools. Usually these programs are not mandatory and do not involve extra fees. Check with individual schools to determine what services they offer, including whether they provide guidance throughout the admissions process.

TABLE 2-4 SCHOOLS WITH LESS FORMAL LEARNING DISABILITY PROGRAMS

University of Alabama	Alabama
American University	Washington, DC
Arizona State University	Arizona
Baker University	Kansas
Bakersfield College	California
Boston College	Massachusetts
Boston University	Massachusetts
Brigham Young University	Utah
Brown University	Rhode Island
California State Polytechnic University–San Luis Obispo	California
California State Polytechnic University–Pomona	California
California State University Chico	California
California State University Northridge	California
California State University San Bernardino	California
University of California Berkeley	California
University of California Los Angeles	California
University of California San Diego	California
University of California Santa Barbara	California
Catholic University of America	Washington, DC
Clark University	Massachusetts
Colgate University	New York
College of William and Mary	Virginia
University of Colorado at Boulder	Colorado
University of Colorado at Colorado Springs	Colorado
University of Connecticut	Connecticut
Cornell University	New York
Davidson College	North Carolina
Dean College	Massachusetts
University of Delaware	Delaware
University of Denver	Colorado

DePaul University	Illinois
Dickinson College	Pennsylvania
Duke University	North Carolina
Eastern Kentucky University	Kentucky
Eastern Washington University	Washington
Emory University	Georgia
Florida A&M University	Florida
University of Florida	Florida
George Washington University	Washington, DC
Georgetown University	Washington, DC
Georgia State University	Georgia
Harding University	Arizona
Hocking College	Ohio
Illinois State University	Illinois
University of Illinois	Illinois
Indiana University	Indiana
Iowa State University	Iowa
University of Iowa	Iowa
Kansas State University	Kansas
Kent State University	Ohio
Lee University	Tennessee
Liberty University	Virginia
Manhattan College	New York
University of Maryland	Maryland
University of Massachusetts	Massachusetts
Miami University	Ohio
Michigan State University	Michigan
University of Michigan	Michigan
University of Nevada	Nevada
New England College	New Hampshire
New York University	New York
North Carolina State University	North Carolina
University of North Carolina	North Carolina
Northern Arizona University	Arizona
Northwestern University	Illinois
Ohio State University	Ohio
University of the Pacific	California
Pennsylvania State University	Pennsylvania

Providence College	Rhode Island
Rocky Mountain College	Montana
St. Bonaventure College	New York
San Diego State University	California
San Francisco State University	California
University of San Francisco	California
San Jose State University	California
Sonoma State University	California
University of South Carolina	South Carolina
University of Southern California	California
State University of New York at Albany	New York
State University of New York at Stony Brook	New York
State University of New York of Technology at Farmingdale	New York
State University of New York of Technology at Delhi	New York
Syracuse University	New York
Temple University	Pennsylvania
University of Tennessee	Tennessee
Unity College	Maine
Wake Forest University	North Carolina
University of Wisconsin	Wisconsin
Xavier University	Ohio

Don't you just wish you had a list of schools that accepted the same application? Even better, wouldn't it be nice if the list told you the deadline for each school *and* whether each school had additional required supplements?

Who's your daddy? That's right, just turn the page to see details about schools that accept the Common Application.*

Then, in Table 2-6, you'll find some schools that don't require you to take the SATs or the ACT. No, really. These schools do not require standardized tests.

*The Common Application, or Common App., is a single application that is accepted by more than two hundred colleges and universities.

TABLE 2-5 SCHOOLS THAT ACCEPT THE COMMON APPLICATION

COMMON APPLICATION™ 2005–2006
College Deadlines, Fees, and Requirements

NOTES:

1 All colleges are coeducational unless marked (W) or (M).
2 Some colleges may charge an alternate fee for international applications. Check institutional application instructions where an asterisk (*) appears in the Fee column.
3 Source for obtaining supplements. Key: (O) online at www.commonapp.org, (W) on college website, (A) in application packet mailed by the college, (M) mailed to student upon receipt of Common App, (C) call the admission office.

4 If English is not your native language, consult institutional information for required testing (TOEFL or other test).
5 Common App forms required. Key: (TE) Teacher Evaluation, (SR) School Report, (MY) Midyear Report. Consult college instructions regarding required letters of recommendation.
6 Most member colleges accept electronic submission via Common App Online™. All accept hardcopy. A few colleges waive/reduce application fees for online submission.

☞ It is important that students review institutional publications or websites for complete application requirements and instructions. For items marked with an asterisk (*), check the appropriate college materials or call the admission office.

☞ Transfer applicants: Not all colleges accept the Common App for transfer students. Check college-specific profiles on Common App Online (http://app.commonapp.org), at the College Info link and/or institutional materials before submitting.

College/University (see note 1)	ED	EA	Regular	Fee (note 2)	Supplement (note 3)	Supplement Due Date	Tests Required (note 4)	TE (#)	SR	MY	Submit Online? (note 6)
Adelphi University		12/1	Rolling	$35	O,W,M	by app deadline	ACT or SAT; TOEFL	1	✓		Yes
Agnes Scott College (W)	11/15		3/1	$35	W,M	by app deadline	ACT or SAT; TOEFL; SAT subj tests recom*	1	✓	✓	Yes (fee waived)
Albertson College		11/15	6/1	$50	None		ACT or SAT; TOEFL	1	✓		Yes (fee $20)
Albion College	11/15	12/1	6/1	$20			ACT or SAT	1	✓	✓	Yes
Albright College			Rolling	$25	None		ACT or SAT; TOEFL	1	✓		Yes (fee waived)
Alfred University	12/1		2/1	$40	None		ACT or SAT	1	✓		Yes (fee waived)
Allegheny College	11/15		2/15	$35	W,M	2/15	ACT or SAT; TOEFL; SAT subject tests recom	1	✓		Yes (fee waived)
American University	11/15		1/15	$45	W**	2/15	ACT (w/writing) or SAT; SAT subj tests recom	2	✓	✓	Yes (fee waived)
Amherst College	11/15		1/1	$55	O,W,A	with CApp	ACT; or SAT & any 2 SAT subj tests; TOEFL*	2	✓	✓	Yes
Antioch College	11/15	12/1	2/1	$35	W	by app deadline	TOEFL of 525	2	✓	✓	Yes
Arcadia University	11/1		Rolling	$30	None		ACT or SAT; TOEFL	1	✓		Yes (fee waived)
Assumption College	11/15		2/15	$50	O	with CApp	ACT or SAT		✓		Yes
Atlantic, College of the	12/1, 1/10		2/15	$45	W,C	by app deadline	TOEFL or verbal SAT for international students	2	✓	✓	Yes
Austin College	12/1	12/1, 1/15	3/1	$35	W	by app deadline	ACT (w/wr) or SAT; TOEFL (or ACT or SAT)	1	✓		Yes
Babson College	11/15	11/15	1/15	$60*	O,W,A	with CApp	ACT or SAT; TOEFL; 2 SAT subj tests recom	1	✓		Yes (fee waived)
Baldwin–Wallace College			Rolling	$25	W	3/1	ACT or SAT	2	✓		Yes
Bard College		11/1	1/15	$50	W	1/15	TOEFL required; ACT/SAT optional	2	✓		Yes
Barnard College (W)	11/15		1/1	$45	W,C	by app deadline	ACT; or SAT & 2 SAT subject tests; TOEFL	2	✓	✓	Yes
Bates College	11/15, 1/1		1/1	$60*	O,W,M	by app deadline	TOEFL required; ACT/SAT optional	2	✓		Yes
Beloit College		11/15, 12/15	1/15	$30	W,M,C	by app deadline	ACT or SAT (writing opt); SAT subj tests opt	1	✓		Yes
Bennington College	11/15, 1/1		1/1*	$60	W,M	by app deadline	ACT or SAT; TOEFL; SAT subj tests recom	2	✓	✓	Yes
Bentley College	11/15	12/1	2/1*	$50*	O,W,M	by app deadline	ACT or SAT; TOEFL or ELPT	2	✓		Yes
Birmingham–Southern College		11/15	1/15	$40	O,W	with CApp	ACT or SAT; TOEFL	1	✓		Yes
Binghamton University–SUNY		12/1	Rolling	$25	None		ACT or SAT; TOEFL of 500 (173 computer)		✓		Yes
Boston College		11/1	1/2	$60*	O,W,A	ASAP	ACT (w/wr); or SAT & 2 SAT subj tests; TOEFL	2	✓	✓	Yes
Boston University	11/1, 1/2		1/2	$70	W	by app deadline	ACT (w/writing) or SAT; 2 SAT subj tests	1	✓	✓	Yes
Bowdoin College	11/15, 1/1		1/1	$60	O,W	with CApp	TOEFL; ACT/SAT optional	2	✓	✓	Yes
Bradley University			Rolling	$35*	None		ACT or SAT	1	✓		Yes (fee waived US)
Brandeis University	11/15		1/15	$55	O,W	by app deadline	ACT or SAT & 2 SAT subj tests; TOEFL recom	2	✓	✓	Yes
Bryant University	11/15		2/15	$50	O,W	by app deadline	ACT; or SAT subject tests; TOEFL*	opt	✓		Yes
Bryn Mawr College (W)	11/15, 1/1		1/15	$50*	W,A*	by app deadline	ACT; or SAT subject tests; TOEFL*	2	✓		Yes
Bucknell University	11/15, 1/1		1/1	$60	O,W,A	by app deadline	ACT or SAT; TOEFL*	1	✓	✓	Yes
Butler University		12/1, 2/1	Rolling	$35*	W,C	by app deadline	ACT or SAT; TOEFL (or ACT or SAT)	1	✓		Yes (fee waived)
California Lutheran University			3/1	$45	None		ACT or SAT; TOEFL		✓		Yes (fee $25)
Carleton College	11/15, 1/15		1/15	$30	O,W,A	by app deadline	ACT or SAT; TOEFL; SAT subj tests optional	2	✓		Yes (fee waived)
Carnegie Mellon University	11/15*		1/1*	$60	O,W,M	with CApp	ACT (w/wr) or SAT; 2 SAT subj tests (incl Math)	1	✓	✓	Yes
Carnegie Mellon University–Qatar			4/1	$60*	W,A	by app deadline	ACT (w/wr) or SAT; 2 SAT subj tests (incl Math); TOEFL	2	✓	✓	Yes

TABLE 2-5 SCHOOLS THAT ACCEPT THE COMMON APPLICATION

College/University (see note 1)	ED	EA	Regular	Fee (note 2)	Supplement (note 3)	Supplement Due Date	Tests Required (note 4)	Forms Required (note 5) TE (#)	SR	MY	Submit Online? (note 6)
Case Western Reserve University		11/1	1/15	$35	W*		ACT (w/writing)or SAT; 3 SAT subj tests optional	1	✓		Yes (fee waived)
Cazenovia College			Rolling	$30	None		Standardized tests not required	1	✓		Yes (fee waived)
Centenary College of Louisiana	12/1	1/15	2/15	$30			ACT or SAT	1*	✓	✓	Yes
Centre College		12/1	2/1	$40	W, M	by app deadline	ACT or SAT; TOEFL of 580	1	✓		Yes (fee waived)
Chatham College (W)			Rolling	$25	None		ACT or SAT; TOEFL	1	✓	✓	Yes (fee waived)
Claremont McKenna College	11/15, 1/2		1/2	$60	O, W, A, M, C	by app deadline	ACT (w/writing) or SAT; SAT subj tests optional	2	✓	✓	Yes
Clark University	11/15		1/15	$50	O, W	by app deadline	ACT or SAT	1	✓	✓	Yes
Clarkson University	12/1, 1/15		3/1	$50	W, M	by app deadline	ACT (writing optional) or SAT; TOEFL	2	✓	✓	Yes (fee waived)
Coe College		12/10	3/1	None	None		ACT or SAT; TOEFL	2	✓	✓	Yes
Colby College	11/15, 1/1		1/1	$55	O, W, A, M	by app deadline	ACT or SAT; TOEFL*; SAT subj tests optional	2	✓	✓	Yes
Colby-Sawyer College		12/15	Rolling	$40	None		ACT or SAT; SAT subject tests optional	1	✓	✓	Yes
Colgate University	11/15, 1/15		1/15	$55	O, W, A	1/15	ACT or SAT	2	✓	✓	Yes (fee waived)
Colorado College	11/15, 1/1		1/15	$50	O, W, M	by app deadline	ACT or SAT; TOEFL of 550	2	✓	✓	Yes
Concordia College–New York	11/15		3/15	$40*	W, A	by app deadline	ACT or SAT; TOEFL	1	✓		Yes
Connecticut College	11/15, 1/1		1/1	$60*	O, W	11/15, 12/15*	ACT or 2 SAT subject tests; TOEFL	1	✓	✓	Yes (fee waived)
Converse College (W)	11/15	12/1	3/1	$40	None		ACT or SAT; TOEFL (SAT also recommended)	1	✓	✓	Yes
Cornell College (Iowa)	11/15	12/15	3/1	$30*	W, M	by app deadline	ACT or SAT; SAT subject tests optional	1	✓	✓	Yes
Cornell University	11/1		1/1	$65	O, W, A	by app deadline	ACT or SAT; SAT subj tests; TOEFL	2	✓	✓	Yes
Dallas, University of		12/1	Rolling	$40	O, M, C	by app deadline	ACT or SAT	1	✓	✓	Yes
Dartmouth College	11/1		1/1	$70*	O, W	by app deadline	ACT or SAT; 2 SAT subj tests; TOEFL recom	2	✓	✓	Yes
Davidson College	11/15, 1/2		1/2	$50*	W, M, C*	by app deadline	ACT (wr recom)or SAT; TOEFL; 2 subj tests rec	2	✓	✓	Yes
Delaware, University of	11/15		1/15	$55	W, M*	by app deadline	ACT or SAT; SAT subj tests rec*; TOEFL / ELPT		✓		Yes
Denison University	11/1, 1/1		12/15, 1/15	$40*	O, W	by app deadline	ACT (w/writing) or SAT; TOEFL	1	✓	*	Yes (fee waived)
Denver, University of		11/1	1/15	$50	W*	by app deadline	ACT or SAT	1	✓		Yes
DePauw University	11/1	12/1	2/1	$40*	O, W	by app deadline	ACT (w/wr) or SAT; TOEFL recom (560 min.)		✓	✓	Yes (fee waived)
Dickinson College	11/15, 1/15	12/1	2/1	$60	O, W	by app deadline	TOEFL; SAT or ACT (for merit scholarships only)	1	✓	✓	Yes (fee waived)
Dominican University of California			Rolling	$40	None		ACT or SAT; TOEFL (or ACT or SAT)	1	✓	✓	Yes
Drew University	12/1, 1/15		2/15	$50	O	by app deadline	ACT (w/writing) or SAT; TOEFL	recom	✓	✓	Yes
Duke University	11/1		1/2	$70	W, A, C	by app deadline	ACT(w/wr)or SAT & 2 subj tests*; TOEFL recom	2	✓	✓	Yes
Earlham College	12/1	1/1	2/15	$30	O, W	2/15	ACT or SAT	1	✓	✓	Yes
Eckerd College			4/1	$35	None		ACT or SAT; TOEFL	1	✓		Yes (fee waived)
Elizabethtown College			Rolling	$30	None		ACT or SAT	1	✓	✓	Yes
Elmira College			Rolling	$50	None		ACT or SAT; TOEFL	2	✓		Yes
Embry-Riddle Aeronautical University			Rolling	$50	None		ACT or SAT; TOEFL	1	✓		Yes
Emmanuel College (Massachusetts)	11/1		3/1	$40	None		ACT or SAT; TOEFL	2*	✓		Yes (fee waived)
Emory University	11/1, 1/1		1/15*	$50	O, W	with CApp	ACT or SAT; 2 subj tests recom; TOEFL recom	1	✓	✓	Yes
Eugene Lang College	11/15		2/1	$50	W	by app deadline	ACT or SAT; TOEFL	1	✓		Yes
Fairfield University	11/15		1/15*	$55	W, A, C	by app deadline	ACT or SAT; TOEFL; SAT subj tests optional	1	✓	✓	Yes
Findlay, University of			Rolling	None	None		ACT or SAT		✓		Yes
Fisk University	12/15		3/1, 10/1	$50*	W*	with CApp	ACT or SAT; TOEFL	1	✓		Yes
Florida Southern College	12/1		4/1	$30	None		ACT or SAT; TOEFL	1	✓		Yes (fee $20)
Fordham University		11/1	1/15	$50	O, W, M	by app deadline	ACT or SAT; SAT subject tests recommended	1*	✓	✓	Yes
Franklin & Marshall College	11/15, 1/15		2/1	$50	O, W	by app deadline	ACT or SAT*; TOEFL (optional for some)	2	✓		Yes (fee $20)
Furman University	11/15		1/15	$40	W, M	by app deadline	ACT or SAT; TOEFL	1	✓	✓	Yes
George Fox University		12/1	2/1	$40	W, M, C	1/15	ACT or SAT	1	✓	✓	Yes
George Washington University	11/15, 1/15		1/15	$60	W	1/15	ACT or SAT; SAT subject tests optional	2*	✓	✓	Yes
Gettysburg College	11/15, 1/15		2/15	$45*	W, C	by app deadline	ACT or SAT; SAT subject tests recommended	1	✓		Yes
Gonzaga University		11/15	2/1	$45	W, C	2/1	ACT or SAT; SAT subj tests considered; TOEFL*	1	✓	✓	Yes (fee $20)
Goucher College		12/1	2/1	$40	W, M	2/1	ACT (w/writing) or SAT	1	✓	✓	Yes
Grinnell College	11/20, 1/1		1/20	$30	O, W, A	by app deadline	ACT or SAT; TOEFL	2	✓	✓	Yes (fee waived)
Guilford College	1/15		2/15	$25	W, M	by app deadline	ACT, SAT, or portfolio; TOEFL	1	✓	✓	Yes (fee waived)
Gustavus Adolphus College	11/1, 12/1		Rolling	None	W, M	by app deadline	ACT or SAT; TOEFL of 550	1	✓	✓	Yes

TABLE 2-5 SCHOOLS THAT ACCEPT THE COMMON APPLICATION

College/University (see note 1)	Application Deadlines			Fee (note 2)	Supplement (note 3)	Supplement Due Date	Tests Required (note 4)	Forms Required (note 5)			Submit Online? (note 6)
	ED	EA	Regular					TE (#)	SR	MY	
Hamilton College	11/15,1/1		1/1	$50	O,W,A*	by app deadline	ACT, SAT, or any 3 tests (consult viewbook)	1	✓	✓	Yes (fee waived)
Hampden–Sydney College (M)	11/15	1/15	3/1	$30	None		ACT (w/writing) or SAT; TOEFL	1	✓	✓	Yes
Hampshire College	11/15	12/1	1/15	$55	O,W,A,M	by app deadline	TOEFL	1	✓	✓	Yes
Hanover College		12/1	3/1	$35*	None		ACT or SAT; TOEFL (or ACT or SAT)	1	✓	✓	Yes (fee waived)
Hartwick College	11/15,1/15		2/15	$35*	W,C		TOEFL; ACT/SAT optional/recommended	1	✓	✓	Yes (fee waived*)
Harvard College		11/1*	1/1	$65	O,W	by app deadline	ACT or SAT; SAT subject tests (any 3)	2*	✓	✓	Yes
Harvey Mudd College	11/15		1/15	$50	W,M	by app deadline	SAT; 2 SAT subj tests incl Math2C; TOEFL recom	2	✓	✓	Yes
Haverford College	11/15		1/15	$60	O,W,M	with CApp	ACT (w/wr) or SAT; 2 SAT subject tests; TOEFL	2	✓	✓	Yes (fee waived)
Hendrix College			Rolling	$40*	W	*	ACT or SAT; TOEFL	recom	✓	✓	Yes (fee waived)
Hiram College		4/15	4/15	$35	None		ACT or SAT; TOEFL	1	✓	✓	Yes (fee waived)
Hobart & William Smith Colleges	11/15,1/1*		2/1	$45	W,A,C	by app deadline	ACT or SAT; TOEFL	1*	✓	✓	Yes (fee waived)
Hofstra University		11/15	Rolling	$50*	W	by app deadline	ACT or SAT; TOEFL	opt	✓	✓	Yes
Hollins University (W)	11/15		2/15	$35	None		ACT or SAT	1	✓	✓	Yes
Holy Cross, College of the	12/15		1/15	$50	None		Standardized tests optional; TOEFL required	1	✓	✓	Yes
Hood College		12/1	2/1	$35	None		ACT or SAT; SAT subject tests optional	2	✓	✓	Yes (fee waived)
Illinois Wesleyan University			Rolling	None	W,M	by app deadline	ACT (wr opt) or SAT; TOEFL (or ACT or SAT)	1*	✓	✓	Yes
Iona College		12/1	2/15	$50	None		ACT or SAT	1	✓	✓	Yes
Ithaca College	11/1		2/1	$55	W	with CApp	ACT (w/writing) or SAT; TOEFL	recom	✓	✓	Yes
John Carroll University			2/1	$25	W,M	by app deadline	ACT or SAT; TOEFL	1	✓	✓	Yes (fee waived)
Johns Hopkins University	11/15		1/1	$60	W,M	by app deadline	ACT (w/writing) or SAT; TOEFL	1	✓	✓	Yes
Juniata College	11/15		4/22	$30	None		ACT or SAT	1	✓	✓	Yes
Kalamazoo College	11/15	12/1,1/15	2/15	$35	W	by app deadline	ACT or SAT	1	✓	✓	Yes
Kenyon College	12/1,1/15		1/15	$45	W	1/15	ACT or SAT; SAT subject tests optional	1	✓	✓	Yes (fee waived)
Knox College		12/1	2/1	$40*	O,W	by app deadline	ACT/SAT optional; TOEFL required	2	✓	✓	Yes
La Roche College			Rolling	$50	None		ACT or SAT; TOEFL recom	2	✓	opt	Yes
La Salle University		11/15	Rolling	$35	None		ACT or SAT; TOEFL	1	✓	✓	Yes
La Verne, University of	Rolling*		Rolling*	$50	W	with CApp	ACT or SAT; 3 SAT subject tests recom	2	✓	✓	Yes (fee waived)
Lafayette College	12/1		1/1	$60	W	with CApp	ACT or SAT; SAT subject tests recom	1	✓	✓	Yes
Lake Forest College	12/1	12/1	2/15	$40	None	by app deadline	ACT or SAT	1	✓	✓	Yes (fee waived)
Lawrence University	11/15	12/1	1/15	$40	O,W,C*	with CApp	ACT/SAT optional; TOEFL, ACT or SAT recom*	1	✓	✓	Yes (fee waived)
Le Moyne College	12/1		2/1	$35	None		ACT or SAT; TOEFL	1	✓	✓	Yes (fee waived)
Lehigh University	11/15,1/1		1/1	$60	O,W	with CApp	ACT or SAT; TOEFL; SAT subj tests recom	1	✓	✓	Yes
Lesley College	12/1		3/1	$40	W	by app deadline	ACT (w/writing) or SAT	2	✓	✓	Yes (fee waived)
Lewis & Clark College	11/15		2/1	$50	W,M	by app deadline	ACT, SAT, Portfolio option*; TOEFL*	1	✓	✓	Yes (fee waived)
Linfield College	11/15		2/15	$40	None		ACT or SAT; TOEFL	1	✓	✓	Yes
Loyola College in Maryland		1/15	1/15	$50	W,M	2/1	ACT or SAT; TOEFL, of 550	1	✓	recom	Yes (fee waived)
Loyola University New Orleans			Rolling	$20	None		ACT or SAT; SAT subject tests optional	1	✓	✓	Yes (fee waived)
Luther College			Rolling	$25*	O,W,M		ACT or SAT; TOEFL, of 550	1	✓	✓	Yes (fee waived)
Macalester College	11/15,1/3		1/15	$40	O,W,A,M	by app deadline	ACT or SAT; TOEFL or ELPT; SAT subj tests opt	2	✓	✓	Yes
Maine at Farmington, University of		12/1	Rolling	$40	None		ACT/SAT optional; TOEFL required	opt	✓	✓	Yes
Maine, University of (Orono)		12/15	Rolling	$40	None		ACT or SAT (preferred)	*	✓	✓	Yes
Manhattan College	11/15		4/15	$40	None		ACT or SAT; TOEFL*	1	✓	✓	Yes
Manhattanville College	12/1		3/1	$50	None		ACT or SAT; TOEFL	2	✓	✓	Yes (fee waived)
Marietta College			4/15	$25*	None		ACT or SAT	1	✓	✓	Yes (fee waived US)
Marlboro College	11/15	1/15	2/15	$50	W	by app deadline	ACT or SAT	2	✓	✓	Yes (fee waived US)
Marquette University			12/1	$30*	W	with CApp	ACT and/or SAT		✓	✓	Yes (fee waived US)
Mary Washington, University of			2/1	$45	W	by app deadline	ACT or SAT; SAT subj tests recom	1	✓	✓	Yes
McDaniel College		12/1	2/1	$50	None		ACT or SAT; 3 SAT subject tests optional	1	✓	✓	Yes
Merrimack College		11/30	2/1	$50	O,W	with CApp	ACT or SAT; TOEFL	1*	✓	✓	Yes
Miami, University of (Florida)	11/1	11/1	12/1,1/1	$65*	W,M	by app deadline	ACT or SAT; TOEFL	1*	✓	✓	Yes (fee $55 US)
Miami University (Ohio)	11/1		12/1,1/31	$45	W	by app deadline	ACT or SAT	1	✓	✓	Yes
Middlebury College	11/15,12/15		12/15	$55	W,A	by app deadline	ACT or SAT; or 3 achv (SAT/AP/IBH); TOEFL*	2	✓	✓	Yes

TABLE 2-5 SCHOOLS THAT ACCEPT THE COMMON APPLICATION

College/University (see note 1)	Application Deadlines			Fee (note 2)	Supplement (note 3)	Supplement Due Date	Tests Required (note 4)	Forms Required (note 5)			Submit Online? (note 6)
	ED	EA	Regular					TE (#)	SR	MY	
Mills College (W)		11/15	3/1	$40	None		ACT or SAT; SAT subj tests recommended	2	✓	✓	Yes
Millsaps College		12/1	2/1	$25	O,W,C	by app deadline	ACT or SAT	1	✓	✓	Yes
Moravian College	1/15		2/15	$40	W,M	by app deadline	ACT or SAT; TOEFL & SAT (for internationals)	1	✓	✓	Yes
Morehouse College (M)	11/15		2/15	$45	None		ACT or SAT	2	✓	✓	Yes
Mount Holyoke College (W)	11/15, 1/1		1/15	$55	W	by app deadline	Standardized tests optional	2	✓	✓	Yes (fee waived)
Mount Saint Vincent, College of		11/1	Rolling	$35	None		ACT or SAT; TOEFL		✓	✓	Yes (fee waived)
Muhlenberg College	2/1		2/15	$45	W,A,M,C		ACT or SAT (or graded paper & interview)	2	✓	✓	Yes
Naropa University			1/15*	$50	W	by app deadline	TOEFL of 550; ACT or SAT recommended	2	✓	✓	Yes
Nazareth College	11/15	12/15	2/15	$40	W	by app deadline	ACT or SAT	2	✓	✓	Yes (fee waived)
New College of Florida			Rolling	$30	W		ACT or SAT; TOEFL	1*	✓	✓	Yes (fee waived)
New England College			Rolling	$30	None		ACT or SAT; TOEFL	1	✓	✓	Yes
New Hampshire, University of		12/1	2/1	*	W	2/1	ACT or SAT; TOEFL		✓	✓	Yes
New Jersey, The College of	11/15		2/15*	$50	W	by app deadline	ACT or SAT (for scholarship); TOEFL	2	✓	✓	No
New York University	11/1		1/15	$65*	O,W	with CApp	ACT (w/wr) or SAT; TOEFL; 2 SAT subj tests*	1	✓	✓	Yes (fee waived)
Northland College			Rolling	$25	None		ACT or SAT; TOEFL		✓	✓	Yes (fee waived)
Northeastern University		11/15	1/15*	$75	O,W	by app deadline	ACT (w/writing) or SAT	1	✓	✓	Yes (fee $65)
Notre Dame de Namur University		12/1	2/1	$40	None		ACT (w/writing) or SAT; TOEFL	1	✓	✓✓	Yes (fee waived)
Notre Dame of Maryland, College of (W)			2/15	$40	None	by app deadline	ACT or SAT; TOEFL	1	✓	✓	No
Oberlin College	11/15, 1/2		1/15	$35	O,W,M	2/1	ACT or SAT; TOEFL; SAT subj tests recom	2	✓	✓	Yes
Occidental College	11/15		1/10	$50	O,W	by app deadline	ACT or SAT; TOEFL/ELPT; 3 subj tests recom	2	✓	✓	Yes
Oglethorpe University		12/5	Rolling	$35	None		ACT or SAT; TOEFL	2	✓	✓	Yes
Ohio Wesleyan University	12/1	12/15	3/1	$35	None		ACT or SAT; TOEFL; SAT subj tests recom	1	✓	✓	Yes
Pace University			Rolling	$45	None		ACT or SAT; subj test (FL) recom; TOEFL recom	2	✓	✓	Yes
Pacific, University of the		11/15	1/15	$60	O,W	with CApp	ACT (w/writing) or SAT; TOEFL	2	✓		Yes (fee $30)
Pitzer College		11/15	1/1	$50	O	by app deadline	ACT/SAT/AP/IB optional	2	✓	✓	Yes
Pomona College	11/15, 12/29		1/1	$60	W,A,C	by app deadline	ACT; or SAT & 2 SAT subject tests	2	✓	✓	Yes
Portland, University of			2/1	$50	None		ACT or SAT	1	✓	✓	Yes
Presbyterian College	12/5		Rolling	$30	M		ACT or SAT; TOEFL	1	✓	✓	Yes (fee waived)
Prescott College	12/1		Rolling	$25	None		ACT or SAT; TOEFL	2	✓		Yes
Princeton University	11/1		1/1	$65	O	by app deadline	ACT (w/wr) or SAT; subj tests*; TOEFL; or SAT*	1	✓	✓	Yes (fee waived)
Providence College		11/1	1/15	$55	O,W	by app deadline	ACT (w/wr) or SAT; TOEFL; subj tests recom	1	✓		Yes
Puget Sound, University of		11/15, 12/15	2/1	$40	None		ACT or SAT	1	✓	✓	Yes
Queens University of Charlotte			Rolling	$40	None		ACT or SAT; 3 SAT subject tests recom	1	✓		Yes
Randolph-Macon College	11/15		3/1	$30	None		ACT or SAT; 3 SAT subject tests recom	1	✓	✓	Yes (fee waived)
Randolph-Macon Woman's College (W)	11/15		3/1	$35	None		ACT or SAT; TOEFL	1*	✓	✓	Yes (fee waived)
Redlands, University of		12/15	Rolling	$40	W,C	with CApp	ACT or SAT	1	✓	✓	Yes
Reed College	11/15, 1/2		1/15	$40	W,A	by app deadline	ACT or SAT (subj tests opt); TOEFL, 3 subj tests*	2	✓	✓	Yes
Regis College (W)		12/1	Rolling	$40	W	with CApp	ACT or SAT; TOEFL	1	✓	*	Yes
Regis University			Rolling	$40	O,W,M	by app deadline	ACT or SAT	1	✓	✓	Yes
Rensselaer Polytechnic Institute	11/15		1/1	$50	O,W,M	by app deadline	ACT or SAT; TOEFL; SAT subj tests (some pgm)	1	✓	✓	Yes
Rhodes College	11/1, 1/1		1/15*	$45	O,W,M	by app deadline	ACT (writing not required) or SAT; TOEFL	1	✓	✓	Yes (fee waived)
Rice University	11/1	12/1	1/10	$50	W,A	by app deadline	ACT (w/writing) or SAT; 2 SAT subj tests*	1*	✓	✓	Yes
Richmond, University of	11/15, 1/15		1/15	$50	W,M	2/15*	ACT or SAT; TOEFL	1	✓	✓	Yes
Rider University		11/15	Rolling	$45	None		ACT or SAT (essay not required); TOEFL	1	✓	✓	Yes
Ripon College			Rolling	$30	None		ACT or SAT; TOEFL	1	✓	✓	Yes
Rochester Institute of Technology	12/1		2/1	$50	O,W,A,M	by app deadline	ACT or SAT; TOEFL/ELPT; SAT subj tests opt	1	✓	✓	Yes (fee waived)
Rochester, University of	11/1		1/20	$50	W,A	by app deadline	ACT or SAT; TOEFL; SAT subj tests recom	1	✓	✓	Yes
Roger Williams University		12/1	Rolling*	$50	None		ACT or SAT	2	✓	✓	Yes
Rollins College	11/15, 1/15		2/15	$50	O,W,M	by app deadline	ACT or SAT; 3 SAT subj tests recom	1	✓	✓	Yes (fee waived)
Saint Anselm College		11/15	3/1	$55	W,M,C	ASAP	ACT or SAT	1	✓	✓	Yes
St. Benedict, College of, & St. John's U			Rolling	None	None		ACT or SAT; SAT subj tests optional	1	✓	✓	Yes
Saint Joseph's College of Maine		11/15	3/1*	$40	None		ACT or SAT; TOEFL; SAT subj tests optional	1	✓	✓	Yes (fee waived)

THE ULTIMATE COLLEGE ACCEPTANCE SYSTEM

2005–2006

TABLE 2-5 SCHOOLS THAT ACCEPT THE COMMON APPLICATION

College/University (see note 1)	Application Deadlines			Fee (note 2)	Supplement (note 3)	Supplement Due Date	Tests Required (note 4)	Forms Required (note 5)			Submit Online? (note 6)
	ED	EA	Regular					TE (#)	SR	MY	
Saint Joseph's University	11/15	11/15	2/1	$55*	None		ACT or SAT	1	✓	recom	Yes
St. Lawrence University	11/15, 1/15	11/15	2/15	$50*	O,W,M	by app deadline	ACT or SAT optional	2	✓	*	Yes
Saint Leo University			Rolling*	None							Yes (fee waived)
Saint Louis University	11/15		Rolling*	$25	None		ACT or SAT	1	✓		Yes (fee waived)
Saint Mary's College (Indiana) (W)		11/30	2/15	$30	M		ACT or SAT; 3 SAT subject tests*	1	✓	✓	Yes (fee waived)
Saint Mary's College of California			2/1	$55	W	by app deadline	ACT or SAT	1	✓	✓	Yes
Saint Michael's College		11/1, 12/1	2/1	$45	W,M	by app deadline	ACT or SAT	1	✓		Yes (fee waived)
St. Norbert College	12/1		4/1	$25	None		ACT or SAT	2	✓		Yes
St. Olaf College	11/1	12/1	2/1	$35	W,M	by app deadline	ACT or SAT; TOEFL	1	✓	✓	Yes
Saint Peter's College		1/15	Rolling*	*	None		ACT or SAT; TOEFL	1	✓		Yes
Saint Vincent College			Rolling*	$25	None		ACT or SAT; TOEFL; SAT subj tests accepted	1	✓		Yes (fee waived)
Salem College (North Carolina) (W)			Rolling	$30	None		ACT or SAT	2	✓	✓	Yes
Salve Regina University		11/1	3/1	$40	W,M	3/1	ACT or SAT; TOEFL (or ACT or SAT)	1	✓	✓	Yes
San Diego, University of		11/15	1/5	$55	O,W	by app deadline	ACT (w/writing) or SAT; TOEFL		✓	✓	Yes (fee waived)
San Francisco, University of		11/15	2/1*	$55*	None		ACT or SAT; TOEFL		✓	✓	Yes
Santa Clara University		11/1	1/15	$55	O,W,C	with CApp	ACT or SAT	1	✓	✓	Yes
Santa Fe, College of			Rolling	$35	None		ACT (w/writing) or SAT; TOEFL	2	✓	✓	Yes
Sarah Lawrence College	11/15, 1/1		1/1	$60	W	1/1	None	2	✓	✓	Yes (fee waived)
Scranton, University of		11/15	3/1	$40	None		ACT or SAT	1	✓	✓	Yes
Scripps College (W)	11/1, 1/1		1/1*	$50	Graded paper	by app deadline	ACT or SAT; SAT subj tests recom; TOEFL	2	✓	✓	Yes (fee waived)
Seattle University			2/1	$45	W,M	by app deadline	ACT or SAT; TOEFL	1	✓	✓	Yes
Seton Hill University			Rolling	$35	None		ACT or SAT; TOEFL	1	✓	✓	Yes (fee waived)
Sewanee (University of the South)	11/15		2/1*	$45	W,M	by app deadline	ACT or SAT; TOEFL recommended	1	✓	✓	Yes
Simmons College (W)		12/1	2/1	$35	W*		ACT or SAT; TOEFL or ELPT	2	✓	✓	Yes (fee waived)
Skidmore College	11/15, 1/15		1/15	$60	O,W,A	by app deadline	ACT or SAT; 2 SAT subj tests recommended	2	✓	✓	Yes (fee waived)
Smith College (W)	11/15, 1/1		1/15	$60	W,A,M	2/1	ACT or SAT; 2 SAT subj tests opt/recom; TOEFL	2	✓	✓	Yes (fee waived)
Southern Maine, University of			2/15*	$40	None		ACT or SAT	recom	✓		Yes
Southern Methodist University		11/1	1/15, 3/15	$50	None		ACT or SAT	1	✓	✓	Yes (fee waived)
Southern New Hampshire University		11/15	Rolling	$35	None		ACT (w/writing) or SAT		✓		Yes (fee waived)
Southwestern University	11/1		2/15	$40	None		ACT or SAT; TOEFL	1	✓	✓	Yes
Spelman College (W)		11/15	2/1	$35	None		ACT or SAT; 2 subj tests (home-schooled only)*	2*	✓	✓	Yes (fee waived)
Spring Hill College		11/1	Rolling	$25	None		ACT or SAT; TOEFL	1	✓	✓	Yes (fee waived)
Stetson University			3/15	$40*	None		ACT or SAT; TOEFL	1	✓	✓	Yes (fee waived)
Stevens Institute of Technology		11/15, 1/15	2/15	$55	None		ACT or SAT; SAT subj tests (accel programs)*	2	✓	✓	Yes (fee waived)
Stonehill College	11/1		1/15	$50	O,W,A	by app deadline	ACT or SAT; TOEFL of 550 (213 computer)	2	✓	✓	Yes
Suffolk University		11/20	3/1	$50	None		ACT or SAT; TOEFL	2	✓	✓	Yes (fee waived)
Susquehanna University	11/15, 1/1		3/1	$35	O,M,C	by app deadline	ACT or SAT; TOEFL; (The Write Option*)	2	✓	✓	Yes (fee waived)
Swarthmore College	11/15, 1/2		1/2	$60	O	by app deadline	ACT or SAT; 2 SAT subj tests; TOEFL*	2	✓	✓	Yes (fee waived)
Sweet Briar College (W)	12/1		2/1	$40	W,M	2/1	ACT or SAT; TOEFL (or SAT)	1	✓	✓	Yes
Syracuse University	11/15		1/1	$60	W,A	by app deadline	ACT or SAT; TOEFL or ELPT	2	✓	✓	Yes
Tampa, University of			Rolling	$35	None		ACT (w/writing) or SAT; TOEFL; or IELTS	1	✓	✓	Yes
TCU (Texas Christian University)		11/15	2/15	$40*	None		ACT or SAT; TOEFL	1	✓		Yes
Transylvania University		12/1	2/1	$30	None		ACT (writing recom) or SAT; or 3 SAT subj tests	1*	✓	✓	Yes (fee waived)
Trinity College (Connecticut)	11/15, 1/1		1/1	$60	W*		ACT or SAT	2	✓		Yes (fee waived)
Trinity University (Texas)	11/1	11/1, 12/15	2/1	$50	W,A,M,C	1/1	ACT (w/wrt; or SAT & 2 SAT subj tests; TOEFL	2	✓	✓	Yes (fee waived)
Tufts University	11/15, 1/1		1/1	$70	W,M		ACT (w/wrt) or SAT or SAT subj tests; TOEFL	1	✓	✓	Yes
Tulane University		11/1	1/15	$55	W,M	by app deadline	ACT or SAT; TOEFL	1*	✓	✓	Yes (fee waived)
Tulsa, University of			Rolling	$35	None		ACT or SAT	1*	✓	✓	Yes (fee waived)
Union College	11/15, 1/15		1/15	$50	O,W,A		ACT; or SAT; or 2 SAT subject tests	1	✓	✓	Yes
Ursinus College	1/15		2/15	$40	M		ACT or SAT	2	✓		Yes
Utica College			Rolling*	$40	W,M*		ACT or SAT; TOEFL	1*	✓	✓	Yes (fee waived)
Valparaiso University		11/1	Rolling	$30	W	with CApp	ACT or SAT		✓	✓	Yes (fee waived)

TABLE 2-5 SCHOOLS THAT ACCEPT THE COMMON APPLICATION

College/University (see note 1)	Application Deadlines ED	EA	Regular	Fee (note 2)	Supplement (note 3)	Supplement Due Date	Tests Required (note 4)	Forms Required (note 5) TE (#)	SR	MY	Submit Online? (note 6)
Vanderbilt University	11/1, 1/3		1/3	$50	W	by app deadline	ACT or SAT; SAT subj tests for placement*	2	✓	✓	Yes
Vassar College	11/15, 1/1		1/1	$60	W	by app deadline	ACT; or SAT & any 2 SAT subject tests; TOEFL	1	✓	✓	Yes
Vermont, University of		11/1	1/15	$45	W	by app deadline	ACT or SAT; TOEFL	1*	✓	✓	Yes
Villanova University		11/1	1/7	$70	W,M	by app deadline*	ACT (w/writing) or SAT		✓		Yes
Wabash College (M)	11/15	12/15	2/1	$30	None		ACT or SAT; TOEFL		✓		Yes
Wagner College	1/1		2/15*	$50*	O,W,A,M	2/15	ACT or SAT; 2 SAT subj tests recom; TOEFL	2	✓	✓	Yes
Wake Forest University	11/15		1/15	$40	O,W	1/15	SAT Reasoning	1	✓	✓	Yes
Washington College	11/15	12/1	2/15	$45	None		ACT or SAT	1	✓		Yes
Washington University in St. Louis	11/15, 1/1		1/15	$55	W,M,C	by app deadline	ACT or SAT; TOEFL	1	✓	✓	Yes
Washington & Jefferson College	12/1	1/15	3/1	$25	None		ACT or SAT; SAT subj tests opt (for placement)	1	✓	✓	Yes (fee waived)
Washington & Lee University	11/15, 1/2		1/15	$40	O,W,M	1/15	ACT (w/writing) or SAT; 2 SAT subject tests*	2	✓	✓	Yes
Webster University			3/1	$35	None		ACT or SAT; TOEFL	1	✓		Yes
Wellesley College (W)	11/1	1/1*	1/15*	$50	O,W	with CApp	ACT(w/wr)or SAT & 2 SAT subj tests; TOEFL	2	✓	✓	Yes (fee waived)
Wells College (W)	12/15	12/15	3/1	$40	None		ACT or SAT; TOEFL, recommended*	2	✓	✓	Yes (fee waived)
Wesleyan University	11/15, 1/1		1/1	$55	W*		ACT; or SAT & 2 SAT subject tests	2*	✓	✓	Yes
Westminster College (Missouri)			Rolling	None	None		ACT or SAT; TOEFL	1	✓		Yes
Westminster College (Pennsylvania)		11/15	5/1	$35	None		ACT or SAT; 3 SAT subject tests optional	2*	✓	✓	Yes
Wheaton College (Massachusetts)	11/15, 1/15		1/15	$55	O,W,A,M	by app deadline	TOEFL required; ACT/SAT optional	2*	✓	✓	Yes
Wheelock College		12/1	3/1	$35*	None		ACT; or SAT; TOEFL	1	✓		Yes (fee $15)
Whitman College	11/15, 1/1		1/15	$45	O,W,A,C	by app deadline	ACT (w/writing) or SAT	1	✓	✓	Yes
Whittier College		12/1	2/1	$50	W,C	by app deadline	ACT (w/writing) or SAT	2	✓	✓	Yes (fee waived)
Widener University		12/1	2/15	$35	None		ACT or SAT; TOEFL of 500 (173 computer)		✓	opt	Yes (fee waived)
Willamette University		11/1, 12/1	2/1	$50	None		ACT or SAT	1	✓	✓	Yes (fee waived)
William & Mary, College of	11/1		1/1	$60	O,W	with CApp	ACT or SAT; SAT subject tests optional		✓	✓	Yes (fee waived)
William Jewell College		12/1	12/1	$25	None		ACT or SAT; TOEFL	1	✓		Yes (fee waived)
Williams College	11/10		1/1	$60	O	by app deadline	ACT (w/writing) or SAT; any 2 SAT subj tests	2	✓	✓	Yes
Wilson College (W)			Rolling	$35	None		ACT or SAT; TOEFL	1	✓	✓	Yes (fee waived)
Wittenberg University	11/15	12/1	3/15	$40	None		ACT or SAT; TOEFL	1	✓		Yes (fee waived)
Wofford College	11/15		2/1	$40	W	by app deadline	ACT or SAT; TOEFL		✓	✓	Yes (fee $20)
Wooster, College of	12/1, 1/15		2/15	$40	O,W,M	by app deadline	ACT or SAT; TOEFL	1/2*	✓	✓	Yes
WPI (Worcester Polytechnic Institute)		11/15, 1/1		$60	None		ACT; or SAT & 3 SAT subj tests; TOEFL*		✓	✓	Yes (fee waived)
Xavier University (Ohio)		12/1	2/1	$35	W,M	with CApp	ACT or SAT	1	✓	✓	Yes
Yale University		11/1*	12/31	$75	O,W	with CApp	ACT; or SAT & 3 SAT subj tests; TOEFL*	2	✓	✓	Yes

Visit www.commonapp.org *today!*

TABLE 2-6 SCHOOLS THAT DON'T REQUIRE TESTS (SAT/ACT)

Antioch College	Lafayette College
Bard College	Lewis and Clark College
Bates College	Middlebury College
Bowdoin College	Mount Holyoke College
Connecticut College	Muhlenberg College
Dickinson College	St. Johns College
Franklin and Marshall College	Susquehanna
Goddard College	Union College
Hampshire College	Wheaton College
Hartwick College	

The table is just a partial list—you can find *many* more schools on the Resource CD.

If you have a GPA between 2.0 and 2.9 and/or SAT scores that range from 450 to 525 for each individual test and (total of 1350 to 1575), look at Table 2-6. It shows some schools that actively recruit and accept students with similar profiles. Again, this isn't a complete list—there are schools in Table 2-0 that fall under this category, and there are many more out there.

TABLE 2-6 SOME SCHOOLS THAT ACCEPT STUDENTS WITH LESS THAN A B AVERAGE

Ashland University	Ohio
Assumption College	Massachusetts
Bemidji State University	Minnesota
Bradford College	Massachusetts
Bryant College	Rhode Island
Castleton State College	Vermont
Catawba College	North Carolina
Cazenovia College	New York
Colby Sawyer College	New Hampshire
Dakota State University	South Dakota
Davis and Elkins College	West Virginia
Delaware Valley College	Pennsylvania
Delta State College	Missouri

Dickinson State College	North Dakota
Eastern New Mexico State University	New Mexico
Eastern Oregon State University	Oregon
Emporia State University	Kansas
Florida Southern University	Florida
Frostburg State University	Maryland
Georgia College	Georgia
University of Hartford	Connecticut
Hawaii Pacific University	Hawaii
Henderson State University	Arkansas
Lake Superior State University	Michigan
Lewis University	Illinois
MacMurry College	Texas
Marian College of Fond du Lac	Wisconsin
Menlo College	California
Monmouth University	New Jersey
Morehead State University	Kentucky
University of New Haven	Connecticut
Nichols College	Massachusetts
Pacific Lutheran College	Washington
Rocky Mountain College	Montana
St. Ambrose College	Iowa
Saint Joseph's College	Indiana
Saint Joseph's College	Maine
Seton Hall University	New Jersey
University of Southern Maine	Maine
Spring Hill College	Alabama
Springfield College	Massachusetts
Unity College	Maine
Utica College of Syracuse	New York
Wayne State College	Nebraska
Wesley College	Delaware
West Virginia Wesleyan	West Virginia
Western State College	Colorado

THE FIRST LIST

List the schools you might be interested in.

Don't worry about putting these schools into "Reaches," "Likelies," or "Safeties" yet. You'll do that in Chapter 4.

Emory University
Washington University (St. Louis)
Columbia University
Yale
Oxford University

CHAPTER THREE
HOW AN ADMISSIONS OFFICE WORKS

WHO ARE THESE PEOPLE?

You're probably thinking admissions officers are stuffy old people with Harvard degrees who were raised by lions and grew up in small, isolated caves. Hey, why else would they hole up in a room for five months, do nothing but read, and then be cruel enough to send those rejection letters?

Let's take a closer look at reality, shall we? Admissions people come in two varieties:

1. The seasoned veterans who have made it their life's work to help run an admissions office.

2. Recent college graduates who need a job and who are a good choice to review files, since they just went through college. These people tend to last about three to five years and then move on by getting a life. (Just kidding—it's actually not a bad job.)

Many admissions people did not actually attend the school for which they are judging you to see if you meet its requirements. The point? Admissions officers are actually caring humans, not gods. They are not looking to be cruel or to admit only the student with a GPA of 4.5 who recently won the Nobel Prize in Chemistry.

Admissions officers want to know you. What you're like. What your passions are. Hell, they *want* to let you into their school, so you can love it, leave it, brag about it, and give them lots of money as an alumnus. That's the game. The problem is they have to determine just who you are by looking at maybe ten pieces of paper—and you are among fifteen thousand students who all want in.

Don't panic! Stop worrying! You *will* show your best side, and they *will* come to know you. I'll help you stand out. That's why you're reading this, right? I am going to show you how to put yourself in an admissions officer's shoes, and read everything about you, as if you didn't know you. By thinking like your audience, you will go from bland to awesome in no time.

PUBLIC VERSES PRIVATE: A STEEL-CAGE MATCH

It is important for you to realize that public colleges evaluate applications differently than private colleges do, and this can affect your chance of being admitted.

In the movie *How I Got into College*, a 1989 comedy starring Lara Flynn Boyle that you must rent someday soon, Lara's dad asks her why she wants to go to a private college instead of the public college where all her sisters went. The dialogue goes something like this:

> LARA: *But Dad, I'm not like my sisters. I want to go to Ramsey College!*
> DAD: *Since Ramsey costs five times more, does Ramsey have a football team that's five times as cute? Is the education five times as good? Is the food at Ramsey five times . . .*

The point is that public schools are not necessarily better or worse than private schools, but the way publics evaluate applications is generally a bit different from the way privates do.

Public schools generally rely more on GPA and test scores than do private schools that often spend more time evaluating all parts of each student's application. This is not to say that public colleges and universities do not value essays, recommendations, and the rest. But because of the sheer number of applicants and the schools' sometimes reduced budgets for admissions, public schools must have a way of accepting or rejecting students immediately. This leaves only the students who are in the middle range of GPA/SAT/ACT scores for further evaluation.

An example is the University of California (UC) system. It has some strict requirements to determine eligibility including mandatory high school courses and choices, GPA, and SATs minimums. Since 2000, the UCs have made an effort to get away from these numbers and evaluate the whole student. But if you don't meet their initial criteria, even a fabulous essay won't stop you from automatically getting rejected. If you want to apply to a public school, make sure you find out the exact qualifications expected.

FLAGS . . . WE'RE NOT JUST TALKIN' FOOTBALL

What the heck is a flag? And why should you care? Ah, good question, grasshopper. A flag means that your application has fallen into a particular school's "special consideration" category.

This does not mean that you are automatically in.

This does not mean that your grades, SATs, essays, recommendations, and the rest don't matter. What it does mean can be illustrated by the following example.

Two students, James and Tamika, both apply to XYZ College. Both are from the same school and have generally the same profile: a 3.2 GPA, 1830 SAT, 1800 combined SAT II, decent essays, strong recommendations, somewhat involved resumes, applied for early decision. Now because everything is exactly the same between these two, they should both either get accepted, denied, or wait-listed. But wait, Tamika is a strong pianist. She has placed second in a national competition. She has sent tapes to XYZ's music department, and she has even corresponded with several professors about her interest in XYZ.

XYZ admissions has been notified by the music department that it is actively seeking musicians, specifically piano players of Tamika's ability, because XYZ has just opened a new music center. After evaluating Tamika's tape, the department puts in a good word on Tamika's behalf.

Tamika's application is now *flagged*. Between James and her, Tamika will now have a better chance of getting in if there is one spot left and XYZ has to decide between the two. Of course, she still has to meet the parameters XYZ uses to accept other students. If she had a 1.2 GPA and a 450 on her SATs, the piano wouldn't help her.

Later, as we discuss CSI, the issue of flags will come up again. Here are some general categories of flags used by admissions officers:

- Minorities

- Athletes

- Legacy students

- Artistic or musical talent

- International Students

- Special case (not used much anymore, but if your dad gave $1 billion to the school or is named George Bush, you're flagged).

Note that although geographical location and choice of major are not flags, they still may influence your chances. More on this in Chapter 4.

COOL AND REFRESHING: SPECIAL PROGRAMS FOR MUSIC, ART, DRAMA, AND LEARNING DISABILITIES

Are you tired of daily homework? Are you really tired of math? Does the thought of chemistry make you want to call up "Ralph" on the big white telephone? Well, for three easy payments of $10,000, you can go to a school that doesn't require any of these things! Yes, friend, we are talking about *special programs*. These include:

- art schools

- drama schools

- music schools

- schools with special programs for students with learning disabilities (Sorry, most of these schools still require academic work—you just get a lot of help!)

Please note: Info about LD programs can be found on page 44, so if you are interested in these programs, turn to that page.

Okay, how do you get in? Before I get to that, I want to make sure you're aware of a couple of things about choosing a special program over a traditional academic college or pre-professional college. Let me use an example of a past student. Tom went to a public high school in Utah. He did okay in most of his classes, pulling Bs and Cs. Now Tom was pretty good at reading and writing, but he missed tons of classes because he ditched school. However, Tom wouldn't go to the beach. No, not Tom. He would go home to work on art! From Claymation movies to six-foot-high watercolors, Tom told me that he wished he could spend all day long being creative. Not only that, but Tom happened to be pretty good at what he did.

When I presented Tom with the options of going to a good college with a strong art program, or to a school where he could primarily focus on art in different mediums, he asked me a good question: "Can I get a job if I go to an art school?" Well, no college guarantees you a job when you get out. But if Tom wanted to pursue art as a hobby but also go into politics, a more traditional school that offered political science and a great art program would be the way for him to go.

As it turned out, Tom wanted to try working in the movie business or possibly graphic design. For these goals, his eventual school, California Institute of the Arts, was perfectly matched to his needs.

Many people think going to a school like Juilliard is a waste of time because these schools don't prepare students for the real world. Well, if your real world centers on your art, whatever it is, and you can't imagine doing anything else, then those people who like to give advice as if they know what they are talking about are actually kind of dumb.

Just remember the following:

- You should have a strong desire to pursue your discipline. Going to a special program simply because you don't want to write any more papers isn't a good enough reason.

- You will need to have an art portfolio (or in the case of acting or music, prepared monologues or songs to audition). It will have to contain your best work because these schools are often very competitive.

- You will probably need a decent GPA and test scores. If you are an amazing jazz musician, your talent and passion will go a long way, but most programs still want evidence of good work in high school. In addition, not all special programs allow you to focus on only your discipline, but still require some academic work. Check each program for its requirements for admission and its requirements for graduation.

- You will most likely have to fill out an application, similar to those from more traditional schools, including essays and letters of recommendation. I have included information about different kinds of programs (pages 23–26), as well as a list of questions targeted to special programs (pages 72–74), so check out these sections for more info.

LEARNING DISABILITY PROGRAMS

Learning disabilities (LDs) are very real. From ADD to auditory and visual discrimination difficulties, hundreds of thousands of students find their academic work and many other parts of their lives are affected simply because they process information differently.

There is nothing to fear or feel bad about. If you have ADD or another LD, you may be ostracized, be made fun of, or more commonly, feel dumb or stupid. You might work ten times harder than everyone else, yet still do poorly in certain subjects, feel pressured on tests, and get hassled by your "friends" about getting extra time. It's no fun, is it?

Well, here's some good news. First, there's nothing wrong with you. Unfortunately, you are in an academic system that emphasizes lecture and memorization. You may rock at creative things, but you never get a chance to prove it because everyone seems to talk only about grades. You need to understand that not only can you do a lot to help your LD, but also that LD is just a stupid label.

The bottom line is, if you have an LD, you have an LD. Big deal. Remember, no matter what your challenges were in the past, you can do or be anything you want—*if you really want to*. Yes, it might take you longer to do certain things. Yes, you might need accommodations and tutoring to help you in academic areas. Remember, there's nothing wrong with getting help in order to become what you want. Isn't that better than having to struggle and be frustrated all the time? Additionally, I'll bet that you have talents that I could only dream of having—you just need the opportunity to showcase them.

In fact, over the last ten years or so, people have begun to wake up and develop programs for students with LDs so they not only can go to a top school, but can also do really well there.

On pages 27–28, I have included lists of schools with different levels of support for students with learning disabilities. Hopefully, you've looked at these lists and found some schools that, in addition to their support services, you also really like. If you haven't done this yet, I encourage you to start taking a look.

WHAT YOU NEED TO KNOW

So what do you need to know about getting into a school with special programs for students with LDs?

- You will probably need to fill out the regular application for admissions first.

- You should contact the office that deals with student disabilities and talk to someone really knowledgeable, like the director of the program. (Chapter 5, College Visits, includes a list of questions you may want to use when talking to this office.) While some schools require only medical documentation of your LD, others have supplemental applications and essays with their own deadlines. Therefore, be sure you ask.

- Most importantly, you must be your own best advocate. This applies whether or not you have an LD, but it is especially important for those with LDs. Don't be afraid to talk about the challenges you have faced. Make sure you convey your desire to attend a certain school in the application, in the essay, and in regular phone calls to the admissions office and to the office of student disabilities. You don't want to be a pest, but with so many thousands of students applying, you have **got to make yourself heard and not allow yourself to fall through the cracks.** Going the extra mile and being absolutely determined often work wonders.

- One question many students ask is how they should let a school know about their LD. Should they write an essay about it to explain their hardship? Well, if you went through absolute hell yet persevered despite your LD, and if you can discuss specific examples of how you developed learning strategies or what you specifically do to succeed academically, an essay might not be a bad idea. It will demonstrate to colleges that you are ready for the next level because of how you have learned to cope with your LD.

- Another way of letting schools know about what you have overcome is to have your counselor mention it in his or her summary. (Often called a "secondary school report," this summary is basically your counselor's recommendation of you and is required by most schools.) This allows colleges to know what difficulties you have had to face and to get an objective explanation for any low grades or test scores in your record.

Many admissions people would rather read your essay to find out other aspects about you. For example, you would stand out more if they knew you were a student interested in chemistry lab research who just happens to have a learning disability, rather than just another student with a learning disability. Some schools ask you to explain about hardships you have overcome or about any learning disabilities. Other schools give you a space to write down any other information you want them to know about. While you want schools to know about your profile, unless your situation is extraordinary, it's best to be brief in your explanations and use the opportunity to discuss other interesting parts of your life.

EARLY ACTION, EARLY DECISION, AND OTHER WACKINESS

"I heard that applying early helps your chances of getting in." True or false?

Time's up! The answer is: true *and* false. Let me explain. *Regular* decision refers to the normal application process that usually requires you to turn in applications around January 1, January 15, or February 1, depending on the school, and lets you know the decision sometime in April. Applying *Early* refers to the following list of application options that offer students certain benefits by getting everything submitted earlier.

EARLY DECISION

Early Decision (ED) means a student submits all his or her application materials, including a shortened financial aid form, to a certain school by early November. Application deadlines are usually November 1 or 15, but schools will often accept test scores from the November dates. The college then responds before Christmas.

The catch is that you have to sign a form that states you will attend that school if you get in early. Therefore, you've got to be sure you want to attend a school before you apply for early decision. You can apply only to one school for Early Decision.

A student can be:

- *Accepted*. You find out in December that you got in, and you also get your financial aid package early.

- *Deferred*. This is limbo land. You are not accepted or rejected. You are put back in with the students who are applying during regular decision, and you will have to wait until April to learn your fate. Note that at the most selective colleges, only about 10 percent of students who get deferred are later admitted. Consequently, it is important to follow the procedures discussed in "Appeals for Rejections and Wait Lists" (page 251), about how to keep a school informed of your progress while you work on increasing your grades, test scores, recommendations, activities, and so on.

- *Rejected*. This is self-explanatory. Again, see page 253 on appeals.

EARLY DECISION II

Early Decision II (ED II) Colleges that do not like losing the best students to other ED I schools have recently developed ED II to give them a second chance to apply early. For example, Vassar offers the choice of applying for Early Decision by November 15 (notifies in December), for ED II by January 1 (notifies in February), or for regular decision by January 1 (notifies in April).

Confused? Here's the simple scoop: Early Decision II is for students who are willing to commit to a school and who want to be notified early. (Note that the ED II application deadline is the same as that for regular decision, but notification is in February rather than April.)

Why would you want to apply for Early Decision II?

- You have applied for an Early Decision at another school, but have been deferred or rejected. Well, guess what? You get another chance for an early decision from schools that offer ED II.

- You want to apply early but still use the first part of your senior year to improve your grades, test scores, or both.

EARLY ACTION

Early Action (EA), is also referred to as Early Notification. With early action, you can apply early, like in ED, but you don't have to go to the school if you get in. Great, right? I agree, but over the years, schools figured out that they like ED better because they lock in their class and don't lose the best students to their competition. Thus, only a few schools offer EA—a few examples include Boston College, Georgetown, and Harvard.

EA can be tricky though. Some schools that offer ED allow you to also apply to schools that offer EA, while others do not. So, if you plan on applying for ED and EA at two different schools, you must find out if they allow this by looking online, asking your counselor, or using a source like *The Insider's Guide to the Colleges*.

Newsflash! Both Yale and Stanford have changed their Early Decision policy to something similar to Early Action, and a binding commitment to attend is not required. The only trick is that if you apply to either of these schools early, you still can't apply anywhere else early, unless you're applying for ED II.

ROLLING ADMISSIONS

Rolling admissions is an option used by many state colleges and some other selective schools—for example, University of Michigan and University of Arizona. These schools allow you to submit applications anytime after they open admissions (usually around November), and they respond to you in a month or two. The schools keep admitting students throughout the year *until the class is full*. There is no early commitment required if you get in. The key is to get your materials in early (if everything is ready and you are happy with your grades, tests, and so on) so that you have a better chance of getting accepted.

SHOULD I APPLY EARLY?

Many people believe that by applying early they will increase their chances of getting accepted because the acceptance rate is higher for this pool of students than for those who apply regular decision. Although this is generally true, you should realize that the students who apply early are usually quite strong in terms of GPA, test scores, and special considerations (flags). Therefore:

- *Only students who are toward the top of the range of a given school's GPA and SAT scores should think about applying early.* Even though acceptance rates are higher, so is the level of competition. For example, although you may not be considered a top prospect at Yale, you may be at the top, say, at Tulane. If Tulane were a college you really wanted to attend and were willing to commit to, applying early there would be a much better idea than applying early to Yale. This would also apply if your choice was between Harvard and Tulane; even though Harvard is EA and doesn't require you to commit, your decision to apply early would still benefit you more at Tulane.

- *Early applicants must be sure their grades and test scores are where they need to be.* Students often get deferred because schools want to wait and see how they do on their senior-year grades. Whether you should apply for early admission depends on where you fit in a school's profile of accepted students. If your stats would be at the top of the class of their recently admitted freshmen, you might apply early, even if you think there is room for improvement during senior year.

- *Early applicants should seek recommendations that give concrete examples of how they match up for that particular school, rather than just a general letter that will serve for all schools.*

- *Early applicants should definitely interview if they can.* If your early-decision school is truly your first choice, you'll want every opportunity to prove it to the admissions staff.

- *Consider your CSI strengths* (page 53). If, for example, one of your parents went to the University of Pennsylvania, which has shown a good deal of preference for legacy status, or if you were recruited for athletics, you might want to apply early even if your numbers are slightly below those of the top applicants.

Remember, you can also apply for Early Decision II at another school that you may have a better chance of getting into.

If you are totally confused about what to do, be sure to consult your high school counselor or call a college's admissions department and ask questions.

CHAPTER FOUR
REFINING YOUR LIST OF SCHOOLS

COLLEGE PROFILE EXTRAVAGANZA

Now that you have an initial list of schools and know how the admissions process works, it's time to figure out if a school belongs on your final list. Here are the steps I suggest.

1. Use the College Profile Extravaganza Form on page 50 to record the name, website, email address, and telephone number of each school on your initial list. Most schools can be found at www.thenameoftheschool.edu (for example, Vassar's website is www.vassar.edu). (Please make copies of the blank form or print it from the Resource CD—you'll need a separate sheet for each school.)

2. Ask each school to send you a viewbook. (A viewbook is a color catalog that describes the school and often contains the application.) Just send the school an email requesting more information, or call the admissions office directly. (A sample email can be found on the Resource CD.)

3. Gather data for each of the College Profile Extravaganza Forms by looking at a school's website, reading a school's viewbook, talking to your counselor, copying information from the college summaries on the Resource CD or from a book like *The Insider's Guide to the Colleges*, calling the admissions office, or looking up a school at www.collegeboard.com. You may have to use multiple sources, but remember that you are researching your potential home for the next four years, so it's wise to take time to read up on each school. The more you research your schools, the more reasons you will find to keep a school on your list or ditch it. By the way, check out page 56 to see the types of things you can get from a school's website.

Once you have gathered the data on your schools, you will be able to evaluate each school and put them into one of the following categories:

- Reaches: Schools you have an outside chance of getting into.

- Likelies: Schools you think you have a 50/50 chance of getting into.

- Safeties: Schools you know you will get into.

This will be your list on which the rest of this book will concentrate.

COLLEGE PROFILE EXTRAVAGANZA FORM

SCHOOL NAME _____

CITY/SETTING (EXAMPLE: URBAN) _____

NO. UNDERGRADS / TOTAL NO. STUDENTS _____

IS SAT I OR ACT REQUIRED? _____

HOW MANY (IF ANY) SAT II SUBJECT TESTS ARE NEEDED? _____

AVERAGE SAT/ACT RANGE _____

AVERAGE GPA _____

PERCENT ADMITTED FROM YOUR STATE _____

OVERALL ACCEPTANCE RATE _____

IS EARLY DECISION (ED) OR EARLY ACTION (EA) OR ROLLING (R) OFFERED? _____

ED/EA/R DEADLINE _____

ED/EA NOTIFICATION DATE _____

REGULAR ADMISSION DEADLINE _____

DO THEY ACCEPT THE COMMON APP? _____

PERSONAL NOTES (EXAMPLES: SPECIAL PROGRAMS, LD PROGRAM, SPECIFIC ACADEMIC PROGRAMS). SEE NEXT PAGE FOR ADDITIONAL QUESTIONS.

_____

_____

_____

_____

MAILING ADDRESS _____

TELEPHONE NUMBER _____

WEBSITE _____

EMAIL ADDRESS _____

WHAT ARE THE SCHOOL'S MOST POPULAR MAJORS? (INCLUDE PERCENTAGES IF POSSIBLE.)

_____

_____

WHAT ARE THE SCHOOL'S LEAST POPULAR MAJORS? (INCLUDE PERCENTAGES IF POSSIBLE.)

_____

_____

WHAT KINDS OF STUDY ABROAD PROGRAMS DOES THE SCHOOL HAVE?

_____

_____

WHAT KINDS OF SPORTS DOES THE SCHOOL OFFER?

- Varsity (Division I, II, or III)
- Club sports (competes against other schools, but teams are usually voluntary)
- Intramural sports (informal competition between dorms or among teams from within the school)

_____

_____

WHAT OUTSIDE ACTIVITIES DOES THE SCHOOL OFFER THAT YOU MAY BE INTERESTED IN?

Art, drama, music? Community service, student government, newspaper, a magazine, a radio station? Others?

_____

_____

WHAT ARE THE ESSAY QUESTIONS ON THE APPLICATION?

_____

_____

ANY MORE STATS YOU THINK ARE IMPORTANT

_____

_____

PERCENTAGE OF STUDENTS ACCEPTED FROM YOUR ETHNIC GROUP _____

PERCENTAGE OF LEGACY STUDENTS ACCEPTED _____

YOUR REVISED LIST OF SCHOOLS

Write down the names of the schools that still interest you, placing each into one of the three categories.

REACHES: SCHOOLS YOU HAVE AN OUTSIDE CHANCE OF GETTING INTO.

_____

_____

_____

LIKELIES: SCHOOLS YOU SHOULD GET INTO.

_____

_____

_____

SAFETIES: SCHOOLS YOU KNOW YOU'LL GET INTO.

_____

_____

_____

NOW WRITE DOWN THE NAMES OF ANY SCHOOLS YOU ARE STILL CONSIDERING OR NEED TO GATHER MORE INFORMATION ON.

_____

_____

_____

_____

_____

_____

_____

_____

CSI (CHARTING YOUR STRENGTHS AS AN INDIVIDUAL)

Remember way back on page 21 when I briefly introduced CSI? Well, now let's look at CSI in depth.

Every applicant has certain experiences or talents that make him or her unique. You may not be president of the math club, student council, honors society, ski team, debate club, or international federation of mimes. But odds are that your profile will match up with one particular school's preferences better than with another's. By doing a little research and listing your advantages, you can better determine where you will get accepted and where you best fit in.

CSI is not meant to make you compare yourself with other students. It is simply a way of identifying whether your interests match up with the schools that are on your list. But what if you're undecided about your major, aren't a legacy, and have only a few extracurriculars? That's okay. Sometimes a student's CSI shows little difference between the schools he wants to go to. Other times, a student realizes that his choices may include too many reaches or too many safeties, and he then has to add or subtract schools.

You should know one thing: *academics (the quality of your grades and the classes you took) is, by far, the most important factor admissions officers use to determine whether to admit you.* If you fall outside a school's range of GPA and SAT/ACT scores, your chances of getting in will be lower than they will be at a school where you *do* fall between the 25th and 75th percentile. Of course, there is a chance that your essays, recommendations, accomplishments, and special categories may help offset your numbers. Remember, there is a mix of students of differing abilities and interests at every school. The institutions that are stingiest about the numbers are typically the ones with the lowest acceptance rates (the schools ranked 3 or 4 on pages 16–20). Schools classified 1 or 2 generally have more flexibility in who they will accept.

WHY DO CSI?

Admissions officers want to put together an incoming class of many different kinds of students. Therefore, they use various criteria or filters to take the pile of applicants and break it into smaller categories.

Let's say there are 18,000 applicants for a class of 1,900. Of these 18,000 prospective students, there are 5,000 with perfect GPAs and 1500 SATs. Well, admissions people want more than just students with perfect numbers, and so they use additional criteria to pick their incoming class.

Essays, recommendations, and extracurricular activities are all tools to identify the unique attributes of individual applicants. However, there are so many students applying that admissions offices generally use different categories to identify qualified students. Notice I said "qualified." Just because you fit into one of these categories does not mean you don't have to meet academic standards. In fact, the majority of incoming students are judged primarily on academics, SATs, and the rest of the usual application. However, to make sure they create balanced student populations, admissions offices can also use the following categories:

- **Minorities**   Most people think minorities are all groups other than whites. However, most schools define minorities to include African Americans, Hispanics, Native Americans, or disadvantaged Asians and whites (also see the underdog factor below). Note that even though it is important to many schools to admit a diverse class, students still have to compete based on their academic achievement.

- **Athletes**   To fit into this category, you generally have to be recruited by a school coach for a specific sports team. While Division I schools in the NCAA usually offer scholarships to attract athletes, other schools—including Ivy League schools—may still recruit athletes; they just don't offer scholarships to entice students to play. Therefore, even at non Division I schools, contacting the coaches may get you some extra consideration.

  For the most part, athletes must meet academic standards. The more selective the school, the more this is generally true.

- **Legacy Students**   You fit into the legacy category at a certain school if one of your parents, grandparents, or relatives went to that school, if you have a brother or sister currently attending, or if your parents or relatives work at the school. Be careful, however, because each school has different rules about who qualifies as a legacy. For example, some schools give you legacy status only if your parents or siblings went there, so be sure to check the rules of your chosen schools before assuming you have legacy status.

  Legacy students generally have a two to three times better chance of admission than do nonlegacy students. Nevertheless, each flagged student will still be competing against other legacy students based on academic achievement.

- **Students with artistic, musical, or other talents** (see page 42, Special Programs)   If you have a special talent or interest that matches a specific or underrepresented program, and if your experiences and record back it up, you may want to emphasize it. For the fine arts or performing arts, you may have to fill out a separate form in addition to the application and submit materials such as photographic slides, videocassettes, or CDs.

  For example, if you are an award-winning violinist and a school you are applying to has a music program that is looking for talent like yours, you will be flagged for special consideration. Or let's say you are fluent in four languages. Then you should get in touch with a school's language department to let them know you are interested in their programs. Of course, you will still need good academic qualifications to compete with the other students.

- **International students**   If you are applying from another country or if you are an American student who has had substantial experience abroad (for example, you have attended an international school), you can get extra consideration. Be sure to write about your international experience in the application and essay.

- **Special cases** Few students fit in the special-case category. Even if your dad donates a lot of money to a college, odds are that you still won't be put in this category. However, if you are the daughter of the president, or you're a movie star, or your grandparents have donated entire wings of buildings, then you might get some extra consideration.

The following factors, while not formal flags, may also help you get into a certain school.

- **State you are applying from** Schools have applicants from many different parts of the country. If you live in an underrepresented area, your chance of getting in goes up, compared to that of someone who lives in a big state that sends a lot of students.

- **Your academic interest** Your choice of major can play a role in whether a college accepts you. The key here is that you shouldn't pick a strange major, like advanced forestry, hoping to change it once you are in. The reason students usually get consideration is that their backgrounds support their desire to study something less popular than the school's most sought-after programs.

- **Underdog factor** You are considered an underdog if you come from an underprivileged background or have overcome huge obstacles. If you had no access to SAT tutoring, college counseling, learning disability resources, and so on, but still succeeded, *or* if you had to persevere to overcome big personal blocks, admissions people give you a bit more consideration. They believe that even if your scores are a bit low, you have a high likelihood of continuing to push yourself and to excel once in college.

- **Ability to pay tuition** Although many schools say their admissions are "need blind"—that is, students' ability to pay has no bearing on whether they get in—some schools can't afford to maintain this policy. In order to offer a quality education, they need to have students who can pay tuition without substantial grants from the school. Therefore, they will give special consideration to those who need little or no financial aid. Schools state their policy outright, and such policies can be found in guidebooks like *The Fiske Guide to Colleges*.

    Despite what you've just read, *do not let a lack of finances stop you from applying to any school you are interested in*. You should apply to several schools and compare financial aid packages to see what you are eligible for. (You can do a lot to raise money for tuition. This will be covered in detail in Chapter 16, Financial Aid.)

Note about state schools. There are a couple of things to know about applying to state schools:

- Because state schools are funded by state funds, they have a charter to admit a certain number of students from "in state." As a result, it is sometimes much harder to get accepted to a state school if you don't live in that state.

- State schools are often subject to political battles, and so they often use GPA and test scores to select students, rather than the categories discussed here.

HOW DOES CSI WORK?

Now let's start learning how to profile a school. Remember, you can get data about schools from their websites, from their viewbooks, or from your counselor.

This information can be very helpful in determining the criteria used by individual schools. For example (these aren't actual numbers), Harvard may accept 25 percent of its class as legacy students, while Yale may accept 35 percent. This means you would have a better chance of going to Yale if one of your parents is an alumnus. While Montana State may enroll 90 percent from Montana, Vanderbilt may only enroll 5 percent, so if you are from Montana, you may have a better chance at Vanderbilt because your state is underrepresented and there will be less competition from your state.

Below is an example from the University of Pennsylvania of what type of information you can pull off a school's website.

INCOMING STUDENT PROFILE: CLASS OF 2009
Taken from the University of Pennsylvania Website

Total applicants	18,824
Total admitted	3,916
Total admit rate	**20.8%**

Early decision applicants	3,420
Total admitted in Dec.	1,169
Early decision admit rate	**34.2%**

Sons and daughters of alumni applicants	1,182
Total admitted	448
Total alumni (legacy) admit rate	**38%**

Freshman Entering	
Male	49.2%
Female	50.8%

Number of high schools in enrolled group	**1,490**
Public	52%
Private	43%
Parochial	5%
Home School	‹1%

GEOGRAPHIC DIVERSITY

States represented   50

Number of enrolled students from different states
(All 50 states were listed on website)

California	204
Oregon	22
Montana	4
North Dakota	1
Texas	65
Florida	84
Alabama	10
Pennsylvania	452
New York	304
Maryland	103
International	288

ETHNIC DIVERSITY

Black	8%
Hispanic	7%
Asian	20%
American Indian	‹1%
Total	35%

ACADEMIC ACHIEVEMENT

(Note 11,567 applicants attended a secondary school that did not provide rank in class.)

Rank	Percent Accepted
Valedictorian	46%
Salutatorian	35%
Other top five percent of class	23%
Second five percent of class	9%
Total top decile (10%) of class	25%
Second decile (10–20%) of class	7%
No rank	21%

DISTRIBUTION OF SAT I SCORES

(17,928 submitted SAT I: reasoning test scores; 428 applicants submitted only ACT)

VERBAL		MATH	
Score	*Percent Admitted*	*Score*	*Percent Admitted*
750–800	30%	750–800	26%
700–740	24%	700–740	22%
650–690	20%	650–690	18%
600–640	17%	600–640	17%
550–590	10%	550–590	10%
500–540	6%	500–540	6%
‹ 500	2%	‹ 500	0%

TESTING MEANS FOR MIDDLE 50% OF ACCEPTED STUDENTS (25TH–75TH PERCENTILES)

SAT I: Verbal	660–760
SAT I: Math	680–780
ACT Composite	30–34

MOST POPULAR MAJORS

1.	Social Sciences	27%
2.	Business/Marketing	21%
3.	Engineering	9%
4.	Biology	6%
5.	Health Professions	6%

FINANCIAL AID

Penn guarantees to meet all demonstrated need and is need-blind in admissions.

- Almost 60% of Penn undergraduates receive some form of financial assistance.

- Nearly 40% of Penn undergraduates are awarded need-based grant aid.

- Approximately 78% of the freshmen who applied for financial aid for the 2004–2005 academic year received a need-based award.

- The average financial aid for incoming aided freshmen in 2004 was $26,300 (combination of grant, loan, and part-time job).

- For 2004–2005, Penn is committing over $70 million of its resources for grant aid to undergraduate students.

These numbers paint a picture that you can match up to your profile and to other schools to see where you might have some advantages. Here are some things you can use from the statistics of incoming freshman.

- Penn only accepted 20.8 percent of its total applicants. However, legacy students are admitted at 38 percent. (Again, each school determines this status differently.)

- Look up your state. Although Penn doesn't necessarily give any preference to specific geographical areas, you can see that bigger states (CA, Florida) and East Coast states (PA, NY) send more students to Penn than do smaller states from the South or the Midwest. This generally means that a lot less people from the South and Midwest submit applications. Consequently, if you live in one of these areas, you may stand out (and face less competition) if a particular college wants to make sure the entire country is represented.

- Penn has a decent percentage of minority students, so depending on your background, you may receive extra consideration.

- Take a look at their "numbers." By comparing your class rank (if your high school computes it), you can roughly determine your chance of getting accepted. (Although as I discuss throughout the book, there are many other factors used besides the numbers, so don't freak out!). In addition, you will see that while the "testing means" for the SAT fall somewhere in the high 600s–low 700s (30–34 for ACT), you might also notice that Penn does accept students with SAT scores in the 500s and 600s.

- Check out the majors. Social sciences, business/marketing, engineering, biology, and health professions are among the most popular. Therefore, if you had a real interest in an area that was not as popular, you'd want to market your strengths and your interests to help you stand out.

- Penn has a need-blind admissions policy, meaning your ability to pay will have no bearing on your acceptance. You will also notice that they award a substantial amount of financial aid and that they guarantee to meet all demonstrated need for accepted students.

CASE STUDY: JENNI

The following case study shows how you can use a college's profile to help you choose schools where you might have an advantage.

Jenni had the following profile:

STRENGTHS

- top 10 percent of the class in a public high school in Arizona

- 2000 SAT

- student body secretary

- captain of the soccer team

- mother graduated from University of Southern California (USC)

COLLEGES SHE WAS INTERESTED IN

Oberlin College, Stanford University, USC, and Williams College

At Oberlin, she had the following advantages: strong academic profile in relation to the other applicants; she was applying from outside the Midwest; a soccer coach at Oberlin's Division III program was very interested in her athletic abilities.

Advantages: 3

At Stanford, she didn't have as many advantages: her academic profile put her in the middle of the applicant pool; she had no advantage with soccer because Stanford has one of the top programs in the country; her home state of Arizona did not give her much of an advantage because three other girls in her school were applying to Stanford.

Advantages: 0

At USC, she had the following advantages: strong academic profile; the legacy of her mom having gone there; a soccer team that showed some interest in her abilities.

Advantages: 3

At Williams, she had some advantages: while her grades put only her in the middle of the applicant pool, Williams gives preference to student athletes who can make a difference on its Division III teams; she was applying from Arizona.

Advantages: 2

OUTCOME

Jenni applied to all four schools. She was accepted by Oberlin and USC, wait-listed at Williams, and rejected by Stanford.

NOW IT'S YOUR TURN

YOUR STRENGTHS

Once you have the college profiles spread in front of you, list the colleges and your strengths on the next page to see how they match up. You may have several matches at some schools, or none at all for others.

Next, you can review your college list from page 52 to see if you need to change any of your reaches, likelies, and safeties or want to add more schools.

EXAMPLE:

COLLEGES I AM INTERESTED IN
Georgetown, Yale, Reed, Stanford, UCSD

MY STRENGTHS
Student government experience, legacy (parents went to Georgetown), geography (I live in Iowa), minority (I am African American), good at foreign languages (looking for programs that have a small percentage of students in language programs), captain of model UN/debate team

SCHOOL	ADVANTAGES	CLASSIFICATION
Stanford	minority, foreign languages	Reach, but possible
Georgetown	student government, legacy, minority, model UN/debate, geography	Also reach but more likely because of advantages

Because this is just an example, I included only two schools rather than all five listed.

MATCHING YOUR STRENGTHS TO COLLEGES

COLLEGES I AM INTERESTED IN

_____

_____

MY STRENGTHS

_____

_____

_____

SCHOOLS	ADVANTAGES	CLASSIFICATION
_____	_____	_____
_____	_____	_____
_____	_____	_____
_____	_____	_____
_____	_____	_____

GETTING APPLICATIONS, INCLUDING THE COMMON APPLICATION

There are a number of options for the format of your application: paper versions, the common application, or online.

NOTE: No matter what method you choose, be sure to print out your applications and make copies of everything.

PAPER APPLICATIONS.

Paper applications are the ones mailed to you from the school, the ones you pick up from an admissions office, or the ones you download from the Internet. You can either fill these out by hand or type them up by cutting and pasting from your computer. Either way, they must be readable. Using the actual paper application is my personal favorite for two reasons:

1. You can show the most individuality.

2. There's no chance of a computer snafu, so you absolutely know they have all your stuff, especially when you mail it using a Certificate of Mailing.

COMMON APPLICATION.

The "Common App" is one single application that is accepted by over two hundred colleges. You go to www.commonapp.org (or get a copy from your counselor), type in all your information once, print it, and send it to schools that accept it. You can submit it online to some schools, but I prefer printing it out, making copies, and sending in a paper version to each school.

Note that many schools require their own Common App Supplement (see list on pages 31–36). Also see Chapter 7 for detailed instructions on how to fill out the Common App.

ONLINE.

To apply online, simply go to a school's website, type in the requested information, and pay the application fee with a credit card. More and more colleges and universities are encouraging students to apply online, but most of them still allow you to use a paper application. While filing online can be convenient and definitely neater than doing everything by hand, just make sure that you fill out the *entire* application. Many forms have multiple parts to fill out, and they often require you to print out recommendation forms that you have to physically mail in.

No matter how you apply, once you've finished all the steps, make sure to get a confirmation email that states your application has been received and is complete. If you don't receive a confirmation, call the school to make absolutely sure.

FURTHER RESEARCH AND RESOURCES

There is an absolute ton of information out there about schools, online applications, scholarships, and test preparation. What should you use?

Don't worry! Danny's here for ya. My goal is to simplify the whole process. Now, having said that, I suggest you use the following resources:

1. This book in its entirety. (My website, www.youcangetin.com, also has resources that support this book.)

2. School websites. From here you can request viewbooks and applications, as discussed. (A large list of school websites is included on the Resource CD.)

3. The test prep resources I recommend (pages 83–85).

Just using these three resources will be enough for you to rock the admissions world. However, the following lists present some other good resources and time-saving web applications, and you might want to check them out.

FINANCIAL AID AND SCHOLARSHIPS

1. *How to Go to College Almost for Free* by Ben Kaplan is a good overall book for finding scholarships and maximizing your chances for financial aid.

2. www.finaid.org is a great place to learn about everything related to financial aid.

3. www.fastweb.com is a big database of scholarships that you can search through.

See Chapter 16 for more info.

MORE INFO ABOUT COLLEGES

1. *The Fiske Guide to Colleges* and *The Insider's Guide to the Colleges* offer more detailed college profiles than those found on the Resource CD. If you can't find a certain school in these books, consult *The College Board College Handbook*, which includes every school in the country. However, it is a bit overwhelming.

2. *The K&W Guide to Colleges for the Learning Disabled* by Marybeth Kravets and Imy F. Wax.

3. *Guide to Performing Arts Programs* by Carole J. Everett and Muriel Topaz.

4. *Arco 100 Colleges Where Average Students Can Excel* by Joe Anne Adler.

INTERNET RESOURCES

1. College Board, www.collegeboard.com. Go to this website to register for the SAT and SAT IIs and to make sure that all your schools are receiving your scores. This site also

includes information on how to get extra time on tests for students with learning disabilities, not to mention a boatload of info on colleges, online applications, and a program that will help you determine your financial aid eligibility. (The learning disability information can also be found on the Resource CD.) *Note:* Using the College Board site, you can request and fill out the CSS PROFILE, a financial aid form required by certain private universities (see Chapter 17).

2. ACT, www.act.org. The ACT is a national college admissions exam. This website is the place to register for—and find out about—the ACT. It also has procedures for getting extra test time for students with learning disabilities. (This information can also be found on the Resource CD.)

3. Common Application, www.commonapp.org. Print out the Common App, or use this website to type in all your info and then print it out. I'll walk you through filling out this application in Chapter 7.

5. Federal Financial Aid Form, www.fafsa.ed.gov. This is the place to get and fill out FAFSA, the form for applying for free federal aid. I discuss it more in Chapter 16.

6. Art Schools, www.artschools.com. This site offers a good beginning list of two- and four-year art schools.

THE FINAL RESOURCE

1. Your school counselor. You may be surprised just how much your school counselor can help you, even if you have never spoken more than two words to him or her. Try to make an appointment, and ask him or her the questions you have. Counselors have to fill out a form about you for each school, so it's a good idea to get to know them. True, some counselors are biased, may not have a lot of time for you, and/or may give you bad advice. But most of the counselors I know generally know their stuff, so go find out.

CHAPTER FIVE
COLLEGE VISITS

HOW TO DITCH YOUR PARENTS AND REALLY LEARN ABOUT A SCHOOL

Note: Some students can visit colleges before they apply, while others will have to wait until after they have been accepted. Either way, this chapter still applies to you. If you can't afford to visit schools, know that once you *are* accepted, schools can arrange for you to visit for free. They don't want to lose you, so contact the admissions office and ask. There are many students in this position every year.

Most students simply visit a college, take the tour, and get a vibe if they like the school or not. Although it is important to trust that vibe—that gut instinct—you have to make sure you are really learning about the campus to get an accurate picture. So if you haven't already visited schools, or if you saw them in the summer when there were no students attending, you may want to follow these guidelines:

- **Ditch your parents.** That's right, tell them you want some time to yourself and that you'll meet up with them later. Take this time to go where the tours don't go—the dorms, the student union (where the stores and the food usually are), and the classes (sit in on one—there's no rule against it, and a professor might enjoy a prospective student, so ask). Most importantly, don't be afraid to talk to the students. I have found that most college students want to brag about their school to a prospective freshman and will often show you around, take you to class, take you to a party, and give you the real dirt on the place. In fact, by calling a school before you visit, you may have the opportunity to stay overnight with a current student.

- **Stop by the admissions office and say howdy.** Even better, call first and tell them you are coming. It's much easier for admissions officers to say yes to a face they have met than to a bunch of papers. Even if the office tells you there are no interviews, or the officers are busy and will not be able to meet you, or you haven't called and so find yourself staring at a student volunteer, make the best of it by doing the following:

- *Know your stuff.* If you are interested in any specific programs or want some admissions numbers for CSI, go ahead and ask. If nothing else, you will come away with more than when you went in.

- *If you don't have an appointment with an admissions officer, ask to introduce yourself to the director.* Yeah, the director, that person whose name you should have pulled off the school's website. Say that you would just like a few seconds to introduce yourself. This is not a horrendous request. After all, the director's job is to get to know prospective students, right? If you have to come back later, do so. You may just get a handshake and a hello, or the director may invite you into the office to get to know you better. You, of course, should look decent—not dressed up, but not in old jeans and a smelly sweatshirt either). Be sure to have questions ready for the director. What questions? Why, the huge list of questions that starts on page 70.

On pages 68 and 69 there is a form on which to log your thoughts when visiting a school. The idea is to record your impressions so that your memories of schools don't all run together. (Example: Was that hot swimmer I met at Yale or Cal State San Bernardino?)

THE PLAN O' ATTACK

Some of you will get to visit schools all over the country, others will just drive around your local area, and still others will get to look only at the viewbooks and the Internet.

If you cannot visit colleges until after you are accepted, make sure you read up on them by consulting such sources as the school's website, the school's viewbook, and books like *The Insider's Guide to the Colleges*. Talk to your counselor about the schools. Meet with on-campus representatives, and ask them questions from the list that starts on page 70. Try to get local interviews. The more you learn about the schools, the more you can make an informed decision about which one to attend.

One option for students who cannot travel is to check out schools in their local area. Even if they are not schools you are interested in, checking out different kinds of institutions will help you get a feel for what is out there. For example, if you live in Colorado, you could visit the University of Colorado at Boulder, a large public university, and then bust on over to the University of Denver, a smaller private school. Remember, each school has its own personality, so don't condemn all small schools just because you didn't like one with the ugly, weird students.

Either way, *make a plan*. If you're going to visit Aunt Mary in Connecticut, make a list of all of the colleges in the area and get out a map to see where they are located. Then during your time in Connecticut, arrange to visit the schools that interest you.

Determine how much time you want to spend at a given school. You might want to hang just a few hours at one, while you might want to stay overnight in a dorm at another.

Now, to get you started on this plan, use the Plan of Attack Worksheet on page 67. I have also included copies of the Plan of Attack Worksheet on the Resource CD. You can use a different sheet for each geographic location—one sheet for all the schools in the West, one for the East, one for the South, and so on.

Then use the Tell Me Why You Love Me Profile on page 68–69 to keep track of your impressions of the school along with any other information about academics, athletics, and student life.

SAMPLE PLAN OF ATTACK WORKSHEET

SCHOOL	LOCATION	CAN I GET AN INTERVIEW AT THE SCHOOL?	AMOUNT OF TIME I WANT TO SPEND THERE	WHEN CAN I GO?
EXAMPLE:				
Tufts	Medford, MA	No	Stay overnight	We could go over winter break to New England and see Tufts, Boston College, Northeastern, and Babson College, in 2–3 days and arrange to stay over at two schools.

TELL ME WHY YOU LOVE ME PROFILE

COLLEGE OR UNIVERSITY:

_____

INTERVIEW: YES OR NO? IF YES, WITH WHOM?

_____

ACADEMICS
- How do the students approach academics?
- How much studying is there?
- How competitive is it?
- How many general education requirements do you have to take your first two years?
- Does it have majors you are interested in?
- What do the students think about the professors?

_____

_____

_____

_____

_____

_____

STUDENTS
- What do you think of the students?
- Are they the kind of people you can see yourself hanging out with?
- How diverse are they?

_____

_____

_____

_____

_____

_____

OTHER IMPORTANT STUFF

- What are the dorms like?
- Do most students live on or off campus?
- How's the food? Where do students hang?
- What do they do for fun?
- What kind of computer facilities are available?
- Will it be easy to meet people? How are the athletics and facilities?

_____

_____

_____

_____

_____

_____

_____

_____

_____

YOUR GRADE

- What did you like most?
- What did you like least?
- Grade the school on a scale from A to F, with A being "I'd sell my kidney to go" and F being "I'd rather stay in high school than go."

_____

_____

_____

_____

_____

_____

_____

_____

_____

OH, THOSE QUESTIONS!

In the following pages you'll find some possible questions to keep in mind and, for gosh sakes, ask. Now, realize that I don't think you should walk around campus with this list in your hand saying, "Excuse me, but I seem to have a few questions left on my list . . . could I have a few minutes of your time . . . ." I wouldn't want you looking too dorky. But do look these over, pick out some you like, and keep them in the back of your mind. When you go to an admissions office, take the list to refer to or take a handwritten version of your questions. Whatever you do, do not be afraid to ask questions. Most people are happy to talk about their school and will even take you around, so ask! You'll note that some of these questions are more formal and are better geared toward adults rather than students, while others are more "hangin' 'round the dorm" questions.

Note: For specific financial aid questions, see Chapter 16. Questions to ask about learning disability programs and art schools can be found at the end of this general list.

ACADEMICS

- What are the strongest programs? What are the weakest? What other opportunities exist for unique academic experiences—study abroad, writing programs, research projects, etc.?

- What are the most popular majors? What are the least popular majors?

- How big are the typical freshman classes? How about classes you'd take as a junior or senior?

- Are there any new programs they are trying to develop?

- Do they have an honors program?

- Do they have "dead week" or "reading days" before finals?

- How many lecture courses will you have to take?

- How available are the professors? (Ask students this one.) How many courses are taught by teaching assistants (TAs)? How good are the TAs?

- Is there a standard structure to class format (that is, do they typically have a midterm and a final)? How long are major tests? 2 hours? 3 hours? Is the grading system the same for all classes?

- Can you drop a class? How long after the start of the term do you have before you can drop? Do they offer classes Pass/No Credit or Credit/No Credit?

- What kind of credit will you get for your Advanced Placement tests? Will they give credit for 3s and 4s?

- What kind of advising program do they have? Will you have an academic adviser all four years?

- Is tutoring available?

- Is there a career counseling and placement center? What services do they offer?

- What makes the school stand out compared to the competition?

- What do the admissions people value most when accepting students?

SOCIAL

- Do most students live on or off campus? Do you have to live on campus your first year? Is housing on campus guaranteed for four years? Do you get to pick your dorm? Do you get to choose your roommate?

- What do the students think about their housing? Are there better dorms or houses than others? Do the dorms have resident assistants (RAs, or upper-class students that oversee things)? Do they have all-freshmen dorms? Four-class dorms? Which do students think are better? Are the dorms coed? Is it by room (men and women live on the same floor)? Is it by floor (men's floor/women's floor)? Are some dorms quieter than others? Are there "theme" dorms?

- How big are sororities and fraternities? Do they have their own housing? Can you rush (try out) your freshman year?

- Do you need to live on campus to be social? Where do students hang out?

- What do students do for fun at night? On the weekends? What cool things does the school offer—concerts, plays, speakers, mud volleyball, and so on?

- How safe is the school? Is crime a concern? Is there campus security? How good is it? Does it provide safe rides home?

- How political is the school? Is it more liberal or conservative? Do students protest?

- Is there alcohol or drug abuse? What is the school's policy on alcohol and drugs? (It'd be interesting to ask both the students and the admissions people this one and see if the answers are the same.)

- Do students date much? Are there surrounding schools where students hang out?

- How diverse are the students in terms of ethnicity? What opportunities exist for different groups? What percentage of students is Hispanic? White? African American? Native American? Asian? International?

- What is the makeup of the student body in terms of geographic origin? How diverse are the students' academic interests? How many students go on to graduate school?

- Are there advantages to the school's size? Disadvantages?

- Is there much political activism? Is there pressure to conform, or can you do your own thing?

- Can you get on-campus jobs if you don't have financial aid?

- What do students like most about the school? What do they like least?

Note: You might ask if the school has additional info and statistics available other than what is on the web or in their viewbook. Sometimes they have longer catalogues available in the admissions office, along with smaller pamphlets and brochures describing specific clubs and programs.

FACILITIES

- How big are the libraries? Do they have libraries that specialize in different subjects? Do they have librarians who can help you? How easy is it to find information? At which libraries do students like to study?

- What are the athletic facilities like?

- What kind of athletic facilities do they have for students who are not varsity athletes?

- How many students have cars on campus? Is it a good idea to bring one? How's the parking situation?

- Is there a student health-care facility? How good is it?

- How is the town surrounding the school? Are stores open late?

- Is there a campus theater? A church? Quiet places to study? A computer lab?

- How wired is the campus? Can you get online easily? Do they have a T1 line or better? Will you need to have your own computer?

- How's the food? What kind of meal plans do they have? How good is the student union (central meeting place for students)? Where's the best pizza place, and how late do they deliver?

QUESTIONS ABOUT FINE ARTS PROGRAMS

Note: Be sure to consult Chapter 16, Financial Aid, for questions you should ask about a school's aid policies. You should also ask about scholarships available through the school and outside scholarships they may recommend, given your individual talent.

- What disciplines and mediums do they offer? Do they specialize in a specific area— say, painting, computer design, or fashion?

- What are the requirements for graduation? Will you have to take certain academic courses in addition to art? Do you have to take classes across art mediums, or can you specialize right away? Do they emphasize classical training, or can you do more experimental work? Do they offer opportunities to study abroad?

- If you major in something like computer graphics, can you also study areas like animation, sculpting, or painting? What opportunities exist for working on independent projects? Do the professors act as mentors for the students?

- What kind of job placement and/or internship assistance does the school provide?

- Will you have an opportunity to showcase your work? What do most of the students do after graduation? Does the school offer graduate programs? If so, what would you have to do to continue your education?

- What are the requirements for admission? Do they want a portfolio? What specifically are they looking for when they evaluate a portfolio? Should your work be submitted on slides? Do they want an artist's statement commenting on the work? Are GPA and test scores part of the admissions process? If so, what is their relative importance compared to the portfolio? If the school requires an essay as part of the application, what are they looking for? Does the school offer an interview?

QUESTIONS ABOUT PERFORMING ARTS PROGRAMS

Note: Be sure to consult Chapter 16, Financial Aid, for questions you should ask about a school's aid policies. You should also ask about scholarships available through the school and outside scholarships they may recommend, given your individual talent.

- What are the requirements for graduation? Will you have to take certain academic courses in addition to dance, music, or drama? Do you have to take classes across disciplines, or can you specialize right away? Do they emphasize classical training, or can you do more experimental work? Do they offer opportunities to direct, choreograph, or conduct? What professional organizations do they cooperate with? Do they offer opportunities to study abroad?

- What opportunities exist for working on independent projects? Do the professors act as mentors for students?

- What kind of job placement and/or internship assistance does the school provide?

- Will you have an opportunity to showcase your work? What do most of the students do after graduation? Does the school offer graduate programs? If so, what would you have to do to continue your education?

- What are the requirements for admission? Will you have to audition? What specifically are they looking for when they evaluate an audition? Are GPA and test scores part of the admissions process? If so, what is their relative importance compared to the audition? If the school requires an essay as part of the application, what are they looking for? Does the school offer an interview?

QUESTIONS ABOUT LEARNING DISABILITY PROGRAMS

- What services does the school provide for students with learning disabilities? Are there professionals on staff who are familiar with different kinds of disabilities? For example, some schools just have available tutors, while other schools have tutors who are coached in techniques to help students with learning issues such as ADD, auditory discrimination difficulties, and visual perception challenges.

- Do they allow for extra time or untimed tests? Do you have to take finals with everyone else, or can you take them alone or in a smaller setting? Do they have materials in large-print format? Are there note takers available, and if so, for what classes? Do they provide writing assistance? What about time management and organization help? Do they have assisted-hearing devices for students with hearing challenges? Can you use a laptop in classes?

- Is there a fee for the school's services?

- How many students at the school have learning disabilities similar to yours? Is there a support network? How do students with disabilities feel about the school environment? Are other students supportive? Is the faculty supportive and understanding? How accessible are professors and teaching assistants in the areas you are interested in?

- Are there educational therapists and/or psychologists on staff? Is there an additional fee for their services?

- Are the admissions requirements different for students with learning disabilities? Does the school welcome students with disabilities? How should you document your challenges? Do they have a separate office in charge of student disabilities? Does their program require an extra application? If you have to apply to a specific program, how does that program communicate with the admissions office? Do you have to first get accepted to the main school, or will the office of student disabilities advocate on your behalf once it receives your application? What can you do to increase your chances of being accepted?

- Who is the director of the learning disability program? Can you talk to him or her? Who is the best person to talk to if you have additional questions?

CHAPTER SIX
STANDARDIZED TESTS

THE REAL DEAL ABOUT ACRONYMS

First question: what the heck is an acronym? Letters, baby, letters. Letters that stand for extreme pain. Letters like SAT and ACT.

Could standardized test companies make it any more stressful on you at the end of your junior year with finals, sports competitions, spring musicals, student government elections, AP tests, and oh yeah, life with a car? The answer is no. No, they really couldn't make it any more stressful. So let's step down a notch, take a deep breath, count to ten, and figure out which of these bad-boy tests you should take and why.

Here's a summary of the exams, followed by a comparison of the SAT and ACT.

SCHOLASTIC APTITUDE TEST (SAT)

Why is there an SAT? Well, the Educational Testing Service and the College Board—aka the authors of the SAT—wanted to create a test that would give colleges an accurate way of comparing students from across the country. Because an A at one high school may be harder to earn than an A at another, this standardized test allows students to showcase their abilities on a level playing field. Of course, it is my opinion that this is somewhat of a crock. I have had brilliant students who bombed on the SAT because their strengths weren't what the SAT tests, yet they totally rocked once they got to college. This was especially true for students who had a talent in the arts and processed information differently than the average math god did. The bottom line is that the SAT does not test how smart you are, how good you are at school, how talented and creative you are, but only how well you can do its silly little problems.

Not to worry! There is some good news.

Although the SAT has questions you have never seen in school, they are incredibly predictable. This means that prepping for it *will* increase your score. But, you've gotta put in the time, or you will not see significant results (see page 79).

Here's how the SAT breaks down:

Total time: 3 hours, 45 minutes. Wrong answers get deducted a quarter of a point.

CRITICAL READING (70 MINUTES)	NO. QUESTIONS
• Sentence completions	19
• Passage-based reading comprehension	48

MATH (70 MINUTES)

- Multiple choice
  (*arithmetic, algebra I and II, geometry*)   44

- Grid-in problems   10

WRITING (60 MINUTES)

- Identifying sentence errors
  (*multiple-choice grammar*)   18

- Improving sentences
  (*multiple-choice grammar*)   25

- Improving paragraphs
  (*multiple-choice grammar*)   6

- One essay (25 minutes)

You might notice that the total time listed above does not add up to 3 hours and 45 minutes. This is because there is an experimental section that I didn't list. It can be an extra critical reading, math, or writing section. Unfortunately, you are not told which section is experimental, so you have to do your best on all of them.

ACT

ACT used to stand for American College Testing, but now it's just ACT. Depending on where you live in the country, either you know about the ACT or you're asking yourself, "There's a test that can get me into college other than the SAT?" The answer, of course, is yes. The ACT, while very popular in the middle of the country, is not used nearly as much on the coasts. It is similar to the SAT, as it is a standardized test with multiple-choice questions and an essay, but the way the questions are written is a bit different. In theory, the ACT is a test that more closely resembles the work you did in school or, as some say, more like the SAT IIs subject tests (which is why some schools accept the ACT in place of both the SAT *and* the SAT IIs). However, it's not an easier test by any means, although some students like it better. Again, prepping for it will up your score.

Here's how the ACT breaks down:

Total time: 3 hours, 25 minutes. No deduction for wrong answers.

ENGLISH (45 MINUTES)	QUESTIONS
• Grammar usage and mechanics (*punctuation and sentence structure*)	40
• Rhetorical skills (*writing strategy, organization, and style*)	35

MATH (60 MINUTES)

• Algebra	33
• Geometry	23
• Trigonometry	4

READING COMPREHENSION (35 MINUTES)

• Passage-based reading comprehension	40

SCIENCE (35 MINUTES)

• Data representation questions	15
• Research summaries	18
• Conflicting viewpoints	07

(*Note:* You don't need to know any science facts for this section. It requires reading charts and graphs and being able to answer multiple-choice questions based on experimental data—think science reading comprehension.)

WRITING TEST (30 MINUTES)

This is an essay, but it's optional. While I suggest you do take this section because colleges often like to see it, it's totally your choice.

WHICH TEST SHOULD I TAKE?

Good question. If I took a random sample of students from across the country, sat them down, and had them take the SAT and the ACT, they would generally score similarly on both—assuming they were taking them cold, without any practice. However, I have had students who really preferred one test over the other, or who scored a lot better on one than on the other. So look at both and even take a practice test of each. If you are going to spend several months studying, you might as well focus on the test that will give you the best chance.

SAT IIs (SUBJECT TESTS)

Until 2005, if a college required SAT IIs, it would often require that three subject tests be taken. With the new SAT I, however, schools are varied. What used to be the SAT II Writing test is now part of the new SAT, and much of the old SAT II Math IC is now part of the new SAT. As a result, most schools want only two SAT IIs in two different subject areas (that is, you can take Chemistry and U.S. History, but not U.S. History and World History). The most selective schools want the same two additional SAT IIs, but some also require that students take the SAT II Math IIC. *Aaagggghhhhh!* The bottom line is that you will need to check each of your desired college's requirements to get the true skinny. Remember, some schools will accept the ACT in place of both the SAT and the SAT IIs. The only good news is that if you have to take these subject tests, you can take up to three at once (they are one hour each) or you can spread them out over different test dates. It's best to take them at the end of the school year when the info is still fresh in your mind.

For certain languages, the College Board offers a listening and a non-listening version. Each have different types of questions, and the listening version is only offered on certain test dates. Check out www.collegeboard.com for more details. Here's how the SAT II subject tests break down:

Total time: 1 hour each

SAT II SUBJECT TEST CHOICES

Literature	French
U.S. History	German
World History	Modern Hebrew
Math Level IC	Italian
Math Level IIC	Japanese
(more "advanced" math than on Level IC including Algebra II, Trig, and Pre-Calculus)	Korean
Biology E/M (You can take either an Ecological or a Molecular test.)	Latin
	Spanish
Chemistry	
Physics	
Chinese	

TIMING IS THE KEY TO COMEDY . . . AND TEST TAKING

For a lot of students, the SAT/ACT/SAT II comes down to timing. You may score great at home, but when it's crunch time in that little smelly room with fifty other students, you may not be able to finish all sections of the test and you'll want to crawl in a hole. Well, here are some suggestions to fight the bastards who put you in the predicament:

- Close yourself in a room, put up a Do Not Disturb sign, lock the door, unplug the phone, get out your watch, and take a full test at one shot. In fact, the more full-length exams you practice at home, the more you will know exactly how fast you can go without making dumb mistakes. With practice, you should get a bit more confident and will be able to do the tests faster.

- If possible, go to the place where you're going to take the exam to check it out before the test day. It's good to sit down by yourself in the space, take some deep breaths, and see yourself just kickin' the pants off the exam. This may seem silly, but visualization can be powerful. Try to see yourself finishing each section and feeling good about your work. In fact, if you visualize this every night before you go to bed and *you believe it will work* (this is key), your brain will try to make it happen on the test day.

- Because the SAT and ACT require you to mark your answer choices by filling in little bubbles on a separate sheet, I suggest the following: Instead of completing a single question and immediately marking the answer in the corresponding bubble, just write the letter of the answer next to the question in the test book until you have completed an entire page. Once you have completed all the questions on a page, you can then fill in all the corresponding bubbles at one time. This allows you to go through the test faster and will prevent you from accidentally filling in a wrong bubble. Remember, though, you have to be careful not to have a full page of answers written on the test booklet, but not bubbled in when the proctor calls time.

- Know the tests. On the SAT and SAT IIs, the questions generally get harder as they go. However, don't just skip no. 25 because it's the hardest. While you practice, figure out which type of hard questions you can do and which you can't. In sentence completion questions, for example, try the questions where you recognize the words, even if it is the last question and it means you will skip the one before it. The same holds true for the ACT, but remember, there is no guessing penalty on the ACT. Therefore, if you run out of time on a section of the ACT, just guess!

- Apply for extra time. If you have a documented learning disability (that is, you have a report from a doctor that says you have an LD), I strongly suggest you talk to your counselor about getting more time. Both the SAT and ACT will look at your request and give you anywhere from an extra hour to an extra three hours. Often, this means you will take the test on a different day and by yourself.

- More than once, I have seen a high school not send in the right documentation to get special accommodations set up on a student's behalf. Therefore, go to www.collegeboard.com or www.act.org, and click on the information for learning disabilities. Learn the process so you can stay on top of everything. (Information about their policies is included on the Resource CD.)

- Many students fear choosing the LD option because colleges will be notified that they have a learning disability. As of 2004, The SAT and the ACT will not report or flag tests that have received extra time. Besides, I have found that reporting an LD has *never* hurt one of my student's chances for admission. In fact, if you do have an LD, I encourage you to advocate for yourself and take advantage of the services provided by colleges. Having an LD does not mean you are needy, nor does it mean you should use your LD as a crutch or an excuse for anything. But using services so you can get the most out of your education makes a lot of sense to me.

First you have to determine whether to focus on the SAT/SAT IIs or the ACT. Although you can and probably should take all of them, I generally find that students can really study for the SAT or the ACT simply because of all the other stuff they have to deal with during junior and senior years. Thus I often recommend taking a practice SAT and a practice ACT to help you decide which will be your priority.

After you've determined which test to take, you have to plan when to take it. Following are the generally recommended times of when to take the tests. There's no simple timeline because there are a lot of options that need to be explained, so hang in there with me. (Now, if you are a senior, ignore the junior-year stuff, and skip to the senior-year plans on page 81.)

IF THE SAT IS YOUR PRIORITY

Junior-Year Plan

- PSAT: October, junior year   Don't worry about signing up for this one—your school will usually just cart you into the cafeteria and make you take it.

- SAT I: March, junior year   First time you should take the SAT.

- SAT IIs: May and June   Because the SAT IIs are becoming more important in admissions, many students now split the subject tests over two test dates or use the June date to retake one or two that they'd like to improve on. Students who do well on the tests in May can retake the SAT I in June if they like. For example, a student takes Chemistry and U.S. History in May. In June, the student takes Chemistry again and takes Literature, *or* he retakes the SAT I.

  Remember, you should take the SAT IIs at the end of the year when the subjects are fresh in your mind. Therefore, if you are a sophomore taking biology, you might want to take the SAT II Biology at the end of tenth grade.

- ACT: June   If you want to give the ACT a shot, you can take it in junior year in June (it's given on a separate day from the SATs) or in October or November of twelfth grade.

Senior-Year Plan

- SAT/SAT II: October/November/January   If you are a senior and want to increase your scores from junior year, or if you still need to take the tests for the first time, don't worry. The last date to take the SATs is November for most early-decision and early-action applications, and January for most regular-decision applications (*check your schools to make sure*). This gives you several more opportunities to improve your score. I suggest you take the SAT at least twice, but not more than three times, unless you have a good reason to believe your scores will go up.

IF THE ACT IS YOUR PRIORITY

Junior-Year Plan

First, determine which of your schools will accept the ACT in place of both the SAT and SAT IIs. Schools such as UCLA still require the SAT IIs (regardless of whether you take the ACT), and this will obviously change how and when you take the tests. Generally, the schedule looks like this:

- The PLAN Test (or practice ACT): October/November, junior year.   Note: Your high school might offer the PSAT rather than the PLAN as the practice test. Ask your counselor where you can go to take the PLAN. Remember, the ACT is accepted by just as many colleges as the SAT; however, your counselor may want you to take both, which as previously discussed, is recommended.

- ACT: March, junior year   First time you should take the ACT.

- ACT: June, junior year   You can take the ACT again if you weren't happy with your scores.

Senior-Year Plan

- ACT: October/December   If you want another shot at the ACT or maybe want to try it for the first time, you can take it during these months and still have it count.

UP YOUR SCORE!

It would take me another whole book to teach you every kind of problem on the SAT/SAT II/ACT; and frankly, there are books and tutors out there that do a pretty good job. So what follows is what students don't usually hear about *how* to do well on standardized tests. I'm convinced that if you do what I suggest, you'll improve your scores.

Please keep in mind that these tests are only pieces of paper with writing on them, not the end of your life. No, they are not fun, and yes, they are looked at by admissions officers. But they are not even close to being the most important factor in admissions, and most of the time they won't make or break your chances. As you will see, I think you should do everything in your power to increase your scores, including studying your butt off. Keep in mind, however, that you can only help yourself, and don't worry if you completely bomb. I know it's easier said than done. But just follow these guidelines, and I will bet that your scores will go up.

Now I have to admit, I stole the title of this section from a book. But somehow I don't think the authors will mind as I am about to promote the heck out of their work. Their book, *Up Your Score: The Underground Guide to the SAT*, is one of the best SAT books I know of. First, it provides an overview and the most essential strategies in a quick and easy-to-understand way. And second, it's freakin' funny, so funny that when I first read it while sitting in a Mexican restaurant eating a burrito, I started laughing out loud and managed to knock everything I was eating onto the floor. Trust me, compared to the five-hundred-page SAT bore-fests, this book is a breath of fresh air. It doesn't have every strategy in it, and it doesn't have practice tests, but if you do pick it up, make sure you check out the words "melancholy" and "puissant" in their word list. I guarantee you will not soon forget either of them.

The other resource you need is *The Official SAT Study Guide* by the College Board. Yeah, that huge blue book. Don't worry about the first 150 pages or so of strategies; trying to read them will cause acute procrastination. What you need this little baby for is the tests. Now, Princeton Review and Kaplan books aren't bad, but I have yet to see a publisher reproduce practice tests like the real thing. If you are going to spend hours studying for the SATs, the best way to do so is to work on the real, past tests.

Why? Because the SAT is extremely predictable. For example, they generally like to put a sequence question in the math test grid-in section at around number 15, and they usually choose answer E in the Writing Test Identifying Sentence Errors Section only three to five times. The only way you are going to know this, however, is if someone shows you or you practice taking the real tests. You might have heard that most students' scores go up the second time they take the SAT. This is true because once students have had the experience of taking the test, they are typically more comfortable and self-confident the second time. Well, what if it was your seventh or eighth time? Do you think your score would go up after you'd taken all eight SATs provided in the official study guide? You better believe it.

This also holds true for the SAT IIs and the ACT. Although the *Real SAT IIs* book is available, it includes only one example of each test—that is, one Math IIC test, one Literature test, etc. The ACT, on the other hand, publishes a book called *The Real ACT Prep Guide*, which includes three real tests. Start with these, and then call the College Board at 609-771-7600 and the ACT at 319-337-1429 to request more practice tests. Once you have taken all the sample tests they have to offer, you can then use practice tests from other publishers, like Princeton Review. They're not exactly the same, but they will still help you.

Warning: Because the SAT changed in 2005, beware of taking practice tests in your brother's or sister's old SAT books. The tests may not the same.

When you are practicing, especially with *The Official SAT Study Guide, Real SAT IIs,* or

The Real ACT Prep Guide, it is important that you grade the tests and spend time going over your mistakes. Don't just say, "Yeah, I got that sentence completion wrong. I didn't know the words. I should have skipped it." Try it again now that you know the right answer. Can you figure out how you could have come up with the right answer the first time? With sentence completions, for example, there are many ways to figure out the answer, even if you don't know the words. In all, the more time you spend with your mistakes, the more you will feel confident about your chances of improving.

In fact, even students who are the biggest standardized-test haters begin to see the tests as a sort of sick game that they can beat. I have heard many students say something like, "Okay, you idiots, you're not tricking me on this question. I've seen it before and I'm takin' it down." This is a good way to think. Too many students on test day get tired and frustrated and say things like, "Ah, forget it, I'll pick B. Who cares anymore?" Well, *you* should! If you spent time preparing, don't let the test makers beat you at the finish line. Believe me, they don't care if you pick B or C, get teed off, or stand up and scream, "I can't take it anymore!" Beat them at their own game. Practice, gain confidence, and kick its butt!

Take as many timed full-length tests as possible before your actual test date. This is the hardest thing for most students to do, because no one wants to spend time on Saturday taking an SAT or ACT if they really don't have to. But suppose you decided to swim a mile when you hadn't been in a pool in five years. Two laps would wear you out. You have to get used to taking a 3 hour plus exam at once, so on the actual day your brain doesn't drip down the side of your neck and leave a stain on the carpet. If you want to do well on these tests, taking practice tests is a must. Of course, if the tests aren't necessary for the schools you're applying to, you can forget about practice tests.

BOOKS, GUIDES, AND OPTIONS TO SCORING WELL ON STANDARDIZED TESTS

Before I give you some recommendations about resources, you should know that there are some schools that do *not* require standardized tests. Here is a partial list—you can find several hundred schools on the Resource CD.

Antioch College	Goddard College	Muhlenberg College
Bard College	Hampshire College	St. John's College
Bates College	Hartwick College	Susquehanna College
Bowdoin College	Lafayette College	Union College
Connecticut College	Lewis and Clark College	Wheaton College
Dickinson College	Middlebury College	
Franklin and Marshall College	Mount Holyoke College	

Over the years, I have pretty much used every book and taught for every company out there. Here are some resources that I recommend.

BOOKS FOR THE SAT AND ACT

Up Your Score: The Underground Guide to the SAT by Larry Berger and others. *Must get. Funny as all hell.*

The Official SAT Study Guide by the College Board. *Must get. Boring as all hell, but necessary.*

The New SAT by Kaplan. *Basically says the same thing as many of the other companies, but the layout is easy to follow.*

The Real ACT Prep Guide by ACT staff. *Must get. The best practice book for the ACT because it has real tests.*

New ACT by Sparknotes. *Sparknotes is the newer kid on the block. Good overall review of strategies, but practice tests aren't exactly the same as the real thing.*

BOOKS FOR THE SAT IIS

There are a number of test prep books available. Following are my recommendations for you to check out. Sit down with two or three, flip through them, and see which ones you like.

Real SAT IIs: Subject Tests by the College Board. Includes only one real practice test for each subject, but is worth picking up for that reason alone.

Princeton Review: They have books on each SAT subject tests. Clear, easy to follow. Not the most thorough, but not too dense either. I specifically like their SAT II Literature book.

Kaplan: They also have books on each of the SAT subject tests. Similar to Princeton Review but their latest revisions are quite good for most subjects. Good general overview. Easy to read.

Sparknotes: They are often prominently featured in Barnes and Noble. I like Sparknotes because the books include extra practice tests. Specifically, their SAT II Math subject test books come closest to writing questions that look like the real thing. Be careful, however, because their questions can actually be harder than the real thing, and their answer explanations can be a bit complicated.

COMPANIES AND COURSES

Kaplan: Along with Princeton Review, known for their classes of about 15 to 20 students. Classes are generally three hours long, once per week. The content is good and it does work, but you have no real choice of who your instructor is, and you have to be ready to do a lot of work on your own. Be prepared to share time for your questions with other students. Kaplan also offers one-on-one, but it's a lot more expensive. Yet it may be worth it if you need someone to crack the whip on you.

Kaplan may offer classes through your school. This can be good because you know the people in your class, but it can be bad because you know the people in your class—if you know what I mean.

Princeton Review: Offers a similar program to Kaplan and has a very good curriculum. If you want to see the difference in philosophy between Princeton Review and Kaplan, pick up their SAT or ACT books and flip through them. With either company, you're going to learn the same general skills and practice like crazy.

Ivy West (*in California*): A popular choice in California because students get one-on-one help for the SAT from two different tutors—one for math, one for verbal. The tutors also come to your house, so it's very convenient. I've had many students who found success with Ivy West. Again, because you have no choice of tutors, some students reported that they had one really good tutor and one not as good. Students also found that there were a lot of "busy work" exercises that they put off until shortly before their tutor showed up. Ivy West's curriculum is a bit dry, and like the others, consists of many rules to remember. But put in the time (especially in combination with practicing real SATs), and their system works wonders.

Local Companies and Private SAT Tutors: In every town there are small companies and lone hired guns like me who teach the tests. Some of these people are great, funny, and flexible—they can focus on your needs rather than stick to a rigid curriculum. But make sure you meet them, get references, and check to see that they have substantial experience. After all, you want results, not just a buddy.

Remember, you will have to put in the time to practice, no matter what method you choose. By practicing the strategies over and over, you will improve your test scores.

PART TWO
COMPLETE AN AWESOME APPLICATION

CHAPTER **SEVEN**
FILLING OUT YOUR APPLICATIONS

APPLICATION HELL . . . ER, FUN

Here's where the real fun begins! So far, you have read and learned a lot, but this chapter introduces the "money," the "juice," the "core," and the "essence" of the Ultimate College Acceptance System. I wrote this to show you the parts of the application process that no one ever helps you with—that is, to show you exactly how to fill out your application, write your essays, put together your resume, and get recommendations, all with the kajillions of deadlines that change from school to school.

A student I know applied to the University of Oregon—or so he thought. Although schools are typically good about telling you if part of your application is missing, in this fellow's case something went screwy. This poor guy was accepted and had started looking for an apartment in Oregon, when he discovered that the school didn't get a few forms in time and gave away his space in the freshman class. Hopefully, he will have to wait only a semester for a space, but it may take a year to go to the school he really wanted to attend, all because of a missed deadline.

I want to make sure this does not happen to you. So I am going to walk you through all the parts of the Common Application (from here on, I'll call it the Common App). **While not every school accepts the Common App, the questions that students ask when filling it out are generally the same as those that come up for school-specific applications.** Therefore, even if you are applying to schools that do not use the Common App, you can still learn some techniques for maximizing your presentation on any application.

Next, using the master of all checklists (MOAC, pronounced "Moke," as in, where the heck is my MOAC? Mom, have you seen my MOAC? It was right here on the table! What do you mean you did some cleaning up today? AHHHHH! I gotta have my MOAC!) you will be able to track the application requirements for each of your schools so nothing is left out.

ALL HAIL THE MOAC—THE MASTER OF ALL CHECKLISTS!

Now since each school has different requirements and deadlines, I have not only devised the MOAC to track your progress, but I've also included it on the Resource CD in case you are applying to more than six schools. Make sure you check off each task as you complete it and

and write down the dates. You may think this is incredibly anal, and it is. But if you just do it, you'll thank me later.

Note: Although there is a trend for students to do much of the application work online, experience has taught me that not all school websites are easy to navigate. As a result, you might overlook an important part (like an application supplement). Therefore, I recommend requesting a school's viewbook and the application by either calling the admissions office, sending the school an e-mail, or contacting your high school's counseling office. That way you'll know everything is complete and in one place. (A sample e-mail is included on the Resource CD.)

The only time you might want to think about doing work online is when you have to fill out three forms:

1. The Common App

2. The FAFSA, the Free Application for Federal Student Aid.

3. The College Scholarship Service (CSS) financial aid form called Profile. (Note: Not all schools require this form, as they do the FAFSA.)

These three forms will all be discussed in detail later on.

For submitting the Common App, I'm a fan of going online, typing and printing out your info and mailing a hard copy to each of your schools with a certificate of mailing at the post office. For the financial aid forms, I suggest submitting both forms online (as long as your parents agree to work online to fill in their data). See Chapter 16. **No matter how you submit your materials, be sure to make copies of them so that you have proof of your work.**

FIGURE 7-1 THE MOAC (MASTER OF ALL CHECKLISTS)

Note: A checked box means it has been completed and/or sent.

	EXAMPLE	SCHOOL 1	SCHOOL 2	SCHOOL 3	SCHOOL 4	SCHOOL 5	SCHOOL 6
School Name	Stanford						
Regular application due date	Dec. 15 ✓						
Early decision or early action? Due date?	EA Nov. 1 (not interested)						
Application fee	$75.00 ✓						
Part 1 or Pre-application Due date?	Yes ✓ Dec. 1						
Common App.?	No						
Common App. Supplement?	No						
SAT/ACT requirement? When is the last accepted date?	SAT or ACT December test date						
SAT IIs? How many?	Yes 2, but Math IIC preferred as third test						
Have you sent your test scores online from collegeboard.com or act.org?	Yes ✓						
Recommendations? How many?	Yes ✓ 2						

	EXAMPLE	SCHOOL 1	SCHOOL 2	SCHOOL 3	SCHOOL 4	SCHOOL 5	SCHOOL 6
Does it require *you* or your *school* to send official transcripts?	Yes, school needs to send ✓						
A midyear report?	Yes, but not done yet						
Counselor or "Secondary School Report" form?	Yes ✓						
Essays?	Yes ✓						
How many?	1 large						
Are there short paragraph essays required?	Yes ✓						
How many?	3						
Taken a tour?	Yes ✓						
Interview?	No						
Do you need to schedule it?							
Sport that you want to play?	Yes						
Have you contacted the coach?	Yes on 9/24 ✓						
FAFSA form?	Yes,						
Due date?	sent to processing agency Feb 1						
PROFILE form?	Yes,						
Due date?	sent to processing agency Dec 15						
Does it have its own financial aid form?	No						
Due date?							

FILLING OUT THE COMMON APP

Note: Even if you are not applying to schools that accept the Common App, you may still want to read this section, as it presents basic principles to keep in mind when filling out college applications. It also answers most questions students have about how to complete these darn things. So tear out the sample application from this book, and put it alongside the instructions that follow to ensure you will complete your applications quickly and effectively.

Figure 7-2 contains a completed Common App. I have used an actual applicant's information (with his name changed) so that you can follow what he did. Much of the application is pretty straightforward, but where I think you might have questions, I have added a number with a circle around it like this: ⑦. This corresponds to the number in the following instructions.

Take a look at the first page of the Common Application for 2005–2006 (it was the latest year available when this book was published—but don't worry, the form rarely changes from year to year). Also note that later in this section I have included an example of a Common App Supplement (see Figure 7-6). To determine if your school requires a supplement, see pages 31–36.

Optional Declaration of Early Decision/Early Action. As the instructions discuss, you should complete this section only if you are applying for Early Decision (ED) or Early Action (EA). It also points out that you must also fill out and submit any EA/ED form provided by the college. For example, figure 7-6 shows a sample form from Agnes Scott College. Note that Agnes Scott calls this form "Part I," although it is actually the Common App Supplement. On the third page of the form, you'll find the Early Decision Honor Pledge. Thus, Agnes Scott has gotten slick and combined everything together in one form. This example is quite common, but can differ from school to school. Some colleges have Common App Supplements separate from their ED form. Therefore pay attention, note any extra forms a school requires, and list them on your MOAC.

No matter what a school calls its additional form, almost all schools require you to send in a check along with the form. Sometimes you can pay a school online when you submit the Common App, and a few schools have waived the fee altogether if you file the form electronically.

Finally, make sure you do not send the Common Application with the ED/EA box filled out to a school to which you are not applying early. In other words, you will send one version of this application only to your early school and one version everywhere else. See #25 on page 98 for more details. Trust me, the rest of my instructions are not this complicated:

1. You will see I have written one above the "legal name" blank on the Common App. Many students ask if they should type or use pen, and it's a good question. I have changed my opinion on this over the years after talking with admissions people. If your handwriting can be read by a normal human being, I suggest using pen. Handwriting makes your application seem more personal, and the admissions people will know you didn't have your mom's secretary type it for you. However, for the Common

App, there is a pretty nifty program at www.commonapp.org that allows you to type in the information and then formats it into a printable application. I recommend using this, especially if your writing looks like your pen exploded onto the page. Regardless of how you complete **the Common App, I do suggest printing it out (instead of submitting it online) and sending it directly to each of your schools with any additional supplements they require.** (See the list on pages 31–36.) Remember, if you do submit the application online rather than printing it and sending it, you can't make changes once it is sent. You will have to write to the school with any changes.

Note: IF YOU USE PEN, YOU MUST USE *BLACK INK* ON THE COMMON APP. (For other applications, I suggest using blue—it's more personal.)

2. *For the term beginning.* Most of you will be starting in the fall (August/September), but there may be a few of you applying for the spring. Just be sure what you put down here is accurate.

3. *Mailing address.* This is generally for students who are not living at home, but want their information sent to them, say, at boarding school. Most of you won't have to worry about this one.

4. *Possible area(s) of concentration/majors.* How the heck are you supposed to know? I agree. However, if you do have an idea, it might help you get in. Let's say, for example, that you want to study modern comparative literature. If this is a new program—or one that does not have a lot of students in it—at a school to which you're applying, the admissions office will take this into consideration. Be careful, however. I don't recommend picking some random major just to give yourself an edge. If, for example, you pick Japanese as your major and you have only two years of language in high school, this choice will seem strange. Your application should back up your choice.

Admissions people have big ol' BS detectors, so be as honest as possible. On the flip side, if you want to major in a subject like economics and you know it is one of the most popular majors at a school to which you're applying, you might want to write down "undeclared." Picking a very popular major won't help you get in and you might change your mind anyway, so I suggest playing it safe.

5. *Special college or division if applicable.* Some schools have specialized undergraduate colleges, such as a dentistry program or an engineering school. Most of you won't have to worry about this, but make sure by checking out the college's viewbook and application instructions.

6. *Possible career or professional plans.* Hey, if you absolutely know you want to be an astronaut, go for it. Putting down "doctor" here won't hurt you either. Just be honest. If you write down something, at least you are showing you have direction.

7. *Will you be a candidate for financial aid?* Unless you know you absolutely will not be applying for financial aid (like if your dad's name is Bill Gates), I suggest you check the yes box. Not only is it free to apply, but many people think they are not eligible, when in fact they are.

If yes, the appropriate form(s) was/will be filed on: This line refers to the FAFSA, the free form you use to apply for federal aid. You can fill out this form at www.fafsa.ed.gov. The FAFSA due date for many schools is February 1, but if you completed it sooner, by all means put down this earlier date.

Note: Some schools also require the PROFILE Form: you can fill out the PROFILE at www.collegeboard.com, which also provides a list of schools that require it. Its due date is typically December 31, and it requires a fee. (*For early action and early decision, it is due in November*) You'll find how to fill out the forms in Chapter 16.

8. *If you wish to be identified with a particular ethnic group, please check all that apply.* If you are white or Asian, just leave this blank. There is no advantage for you in marking a box. However, if, you fit into one of the other categories, I suggest marking the appropriate box so that your application can be flagged for underrepresented status, as discussed previously.

9. *Date of entry.* Simply write down the month and year you started the high school you are now attending. The day doesn't matter.

10. *CEEB/ACT code.* Get this number from your counselor or school administrator. You will be using it several times.

11. *The official scores from the appropriate testing agency must be submitted to each institution as soon as possible.* Remember when you signed up for those standardized tests like the SAT/SAT II and ACT and they made you fill in all those little bubbles? Remember when they wanted you to list the schools you were applying to and you thought, "Ah, I'll just do this later"? Well, Bunky, that time has come. You need to make sure all your scores were sent to all your schools. If you have to get them to the schools quickly, you can pay to have a "rush report" sent in two days. (Note, however, that not all schools will accept rushed reports.) To check and send your scores, go to www.collegeboard.com/sat/html/sat_scores.html or www.act.org/aap/scores/asr_current.html.

12. *Look, there is this nifty extra white space here.* Here you can list any test scores that don't fit in the spaces provided. This includes extra SAT/SAT II/ACT and, most importantly, AP tests. Even if you didn't score a 4 or a 5, I recommend you put down your AP scores if you passed. Your AP tests show you took the most demanding curriculum possible. If you passed, they also show competency in that academic area. Therefore, if you got a 480 on the SAT II Chemistry, but got a 5 on the Chem AP, it tells admissions that the SAT II score may not be representative of your ability. In other words, APs will help you out.

13. *Parents' Occupations.* Okay, some advice here. Never be ashamed to write down what your parents do, even if they stay at home. And never "talk up" your parents' job titles as if their positions of influence will help get you admitted. Now, if your dad's name is Bill Clinton, ex-president, be my guest. But if you talk up your family's position, admissions people may have a slight bias against you. Why? Well, if you have every ad-

vantage available—best schools, wealthy parents, SAT tutors, private tutors, college counselors—then admissions people will expect that everything about you is tops. If, however, you come from a background where you don't have access to all these things and have had to achieve despite your lack of choices, you may be given some leeway with things like test scores. Don't feel bad for what you have or don't have. Don't apologize for being you. However, if you have the choice of writing "head research physician of world-renowned cancer facility" or "doctor," keep it simple.

14. *Parents' College.* Indicate where your parents went to school, especially if you are applying to the same school. While many schools flag your application only if a parent went to the school as an undergraduate, there are some exceptions. Therefore, include your parents' professional or graduate school in the appropriate spaces as well.

15. *Degree.* Indicate the degree each parent earned, if applicable. If there's no answer here (say, your dad didn't go to college), write "N/A" or "not applicable." This will show you didn't overlook this item.

16. *With whom do you make your permanent home?* Many students split time between parents. So list the parent or guardian you spend the most time with.

17. *Please give names and ages of your brothers and sisters. If they have attended college, give the names of the institutions attended, degrees, and approximate dates.* Pretty self-explanatory. If you have siblings who are currently attending college, simply list the date they entered as freshmen and the approximate date when they will graduate.

18. Please complete this section even if you plan to attach a resume. Almost all college applications have a section for extracurricular activities. On most applications (but not the Common App), you will write, "Please see attached resume," because in Chapter 8 you will learn how to make a resume that will showcase your activities. However, for the Common App, you must fill out this activities section, even though you will attach your full resume to cover the Work Experience and Academic Honors sections. **(Note: If you enter your information online, I still suggest printing out the form and sending it to individual schools. If you submit it online, you will not be able to attach a resume and so you will have to complete the Work Experience and Academic Honors sections.)**

The bottom line is that for this activities section, you should simply copy the information that appears on your resume like I have shown in the example. Make sure, however, that you fill in each box accurately. For example, do not write that you participated in an activity 60 hours a week for 60 weeks! There is only so much time in a day and only 52 weeks in a year. Also, be honest about whether you want to pursue an interest in college. If the answer is yes, you will probably talk about this activity at some point in an essay or in describing reasons why you want to attend the school.

19. *Briefly list or describe any scholastic distinctions or honors you have won since the ninth grade.* You will have completed this info as part of your resume (see Chapter 8). If you plan to submit online, then you will have to copy the info. from you resume. If you are using pen, just attach the resume and simply write, "Please see attached sheet."

20. *Work experience.* This will be listed on your resume, so write, "Please see attached sheet."

21. *Please describe which of your activities (extracurricular and personal activities or work experience) has been most meaningful and why.* We will be covering how to write an answer to this question in Chapter 12.

22. *Personal essay.* Again, you are one lucky student. You will have already written this essay after having gone through the upcoming sections. Much of the time, students take their big essay and use it for choice 6, topic of your choice. Writing about a topic of your choice obviously gives you the most room for creativity and freedom. If, however, your big essay fits one of the other four categories, then use it. Just make sure that it answers the question you are choosing. If you choose no. 6 you might want to think about writing a title on your essay that shows the topic you are writing about. "A Personal Story" is not quite as strong a hook as "How My Obsession with Stamps Helped Me Become Interested in Dinosaurs." Okay, that's a ridiculous comparison, but my point is, if you do write in a title, make it personally relevant to your essay and make it interesting. Remember, admissions people want an essay that reveals more about who you are and that expands on the rest of your application. Therefore, the topic doesn't really matter that much. You can either choose to cut and paste your essay or use our favorite saying, "Please see attached sheet." Also, don't worry if your essay is slightly more than 500 words (like 520). But don't shrink the font down to 9 and decrease the margins to fit in 700 words. Some of the best essays are the ones that are the most concise, and I have read many a good essay that is less than 500 words.

23. *Application fee payment.* Make sure you send a check or money order or a Counselor-approved Fee Waiver to each school you are applying to, along with a copy of the Common App and any supplements the school requires. A fee waiver form can be found on a school's website or obtained from your counselor; it says that you are exempt from paying application fees. The cost of applying to several schools can reach into the hundreds of dollars, but do not let finances or a lack of them dictate where you apply. There are means available to help you to apply and to be able to attend. Just make sure you ask (and read Chapter 16, Financial Aid).

24. *Required signature.* You would be surprised at how many students do all this work and then forget to sign the application. Please sign it *now*.

25. *If applying via early decision or early action.* Make sure you complete the "Optional Declaration of Early Decision/Early Action" box at the very beginning of the first page of the application. If you do decide to apply early to a Common App school, you must

send the version of the Common App with the completed Optional Declaration section to that school only. Any additional Common App schools must receive a version where this section is blank. There are two ways to do this. For online submissions, you must first send the early application to the one school by selecting only that school under the "My Colleges" tab. You can then save a separate version by giving it a different name. This will allow you to clear the Optional Declaration section and submit the changed version to your other schools. For paper submissions, simply print (or write) out one version without the Optional Declaration section completed, from which you can then make copies to mail. Then create a version where you complete the Optional Declaration section and send it to the school to which you want to apply early.

26. *School Report.* The school report is one of two forms in the Common App you will need to give to your counselor. Remember, your schools might require other supplemental forms—check their applications. (A list of which schools require supplements appears on pages 31–36.)

27. *To the applicant:* Make sure you fill in all the personal information at the top.

28. *Current Year Courses—please indicate title, level (AP, IB, advanced honors, etc.) and credit value of all courses you are taking this year.* This is pretty self-explanatory. Be sure you include your senior-year classes here and—very important—titles like AP, honors, or IB. Use the first two columns if your high school is on the semester system, or all three columns if your school is on the trimester system.

29. This is the first Teacher Recommendation form (Figure 7-4). (See chapter 14 for more info.)

30. *To the applicant:* Make sure you fill in all the personal information at the top.

31. There is no 31. I just wanted to make sure you were paying attention and to let you know that there are actually two identical Teacher Recommendation forms as part of the Common App. I have only included one as an example. Please make sure you give each of the forms to two different teachers.

32. *Midyear report.* Remember when I said you would have two forms to give to your counselor? The midyear report is number two. (See Figure 7-5).

33. *To the Applicant.* Do I really need to remind you to fill in this part?

That's it. You're done!!

FIG 7-2 **COMMON APPLICATION**

Adelphi · Agnes Scott · Albertson · Albion · Albright · Alfred · Allegheny · American · Amherst · Antioch · Arcadia · Assumption · College of the Atlantic · Austin College · Babson · Baldwin–Wallace · Bard · Barnard · Bates · Beloit · Bennington · Bentley · Binghamton · Birmingham–Southern · Boston College · Boston U · Bowdoin · Bradley · Brandeis · Bryant · Bryn Mawr · Bucknell · Butler · California Lutheran · Carleton · Carnegie Mellon · Case Western Reserve · Cazenovia · Centenary (La.) · Centre · Chatham · Claremont McKenna · Clark U · Clarkson U · Coe · Colby · Colby–Sawyer · Colgate · Colorado College · Concordia College (N.Y.) · Connecticut College · Converse · Cornell College · Cornell U · U of Dallas · Dartmouth · Davidson · U of Delaware · Denison · U of Denver · DePauw · Dickinson · Dominican (Calif.) · Drew · Duke · Earlham · Eckerd · Elizabethtown · Elmira · Embry–Riddle · Emmanuel College (Mass.) · Emory · Eugene Lang · Fairfield · Findlay · Fisk · Florida Southern · Fordham · Franklin & Marshall · Furman · George Fox · George Washington · Gettysburg · Gonzaga · Goucher · Grinnell · Guilford · Gustavus Adolphus · Hamilton · Hampden–Sydney · Hampshire · Hanover · Hartwick · Harvard · Harvey Mudd · Haverford · Hendrix · Hiram · Hobart & William Smith · Hofstra · Hollins · Holy Cross · Hood · Illinois Wesleyan · Iona · Ithaca · John Carroll · Johns Hopkins · Juniata · Kalamazoo · Kenyon · Knox · La Roche · La Salle · La Verne · Lafayette · Lake Forest · Lawrence · Le Moyne · Lehigh · Lesley · Lewis & Clark · Linfield · Loyola College · Loyola U (La.) · Luther · Macalester · U of Maine (Farmington) · U of Maine (Orono) · Manhattan · Manhattanville · Marietta · Marlboro · Marquette · Mary Washington · McDaniel · Merrimack · U of Miami (Fla.) · Miami U (Ohio) · Middlebury · Mills · Millsaps · Moravian · Morehouse · Mount St Vincent · Mt Holyoke · Muhlenberg · Naropa · Nazareth · New College (Fla.) · New England College · U of New Hampshire · College of New Jersey · New York U · Northeastern U · Northland · Notre Dame (Md.) · Notre Dame de Namur · Oberlin · Occidental · Oglethorpe · Ohio Wesleyan · Pace · U of the Pacific · Pitzer · Pomona · U of Portland · Presbyterian · Prescott · Princeton · Providence · Puget Sound · Queens U (N.C.) · Randolph–Macon · Randolph–Macon Woman's · Redlands · Reed · Regis College · Regis U · Rensselaer · Rhodes · Rice · U of Richmond · Rider · Ripon · U of Rochester · Rochester Inst of Tech · Roger Williams · Rollins · St Anselm · St Benedict & St John's · St Joseph's College (Me.) · St Joseph's U · St Lawrence · St Leo · St Louis U · St Mary's College (Calif.) · St Mary's College (Ind.) · St Michael's · St Norbert · St Olaf · St Peter's · St Vincent · Salem (N.C.) · Salve Regina · U of San Diego · U of San Francisco · Santa Clara · College of Santa Fe · Sarah Lawrence · Scranton · Scripps · Seattle U · Seton Hall · Sewanee · Simmons · Skidmore · Smith · Southern Maine · Southern Methodist · Southern New Hampshire · Southwestern U · Spelman · Spring Hill · Stetson · Stevens Inst of Tech · Stonehill · Suffolk · Susquehanna · Swarthmore · Sweet Briar · Syracuse · U of Tampa · TCU · Transylvania · Trinity College (Conn.) · Trinity U · Tufts · Tulane · Tulsa · Union College (N.Y.) · Ursinus · Utica · Valparaiso · Vanderbilt · Vassar · U of Vermont · Villanova · Wabash · Wagner · Wake Forest · Washington College · Washington (Mo.) · Washington & Jefferson · Washington & Lee · Webster · Wellesley · Wells · Wesleyan · Westminster (Mo.) · Westminster (Pa.) · Wheaton (Mass.) · Wheelock · Whitman · Whittier · Widener · Willamette · William & Mary · William Jewell · Williams · Wilson · Wittenberg · Wofford · Wooster · WPI · Xavier (Ohio) · Yale

COMMON APPLICATION™
2005–2006

APPLICATION FOR UNDERGRADUATE ADMISSION

The member colleges and universities listed above fully support the use of this form. No distinction will be made between it and the college's own form. Please type or print in black ink.

Be sure to follow the instructions on the cover page of the Common Application booklet to complete, copy, and file your application with any one or several of the member colleges and universities.

OPTIONAL DECLARATION OF EARLY DECISION/EARLY ACTION

Complete this section **ONLY** for the individual college to which you are applying ED or EA. It is your responsibility to follow that college's instructions regarding early admission, including obtaining and submitting any ED/EA form provided by that college. **Do NOT** complete this ED/EA section on copies of your application submitted to colleges for Regular Decision or Rolling Admission.

College Name: SYRACUSE UNIVERSITY   Deadline: NOV 15

[X] Early Decision   [ ] Early Action   [ ] EASC

PERSONAL DATA

Legal Name: HAYES (Last/Family) CHRISTOPHER (First) DANIEL (Middle (complete)) ___ (Jr. etc.) M (Gender)   ①
Enter name exactly as it appears on passports or other official documents.

Nickname (choose only one): CHRIS   Former last name(s) if any: ___

Are you applying as a [X] freshman or [ ] transfer student?   For the term beginning FALL 2006 ②

Birthdate: 01 / 08 / 1988 (mm/dd/yyyy)   E-mail Address: ch1234@yahoo.com

Permanent Home Address: 1234 BEVERLY LANE (Number and Street)
CAMARILLO (City or Town)   CA (State/Province)   USA (Country)   90132 (Zip Code or Postal Code)

Permanent Home Phone (805) 987-6543

If different from above, please give your mailing address for all admission correspondence.

Mailing Address (from __/__ (mm/yyyy) to __/__ (mm/yyyy)) ③ ___ (Number and Street)
___ (City or Town)   ___ (State/Province)   ___ (Country)   ___ (Zip Code or Postal Code)

Phone at mailing address (___) ___ (Area Code / Number)   Cell phone (___) ___ (Area Code / Number)

Citizenship: [X] US citizen   [ ] Dual US citizen; please specify other country of citizenship ___

[ ] US Permanent Resident visa; citizen of ___   Alien Registration Number ___

[ ] Other Citizenship ___ (Country(ies))   ___ (Visa type)

If you are not a US citizen and live in the United States, how long have you been in the country? ___

Possible area(s) of academic concentration/major(s): POLITICAL SCIENCE ④   or undecided [ ]

Special college or division if applicable: ___ ⑤

Possible career or professional plans: LAWYER ⑥   or undecided [ ] ⑦

Will you be a candidate for financial aid? [X] Yes [ ] No   If yes, the appropriate form(s) was/will be filed on JAN 15, 2006

The following items are *optional*. No information you provide will be used in a discriminatory manner.

Place of birth: SANTA MONICA (City) CA (State/Province) USA (Country)   Social Security Number (if any): 123-45-6789

First language, if other than English ___   Language spoken at home ___

If you wish to be identified with a particular ethnic group, please check all that apply ⑧

[ ] African American, Black
[ ] Native American, Alaska Native (tribal affiliation ___ enrolled ___)
[ ] Asian American (countries of family's origin ___)
[ ] Asian, including Indian Subcontinent (countries ___)
[ ] Hispanic, Latino (countries ___)

[ ] Mexican American, Chicano
[ ] Native Hawaiian, Pacific Islander
[ ] Puerto Rican
[X] White or Caucasian
[ ] Other (specify ___)

2005–2006   Common App Online **AP-1**

FIG 7-2 **COMMON APPLICATION**

EDUCATIONAL DATA

Secondary school you now attend (or from which you graduated) _CAMARILLO HIGH SCHOOL_ ⑨ Date of entry _9/2002_

Address _1234 MAPLE AVE_
      Number and Street   CEEB/ACT code _123456_ ⑩

CAMARILLO   _CA_   _USA_   _93010_
City or Town   *State/Province*   *Country*   *Zip Code or Postal Code*

Date of secondary graduation _6/2006_   Type of school ☑ public ☐ private ☐ parochial ☐ home school

Guidance Counselor's Name _EILEEN SMITH_   Counselor's E-mail _esmith@gmail.com_

Position _Counselor_   Phone (_805_) _999-9999_   Fax (_805_) _444-4444_
                        Area Code *Number* *Ext.*   *Area Code* *Number*

List all other secondary schools, including summer schools and programs you have attended beginning with ninth grade.

Name of School	Location (City, State/Province, Zip, Country)	Dates Attended

List all colleges/universities at which you have taken courses for credit; list names of courses taken and grades earned on a separate sheet.
Please have an official transcript sent from each institution as soon as possible.

Name of College/University & CEEB/ACT Code	Location (City, State/Province, Zip, Country)	Degree Candidate?	Dates Attended
		☐	
		☐	
		☐	

☐ Not currently attending school   ☐ Graduated from secondary school early.
Describe in detail, here or on a separate sheet, your activities since last enrolled.

TEST INFORMATION

Be sure to note the tests required for each institution to which you are applying. The official scores from the appropriate testing agency ⑪ must be submitted to each institution as soon as possible. Please list your test plans below.

AP TESTS ⑫

5/05 US HISTORY - 3
5/05 CHEMISTRY - 4

ACT

Date taken/ to be taken	English	Reading	Math	Science	Composite	Combination English/Writing
6/05	27	29	24	22	26	

SAT I or SAT Reasoning Tests

Date taken/ to be taken	Verbal/Critical Reading	Math	Writing	Date taken/ to be taken	Verbal/Critical Reading	Math	Writing	Date taken/ to be taken	Verbal/Critical Reading	Math	Writing
5/05	610	620	570	3/05	580	580	540				

SAT II or Subject Tests

Date taken/ to be taken	Subject	Score	Date taken/ to be taken	Subject	Score	Date taken/ to be taken	Subject	Score
6/04	BIOLOGY	600	6/05	US HISTORY	630	6/05	LITERATURE	510

Test of English as a second language (TOEFL or other exam)

Test	Date taken/ to be taken	Score	Test	Date taken/ to be taken	Score

AP-2

Common App Online   2005–2006

FIG 7-2 **COMMON APPLICATION**

FAMILY

Parent 1 _HAYES_ _BRUCE_ _____
Last/Family — First — Middle — Gender

Living? ☒ Yes ☐ No (Date deceased _____)

Home address if different from yours

2222 HOPKINS COURT
SAN DIEGO, CA 91111

Home phone (619) 555-4211

E-mail 02bhayes @ yahoo.com

Occupation SELF EMPLOYED / OWNER ⑬

Name of employer FAST TIMES MOTORCYCLES

Work phone (619) 555-2222

Work e-mail N/A

College (if any) NONE

Degree N/A Year N/A

Graduate school (if any) N/A

Degree N/A ⑮ Year N/A

Parent 2 _HAYES_ _MAY_ _____
Last/Family — First — Middle — Gender

Living? ☒ Yes ☐ No (Date deceased _____)

Home address if different from yours

Home phone (805) 555-1674

E-mail M1694H @ hotmail.com

Occupation PHYSICIAN

Name of employer CONEJO MEDICAL PRACTICE

Work phone (805) 555-3333

Work e-mail N/A

College (if any) ⑭ STANFORD UNIVERSITY

Degree B.S. BIOLOGY Year 1974

Graduate school (if any) JOHNS HOPKINS

Degree M.D. Year 1979

Parents' marital status: ☐ married ☐ separated ☒ divorced (date 5/02) ☐ never married ☐ widowed

With whom do you make your permanent home? ☐ Parent 1 ☒ Parent 2 ☐ Both ☐ Legal Guardian ☐ Other relation
⑯

Legal guardian's name/address

Please give names and ages of your brothers or sisters. If they have attended college, give the names of the institutions attended, degrees, and approximate dates. NONE ⑰

EXTRACURRICULAR, PERSONAL, AND VOLUNTEER ACTIVITIES (including summer)

Please list your **principal** extracurricular, community, and family activities and hobbies **in the order of their interest to you.** Include specific events and/or major accomplishments such as musical instrument played, varsity letters earned, etc. Check (✓) in the right column those activities you hope to pursue in college. **To allow us to focus on the highlights of your activities, please complete this section even if you plan to attach a résumé.** ⑱

Activity	Grade level or post-secondary (PS) 9 10 11 12 PS	Hours per week	Weeks per year	Positions held, honors won, or letters earned	Do you plan to participate in college?
MOCK TRIAL	☐☐☐☒☐	12	12	FOUNDER- LEAD DEFENSE ATTORNEY	☒
STUDENT GOVERNMENT	☐☐☒☒☐	8	32	ASB V.P-11th SENIOR CLASS PRES -12th	☒
SWIMMING	☒☒☒☒☐	12	30	VARSITY-4YRS CAPTAIN 12th	☐
WATER POLO	☐☒☒☒☐	12	15	VARSITY-2YRS CAPTAIN 12th	☐
BOY SCOUTS	☒☒☐☐☐	2-4	40	EAGLE SCOUT	☐
RED CROSS VOLUNTEER	☐☒☒☒☐	2	10	TAUGHT CPR TO 8th GRADERS	☐
SCHOOL TUTOR/MENTOR	☐☐☒☒☐	4	40	GEOMETRY TUTOR	☐

ACADEMIC HONORS

Briefly list or describe any scholastic distinctions or honors you have won since the ninth grade (e.g., National Merit, Cum Laude Society).

PLEASE SEE ATTACHED SHEET ⑲

FIG 7-2 COMMON APPLICATION

WORK EXPERIENCE

List any job (including summer employment) you have held during the past three years.

Specific nature of work (20)	Employer	Approximate dates of employment	Approximate no. of hours spent per week
PLEASE SEE ATTACHED SHEET			

SHORT ANSWER

Please describe which of your activities (extracurricular and personal activities or work experience) has been most meaningful and why (150 words or fewer).

PLEASE SEE ATTACHED SHEET (21)

PERSONAL ESSAY

This personal statement helps us become acquainted with you in ways different from courses, grades, test scores, and other objective data. It will demonstrate your ability to organize thoughts and express yourself. We are looking for an essay that will help us know you better as a person and as a student. Please write an essay (250–500 words) on a topic of your choice or on one of the options listed below. *Please indicate your topic by checking the appropriate box below.*

☐ 1 Evaluate a significant experience, achievement, risk you have taken, or ethical dilemma you have faced and its impact on you.

☐ 2 Discuss some issue of personal, local, national, or international concern and its importance to you.

☐ 3 Indicate a person who has had a significant influence on you, and describe that influence.

☐ 4 Describe a character in fiction, an historical figure, or a creative work (as in art, music, science, etc.) that has had an influence on you, and explain that influence.

☐ 5 A range of academic interests, personal perspectives, and life experiences adds much to the educational mix. Given your personal background, describe an experience that illustrates what you would bring to the diversity in a college community, or an encounter that demonstrated the importance of diversity to you.

☒ 6 Topic of your choice. (22)

☞ Your essay will appear on an additional page at the end of this form.

APPLICATION FEE PAYMENT   ☐ Check/money order attached   ☒ Counselor-approved Fee Waiver attached (23)

REQUIRED SIGNATURE Your signature is required whether you are an ED, EA, EASC, or regular decision candidate.
I certify that all information in my application, including my Personal Essay, is my own work, factually true, and honestly presented.

Signature _C Hayes_ (24)   Date _10/2/05_

IF APPLYING VIA EARLY DECISION OR EARLY ACTION (1) Complete the Optional ED/EA/EASC Declaration for your early application *only.* (2) Submit the college's required ED/EA/EASC form, if any. (3) Understand that it is your responsibility to report any changes in your schedule to the colleges to which you are applying. (25)

These colleges are committed to administer all educational policies and activities without discrimination on the basis of race, color, religion, national or ethnic origin, age, handicap, or gender.

AP-4   Common App Online 2005–2006

FIG 7-3 SCHOOL REPORT

Adelphi · Agnes Scott · Albertson · Albion · Albright · Alfred · Allegheny · American · Amherst · Antioch · Arcadia · Assumption · College of the Atlantic · Austin College · Babson · Baldwin—Wallace · Bard · Barnard · Bates · Beloit · Bennington · Bentley · Binghamton · Birmingham—Southern · Boston College · Boston U. · Bowdoin · Bradley · Brandeis · Bryant · Bryn Mawr · Bucknell · Butler · California Lutheran · Carleton · Carnegie Mellon · Case Western Reserve · Cazenovia · Centenary (La.) · Centre · Chatham · Claremont McKenna · Clark U. · Clarkson U. · Coe · Colby · Colby—Sawyer · Colgate · Colorado College · Concordia College (N.Y.) · Connecticut College · Converse · Cornell College · Cornell U. · U. of Dallas · Dartmouth · Davidson · U. of Delaware · Denison · U. of Denver · DePauw · Dickinson · Dominican U. (Calif.) · Drew · Duke · Earlham · Eckerd · Elizabethtown · Elmira · Embry—Riddle · Emmanuel College (Mass.) · Emory · Eugene Lang · Fairfield · Findlay · Fisk · Florida Southern · Fordham · Franklin & Marshall · Furman · George Fox · George Washington · Gettysburg · Gonzaga · Goucher · Grinnell · Guilford · Gustavus Adolphus · Hamilton · Hampden—Sydney · Hampshire · Hanover · Hartwick · Harvard · Harvey Mudd · Haverford · Hendrix · Hiram · Hobart & William Smith · Hofstra · Hollins · Holy Cross · Hood · Illinois Wesleyan · Iona · Ithaca · John Carroll · Johns Hopkins · Juniata · Kalamazoo · Kenyon · Knox · La Roche · La Salle · La Verne · Lafayette · Lake Forest · Lawrence · Le Moyne · Lehigh · Lesley · Lewis & Clark · Linfield · Loyola College · Loyola U (La.) · Luther · Macalester · U. of Maine (Farmington) · U. of Maine (Orono) · Manhattan · Manhattanville · Marietta · Marlboro · Marquette · Mary Washington · McDaniel · Merrimack · U. of Miami (Fla.) · Miami U. (Ohio) · Middlebury · Mills · Millsaps · Moravian · Morehouse · Mount St Vincent · Mt Holyoke · Muhlenberg · Naropa · Nazareth · New College (Fla.) · New England College · U. of New Hampshire · College of New Jersey · New York U. · Northeastern U. · Northland · Notre Dame (Md.) · Notre Dame de Namur · Oberlin · Occidental · Oglethorpe · Ohio Wesleyan · Pace · U. of the Pacific · Pitzer · Pomona · U. of Portland · Presbyterian · Prescott · Princeton · Providence · Puget Sound · Queens U (N.C.) · Randolph—Macon · Randolph—Macon Woman's · Redlands · Reed · Regis College · Regis U · Rensselaer · Rhodes · Rice · U. of Richmond · Rider · Ripon · U. of Rochester · Rochester Inst of Tech · Roger Williams · Rollins · St Anselm · St Benedict & St John's · St Joseph's College (Me.) · St Joseph's U · St Lawrence · St Leo · St Louis U · St Mary's College (Calif.) · St Mary's College (Ind.) · St Michael's · St Norbert · St Olaf · St Peter's · St Vincent · Salem (N.C.) · Salve Regina · U. of San Diego · U. of San Francisco · Santa Clara · College of Santa Fe · Sarah Lawrence · Scranton · Scripps · Seattle U. · Seton Hall · Sewanee · Simmons · Skidmore · Smith · Southern Maine · Southern Methodist · Southern New Hampshire · Southwestern U · Spelman · Spring Hill · Stetson · Stevens Inst of Tech · Stonehill · Suffolk · Susquehanna · Swarthmore · Sweet Briar · Syracuse · U. of Tampa · TCU · Transylvania · Trinity College (Conn.) · Trinity U. · Tufts · Tulane · Tulsa · Union College (N.Y.) · Ursinus · Utica · Valparaiso · Vanderbilt · Vassar · U. of Vermont · Villanova · Wabash · Wagner · Wake Forest · Washington College · Washington U (Mo.) · Washington & Jefferson · Washington & Lee · Webster · Wellesley · Wells · Wesleyan · Westminster (Mo.) · Westminster (Pa.) · Wheaton (Mass.) · Wheelock · Whitman · Whittier · Widener · Willamette · William & Mary · William Jewell · Williams · Wilson · Wittenberg · Wofford · Wooster · WPI · Xavier (Ohio) · Yale

SCHOOL REPORT

The member colleges and universities listed above fully support the use of this form. No distinction will be made between it and the college's own form. (26)
Please type or print in black ink.

TO THE APPLICANT

After filling in the information below, give this form to your guidance counselor. (27)

Birthdate __01_ / _08_ / _1988___   Gender ___MALE_____   Social Security No. _123-45-6789_
mm/dd/yyyy   (Optional)

Student Name ___HAYES_____ ___CHRISTOPHER___ ___DANIEL_____
                  Last/Family   First   Middle (complete)   Jr., etc.

Address ___1234 BEVERLY LANE_____ ___CAMARILLO___ __CA__ __USA__ __90132__
           Number and Street   City or Town   State/Province Country Zip Code or Postal Code

Current year courses—please indicate title, level (AP, IB, advanced honors, etc.) and credit value of all courses you are taking this year. (28)

First Semester/Trimester		Second Semester/Trimester		Third Trimester
CALCULUS AB	AP 5	CALCULUS AB	AP 5	
PHYSICS	5	PHYSICS	AP 5	
ENGLISH 12	AP 5	ENGLISH 12	AP 5	
EUROPEAN HIS	AP 5	EUROPEAN HIS	AP 5	
STUDENT COUNCIL	5	STUDENT COUNCIL	5	
ECONOMICS	5	GOVERNMENT	5	

TO THE SECONDARY SCHOOL GUIDANCE COUNSELOR

Attach applicant's official transcript, including courses in progress, a school profile, and transcript legend. (Please check transcript copies for readability.) After filling in the blanks below, use both sides of this form to describe the applicant. Please provide all available information for this candidate. *Be sure to sign below.*

Class rank _____ in a class of _____, covering a period from _____ to _____   **S.S. graduation date** _____
                                                            (mm/yyyy)   (mm/yyyy)

The rank is ○ weighted   ○ unweighted. How many students share this rank? _____

If a precise rank is not available, please indicate rank to the nearest tenth from the top _____

Cumulative GPA _____ on a _____ scale, covering a period from _____ to _____
                                                                (mm/yyyy)   (mm/yyyy)

This GPA is ○ weighted   ○ unweighted. The school's passing mark is _____

Percentage of graduating class attending: _____ four-year _____ two-year institutions

In comparison with other college preparatory students *at our school,* the applicant's course selection is
○ most demanding   ○ very demanding   ○ demanding   ○ average   ○ less than demanding

Are classes taken on a block schedule?
○ yes   ○ no

If yes, in what year did _____
block scheduling begin?

Highest grade/GPA in class _____

Counselor's Name Mr./Mrs./Ms _____
                              Please print or type

Signature _____   *Date* _____

Position _____   School _____

Counselor's Address _____

Counselor's Phone (_____) _____   Counselor's Fax (_____) _____
                    Area Code   Number   Ext.   Area Code   Number

Secondary School CEEB/ACT Code _____   Counselor's E-mail _____

2005–2006 COMMON APPLICATION ™   SR-1

FIG 7-3 **SCHOOL REPORT**

EVALUATION Please write whatever you think is important about this student, including a description of academic and personal characteristics. We are particularly interested in the candidate's intellectual promise, motivation, maturity, integrity, independence, originality, initiative, leadership potential, capacity for growth, special talents, enthusiasm, concern for others, respect accorded by faculty, and reaction to setbacks. We welcome information that will help us to differentiate this student from others.

How long have you known this student and in what context? _____

_____

What are the first words that come to your mind to describe this student? _____

_____

RATINGS

Compared to other students in his or her class year, how do you rate this student in terms of:

No basis		Below Average	Average	Good (above average)	Very Good (well above average)	Excellent (top 10%)	Outstanding (top 5%)	One of the top few encountered in my career
	Academic achievement							
	Extracurricular accomplishments							
	Personal qualities and character							
	Creativity							

I recommend this student: ☐ With reservation ☐ Fairly strongly ☐ Strongly ☐ Enthusiastically

CONFIDENTIALITY We value your comments highly and ask that you complete this form in the knowledge that it may be retained in the student's file should the applicant matriculate at a member college. In accordance with the Family Educational Rights and Privacy Act of 1974, matriculating students *do* have access to their permanent files, which may include forms such as this one. Unless required by state law, colleges may not provide access to admission records to applicants, those students who are denied admission, or those students who decline an offer of admission. Again, your comments are important to us and we thank you for your cooperation. These colleges are committed to administer all educational policies and activities without discrimination on the basis of race, color, religion, national or ethnic origin, age, handicap, or gender.

SR-2

COMMON APPLICATION ™ 2005–2006

FIG 7-4 **TEACHER EVALUATION**

Adelphi · Agnes Scott · Albertson · Albion · Albright · Alfred · Allegheny · American · Amherst · Antioch · Arcadia · Assumption · College of the Atlantic · Austin College · Babson · Baldwin—Wallace · Bard · Barnard · Bates · Beloit · Bennington · Bentley · Binghamton · Birmingham–Southern · Boston College · Boston U. · Bowdoin · Bradley Brandeis · Bryant · Bryn Mawr · Bucknell · Butler · California Lutheran · Carleton · Carnegie Mellon · Case Western Reserve · Cazenovia · Centenary (La.) · Centre · Chatham · Claremont McKenna · Clark U. · Clarkson U. · Coe · Colby · Colby–Sawyer · Colgate · Colorado College · Concordia College (N.Y.) · Connecticut College · Converse Cornell College · Cornell U. · U. of Dallas · Dartmouth · Davidson · U. of Delaware · Denison · U. of Denver · DePauw · Dickinson · Dominican U (Calif.) · Drew · Duke · Earlham · Eckerd · Elizabethtown · Elmira · Embry–Riddle · Emmanuel College (Mass.) · Emory · Eugene Lang · Fairfield · Findlay · Fisk · Florida Southern · Fordham Franklin & Marshall · Furman · George Fox · George Washington · Gettysburg · Gonzaga · Goucher · Grinnell · Guilford · Gustavus Adolphus · Hamilton · Hampden–Sydney Hampshire · Hanover · Hartwick · Harvard · Harvey Mudd · Haverford · Hendrix · Hiram · Hobart & William Smith · Hofstra · Hollins · Holy Cross · Hood · Illinois Wesleyan · Iona Ithaca · John Carroll · Johns Hopkins · Juniata · Kalamazoo · Kenyon · Knox · La Roche · La Salle · La Verne · Lafayette · Lake Forest · Lawrence · Le Moyne · Lehigh · Lesley Lewis & Clark · Linfield · Loyola College · Loyola U. (La.) · Luther · Macalester · U. of Maine (Farmington) · U. of Maine (Orono) · Manhattan · Manhattanville · Marietta Marlboro · Marquette · Mary Washington · McDaniel · Merrimack · U. of Miami (Fla.) · Miami U. (Ohio) · Middlebury · Mills · Millsaps · Moravian · Morehouse · Mount St Vincent Mt Holyoke · Muhlenberg · Naropa · Nazareth · New College (Fla.) · New England College · U. of New Hampshire · College of New Jersey · New York U. · Northeastern U · Northland Notre Dame (Md.) · Notre Dame de Namur · Oberlin · Occidental · Oglethorpe · Ohio Wesleyan · Pace · U. of the Pacific · Pitzer · Pomona · U. of Portland · Presbyterian Prescott · Princeton · Providence · Puget Sound · Queens U (N.C.) · Randolph–Macon · Randolph–Macon Woman's · Redlands · Reed · Regis College · Regis U. · Rensselaer · Rhodes Rice · U. of Richmond · Rider · Ripon · U. of Rochester · Rochester Inst of Tech · Roger Williams · Rollins · St Anselm · St Benedict & St John's · St Joseph's College (Me.) · St Joseph's U · St Lawrence · St Leo · St Louis U · St Mary's College (Calif.) · St Mary's College (Ind.) · St Michael's · St Norbert · St Olaf · St Peter's · St Vincent · Salem (N.C.) Salve Regina · U. of San Diego · U. of San Francisco · Santa Clara · College of Santa Fe · Sarah Lawrence · Scranton · Scripps · Seattle U · Seton Hill · Sewanee · Simmons · Skidmore · Smith · Southern Maine · Southern Methodist · Southern New Hampshire · Southwestern U · Spelman · Spring Hill · Stetson · Stevens Inst of Tech Stonehill · Suffolk · Susquehanna · Swarthmore · Sweet Briar · Syracuse · U. of Tampa · TCU · Transylvania · Trinity College (Conn.) · Trinity U · Tufts · Tulane · Tulsa · Union College (N.Y.) · Ursinus · Utica · Valparaiso · Vanderbilt · Vassar · U. of Vermont · Villanova · Wabash · Wagner · Wake Forest · Washington College · Washington U (Mo.) Washington & Jefferson · Washington & Lee · Webster · Wellesley · Wells · Wesleyan · Westminster (Mo.) · Westminster (Pa.) · Wheaton (Mass.) · Wheelock · Whitman · Whittier · Widener · Willamette · William & Mary · William Jewell · Williams · Wilson · Wittenberg · Wofford · Wooster · WPI · Xavier (Ohio) · Yale

TEACHER EVALUATION

The member colleges and universities listed above fully support the use of this form. No distinction will be made between it and the college's own form.
Please type or print in black ink. (29)

TO THE APPLICANT

Fill in the information below and give this form and a stamped envelope, addressed to each college to which you are applying that requests a Teacher Evaluation, to a teacher who has taught you an **academic subject.** (30)

Birthdate 01 / 08 / 1988   Gender MALE   Social Security No. 123-45-6789
     mm/dd/yyyy   *(Optional)*

Student Name ___ HAYES   CHRISTOPHER   DANIEL ___
     Last/Family   *First*   *Middle (complete)*   *Jr., etc.*

Address ___ 1234   BEVERLY LANE   CAMARILLO   CA   USA   90132 ___
     Number and Street   *City or Town*   *State/Province*   *Country*   *Zip Code or Postal Code*

School you now attend ___ CAMARILLO HIGH SCHOOL ___   CEEB/ACT code 1 2 3 4 5 6

TO THE TEACHER

The Common Application group of colleges finds candid evaluations helpful in choosing from among highly qualified candidates. We are primarily interested in whatever you think is important about the applicant's academic and personal qualifications for college.

Please submit your references promptly. A photocopy of this reference form, or another reference you may have prepared on behalf of this student, is acceptable. You are encouraged to keep the original of this form in your private files for use should the student need additional recommendations. Please return it to the appropriate admission office(s) in the envelope(s) provided you by this student. We are grateful for your assistance. ***Be sure to sign below.***

Teacher's Name Mr./Mrs./Ms _____ Position _____
                     Please print or type

Secondary School _____

School Address _____

Teacher's Phone (_____) _____ _____ Teacher's E-mail _____
          Area Code   *Number*   *Ext.*

Signature _____ *Date* _____

BACKGROUND INFORMATION

How long have you known this student and in what context? _____

_____

What are the first words that come to your mind to describe this student? _____

_____

List the courses you have taught this student, noting for each the student's year in school (10th, 11th, 12th; first-year, sophomore; etc.) and the level of course difficulty (AP, accelerated, honors, IB, elective; 100-level, 200-level, etc.).

_____

_____

_____

_____

_____

2005–2006 COMMON APPLICATION ™   **TEACHER EVALUATION I**   TE-1

FIG 7-4 TEACHER EVALUATION

EVALUATION Please write whatever you think is important about this student, including a description of academic and personal characteristics. We are particularly interested in the candidate's intellectual promise, motivation, maturity, integrity, independence, originality, initiative, leadership potential, capacity for growth, special talents, enthusiasm, concern for others, respect accorded by faculty, and reaction to setbacks. We welcome information that will help us to differentiate this student from others.

RATINGS

Compared to other students in his or her class year, how do you rate this student in terms of:

No basis		Below Average	Average	Good (above average)	Very Good (well above average)	Excellent (top 10%)	Outstanding (top 5%)	One of the top few encountered in my career
	Creative, original thought							
	Motivation							
	Self-confidence							
	Independence, initiative							
	Intellectual ability							
	Academic achievement							
	Written expression of ideas							
	Effective class discussion							
	Disciplined work habits							
	Potential for growth							

CONFIDENTIALITY We value your comments highly and ask that you complete this form in the knowledge that it may be retained in the student's file should the applicant matriculate at a member college. In accordance with the Family Educational Rights and Privacy Act of 1974, matriculating students *do* have access to their permanent files, which may include forms such as this one. Unless required by state law, colleges may not provide access to admission records to applicants, those students who are denied admission, or those students who decline an offer of admission. Again, your comments are important to us and we thank you for your cooperation. These colleges are committed to administer all educational policies and activities without discrimination on the basis of race, color, religion, national or ethnic origin, age, handicap, or gender.

TE-2   **TEACHER EVALUATION I**   COMMON APPLICATION ™ 2005–2006

FIG 7-5 **MIDYEAR REPORT**

Adelphi · Agnes Scott · Albertson · Albion · Albright · Alfred · Allegheny · American · Amherst · Antioch · Arcadia · Assumption · College of the Atlantic · Austin College · Bobson · Baldwin—Wallace · Bard · Barnard · Bates · Beloit · Bennington · Bentley · Binghamton · Birmingham—Southern · Boston College · Boston U. · Bowdoin · Bradley · Brandeis · Bryant · Bryn Mawr · Bucknell · Butler · California Lutheran · Carleton · Carnegie Mellon · Case Western Reserve · Cazenovia · Centenary (La.) · Centre · Chatham · Claremont McKenna · Clark U. · Clarkson U. · Coe · Colby · Colby—Sawyer · Colgate · Colorado College · Concordia College (N.Y.) · Connecticut College · Converse · Cornell College · Cornell U. · U. of Dallas · Dartmouth · Davidson · Denison · U. of Denver · DePauw · Dickinson · Dominican U. (Calif.) · Drew · Duke · Earlham · Eckerd · Elizabethtown · Elmira · Embry—Riddle · Emmanuel College (Mass.) · Emory · Eugene Lang · Fairfield · Findlay · Fisk · Florida Southern · Fordham · Franklin & Marshall · Furman · George Fox · George Washington · Gettysburg · Gonzaga · Goucher · Grinnell · Guilford · Gustavus Adolphus · Hamilton · Hampden—Sydney · Hampshire · Hanover · Hartwick · Harvard · Harvey Mudd · Haverford · Hendrix · Hiram · Hobart & William Smith · Hofstra · Hollins · Holy Cross · Hood · Illinois Wesleyan · Iona · Ithaca · John Carroll · Johns Hopkins · Juniata · Kalamazoo · Kenyon · Knox · La Roche · La Salle · La Verne · Lafayette · Lake Forest · Lawrence · Le Moyne · Lehigh · Lesley · Lewis & Clark · Linfield · Loyola College · Loyola U (La.) · Luther · Macalester · U. of Maine (Farmington) · U. of Maine (Orono) · Manhattan · Manhattanville · Marietta · Marlboro · Marquette · Mary Washington · McDaniel · Merrimack · U. of Miami (Fla.) · Miami U (Ohio) · Middlebury · Mills · Millsaps · Moravian · Morehouse · Mount St Vincent · Mt Holyoke · Muhlenberg · Narapa · Nazareth · New College (Fla.) · New England College · U. of New Hampshire · College of New Jersey · New York U. · Northeastern U. · Northland · Notre Dame (Md.) · Notre Dame de Namur · Oberlin · Occidental · Oglethorpe · Ohio Wesleyan · Pace · U. of the Pacific · Pitzer · Pomona · U. of Portland · Presbyterian · Prescott · Princeton · Providence · Puget Sound · Queens U (N.C.) · Randolph—Macon · Randolph—Macon Woman's · Redlands · Reed · Regis College · Regis U · Rensselaer · Rhodes · Rice · U. of Richmond · Rider · Ripon · U. of Rochester · Rochester Inst of Tech · Roger Williams · Rollins · St Anselm · St Benedict & St John's · St Joseph's College (Me.) · St Joseph's U · St Lawrence · St Leo · St Louis U · St Mary's College (Calif.) · St Mary's College (Ind.) · St Michael's · St Norbert · St Olaf · St Peter's · St Vincent · Salem (N.C.) · Salve Regina · U. of San Diego · U. of San Francisco · Santa Clara · College of Santa Fe · Sarah Lawrence · Scranton · Scripps · Seattle U · Seton Hill · Sewanee · Simmons · Skidmore · Smith · Southern Maine · Southern Methodist · Southern New Hampshire · Southwestern U · Spelman · Spring Hill · Stetson · Stevens Inst of Tech · Stonehill · Suffolk · Susquehanna · Swarthmore · Sweet Briar · Syracuse · U. of Tampa · TCU · Transylvania · Trinity College (Conn.) · Trinity U · Tufts · Tulane · Tulsa · Union College (N.Y.) · Ursinus · Utica · Valparaiso · Vanderbilt · Vassar · U. of Vermont · Villanova · Wabash · Wagner · Wake Forest · Washington College · Washington U (Mo.) · Washington & Jefferson · Washington & Lee · Webster · Wellesley · Wells · Wesleyan · Westminster (Mo.) · Westminster (Pa.) · Wheaton (Mass.) · Wheelock · Whitman · Whittier · Widener · Willamette · William & Mary · William Jewell · Williams · Wilson · Wittenberg · Wofford · Wooster · WPI · Xavier (Ohio) · Yale

MIDYEAR REPORT

The member colleges and universities listed above fully support the use of this form. No distinction will be made between it and the college's own form.
Please type or print in black ink. (32)

TO THE APPLICANT

Check institutional instructions to see if your selected colleges require this form. After filling in the information below, give this form to your guidance counselor. (33)

Birthdate _01_ / _08_ / _1988_ Gender _MALE_ Social Security No. _123-45-6789_
    mm/dd/yyyy *(Optional)*

Student Name _HAYES_   _CHRISTOPHER_   _DANIEL_
    Last/Family   *First*   *Middle (complete)*   *Jr., etc.*

Address _1234 BEVERLY LANE_   _CAMARILLO_   _CA_   _USA_   _90132_
    Number and Street   *City or Town*   *State/Province*   *Country*   *Zip Code or Postal Code*

TO THE SECONDARY SCHOOL GUIDANCE COUNSELOR

Please submit this form when midyear senior grades are available (end of first semester or second trimester). Please complete the grid below or, if you prefer, attach your own grade report form or a copy of the secondary school transcript. Feel free to provide additional comments about the candidate on the reverse of this form or on a separate sheet of paper. *Be sure to sign below.*

Where possible, please provide IB and A-level predictions, as well as the grades for the trimester or semester.

Indicate if marking period is ☐ first semester   ☐ second trimester   S.S. graduation date _____

Course (include title and level)	Grade	Remarks

If available, please provide updated class rank or cumulative GPA through the senior fall semester/trimester.

Class rank _____ in a class of _____, covering a period from _____ to _____
      (mm/yyyy) *(mm/yyyy)*

   The rank is ☐ weighted ☐ unweighted. How many students share this rank? _____

   If a precise rank is not available, please indicate rank to the nearest tenth from the top _____

Cumulative GPA _____ on a _____ scale, covering a period from _____ to _____
      (mm/yyyy) *(mm/yyyy)*

   This GPA is ☐ weighted ☐ unweighted. The school's passing mark is _____

> Have there been any substantial additions to or changes in this candidate's academic or extracurricular record since your previous report? ☐ yes ☐ no
>
> If yes, or if your recommendation for this student has changed since the School Report was submitted, please comment on reverse.

Counselor's Name Mr./Mrs./Ms _____
            Please print or type

Signature _____   *Date* _____

Position _____ School _____

Secondary School CEEB/ACT Code _____

2005–2006 COMMON APPLICATION ™   MY-1

FIG 7-5 MIDYEAR REPORT

Please use the space below, or a separate sheet of paper, for additional comments.

FIG 7-6 COMMON APPLICATION SUPPLEMENT

Application for Admission

**PART I OF II
2005–2006**

Agnes Scott uses a two-part application process. This is Part I, which should be completed as indicated below. Part II consists of the Common Application.

Please note that the $35 application fee must accompany the paper version of Part I of the application for admission. Checks should be made to Agnes Scott College. An online version of this form is available at www.agnesscott.edu/~apply. The application fee is waived for online applications.

Agnes Scott

THE WORLD FOR WOMEN

AGNES SCOTT COLLEGE
Office of Admission
141 E. College Ave.
Decatur, GA 30030-3797

PHONE: 404 471-6285
TOLL-FREE: 800 868-8602
FAX: 404 471-6414

E-MAIL: *admission@agnesscott.edu*

WEB SITE: *www.agnesscott.edu*

This is a four page form, do not tear along this edge

Decision Plans

I expect to enter ASC in the ☐ fall ☐ spring of 20 ____. High school graduation ____ /____
MONTH / YEAR

I am applying under the following plan (please check appropriate box):

☐ Early Decision –
Deadline: November 15

☐ Scholarship Decision –
Deadline: January 15

☐ Regular Decision –
Priority Deadline: March 1

☐ Transfer – Fall
Priority Deadline: March 1

☐ Transfer – Spring
Priority Deadline: November 1

☐ International Candidate
Priority Deadline: January 1

Are you an Early Admission Candidate (*leaving school after grade 11*)? ☐ Yes ☐ No

Are you currently enrolled in a college/university? ☐ Yes ☐ No

If yes, name of institution: _____

Personal Information

Name _____
FIRST　　　　　　MIDDLE　　　　　LAST　　　　　PREFERRED NAME

Permanent home address _____
NUMBER　STREET

_____
CITY　　　　STATE　　　　COUNTRY　　ZIP/POSTAL CODE

Mailing address _____
NUMBER　STREET　　　　　　CITY

_____
STATE　　　　COUNTRY　　ZIP/POSTAL CODE　　PHONE

E-mail address _____ Home phone _____

Social security number (optional) _____ Marital status _____

Religious affiliation (optional) _____

High school _____
NAME　　　　　　　　NUMBER & STREET ADDRESS

_____
CITY　　　　　　STATE　　　　　ZIP/POSTAL CODE

Ethnicity (optional)

☐ African American, Black　　☐ Native American, Alaska Native　☐ Asian American

☐ Asian, including Indian Subcontinent　☐ Hispanic, Latina　☐ Mexican American

☐ Native Hawaiian, Pacific Islander　☐ Puerto Rican　　☐ White, Caucasian

☐ Other (specify) _____

Citizenship

☐ U.S. Citizen ☐ Dual U.S. Citizen; please specify other country of citizenship: _____

☐ U.S. Permanent Resident visa; citizen of: _____

☐ Other citizenship: Countries _____ Visa type _____

Alien registration number: _____

If you are not a U.S. citizen and live in the U.S., how long have you been in the country? _____

Profile

Do you plan to ☐ Board or ☐ Commute?

Other colleges/universities to which you are applying? _____

Have you ever been placed on probation or convicted in court (other than for traffic violations)?
☐ Yes ☐ No　　　If yes, please attach a complete explanation.

Have you ever been suspended or expelled from school or found guilty of an honor-code violation?
☐ Yes ☐ No　　　If yes, please attach a complete explanation.

Has your education ever been interrupted for any reason?
☐ Yes ☐ No　　　If yes, please attach a complete explanation.

PART I APPLICATION FOR ADMISSION/PAGE 1 OF 3

FIG 7-6 **COMMON APPLICATION SUPPLEMENT**

Family Information

Parent 1 _____   Parent 2 _____

Living?   ☐ Yes   ☐ No   Living?   ☐ Yes   ☐ No

If no, legal guardian?   ☐ Yes   ☐ No   If no, legal guardian?   ☐ Yes   ☐ No

Gender   ☐ Male   ☐ Female   Gender   ☐ Male   ☐ Female

_____   _____
STREET ADDRESS   STREET ADDRESS (IF DIFFERENT)

_____   _____
CITY   STATE   ZIP   CITY   STATE   ZIP

_____   _____
HOME PHONE   WORK PHONE   HOME PHONE   WORK PHONE

_____   _____
E-MAIL   E-MAIL

Who should we mail parent information to: ☐ Joint   ☐ Parent 1   ☐ Parent 2   ☐ Legal guardian

Are your parents?   ☐ Married   ☐ Divorced   ☐ Separated

Are you or a sibling the first in your family to attend college?   ☐ Yes   ☐ No

Relatives/friends who are Agnes Scott alumnae or current students

Name _____
                                    RELATIONSHIP   CLASS YEAR

Relatives who are employed by Agnes Scott

Name _____
                                    RELATIONSHIP   DEPARTMENT

Academic Interest

Please list your intended major/area of academic interest (if known).

☐ Undecided   ☐ English Literature –   ☐ Religious Studies/
☐ Africana Studies   Creative Writing   Social Justice
☐ Art History   ☐ Environmental Studies   ☐ Sociology and Anthropology
☐ Art – Studio Art   ☐ French   ☐ Spanish
☐ Astrophysics   ☐ German Studies   ☐ Theatre
☐ Biochemistry and   ☐ History   ☐ Women's Studies
   Molecular Biology   ☐ International Relations   ☐ Other:_____
☐ Biology   ☐ Mathematics
☐ Chemistry   ☐ Mathematics – Economics   PRE-PROFESSIONAL PROGRAMS
☐ Classical Civilization   ☐ Mathematics – Physics   ☐ Pre-Health
☐ Classical Languages   ☐ Music   ☐ Pre-Law
   and Literatures   ☐ Philosophy   ☐ Pre-Medical
☐ Dance   ☐ Physics
☐ Economics   ☐ Political Science   DUAL DEGREE PROGRAMS
☐ Economics and Business   ☐ Psychology   ☐ Engineering
☐ English   ☐ Nursing
                                                         ☐ Architecture

Please select any scholarships or awards you have received.

☐ National Achievement Finalist   ☐ National Merit Semifinalist/Finalist

☐ National Achievement Commended Scholar   ☐ National Merit Commended Scholar

☐ National Honor Society   ☐ National Hispanic Scholar Semifinalist

What activities/sports do you plan to participate in at ASC? _____

PART I APPLICATION FOR ADMISSION/PAGE 2 OF 3

FIG 7-6 **COMMON APPLICATION SUPPLEMENT**

Contact
(Check all sources that influenced your decision to apply.)

How did you learn about Agnes Scott College? _____

☐ Admission event
_____
SPECIFY DATE

☐ Hotel Interview/Dessert & Discussion
_____
SPECIFY CITY

☐ General campus event
_____
SPECIFY DATE

☐ Campus visit including an individual interview and/or tour
_____
SPECIFY DATE

☐ College fair program

☐ Letter from admission office before I actually requested information

☐ Letter from admission office after I requested information

☐ Visit by an Agnes Scott representative at my high school

☐ Contact with athletic department/coaches
_____
SPECIFY

☐ Other
_____
SPECIFY

☐ Agnes Scott student

☐ Agnes Scott faculty

☐ Agnes Scott alumna

☐ College counselor

☐ Web site

☐ E-mail from office of admission

Honor Pledge
(All applicants must sign.)

The honor system is fundamental to all aspects of student life at Agnes Scott. In choosing Agnes Scott, I formally adopt the Honor System by the following pledge: As a member of the student body of Agnes Scott College, I consider myself bound by honor to develop and uphold high standards of honesty and behavior; to strive for full intellectual and moral stature; and to realize my social and academic responsibilities in the community. To attain these ideals, I do therefore accept this Honor System as my way of life.

My signature indicates that all information contained in my application is complete, factually correct and honestly presented. Falsification of information on this application could jeopardize acceptance and enrollment. I hereby request admission to Agnes Scott College on the basis of the terms listed above.

Signature of applicant _____
DATE

Early Decision Honor Pledge
(Early Decision applicants must sign.)

After careful consideration, I have decided to apply to Agnes Scott as an Early Decision – First Choice candidate. If admitted under this plan, I will accept Agnes Scott's offer of admission by submitting the nonrefundable enrollment deposit by January 15, withdraw admission applications from any other colleges or universities, including those to which I have applied for Early Action, and initiate no new applications to any other colleges or universities.

Signature of applicant _____
DATE

Signature of parent of guardian _____
DATE

Signature of college counselor _____
DATE

PART I APPLICATION FOR ADMISSION/PAGE 3 OF 3

CHAPTER EIGHT
MARKETING YOUR STRENGTHS

YOUR PACKAGE: WHY EVERYONE SHOULD WANT YOU

I hate the word "marketing." After all, shouldn't you just be you without having to package and sell yourself? Yes and no.

You should be absolutely honest and present who you are as an individual. As I've said before, there is only one applicant with your personality, your accomplishments, your qualities, and your weird taste for pudding and pickles.

However, there may be up to twenty thousand applicants all trying to get accepted to a limited number of spaces in a freshman class. Therefore, you need to showcase your strengths so that you stand out from those ten or so pieces of paper that make up your—and everyone else's—application.

Back in the day, interviews were a major factor in helping an applicant stand out. Now, however, interviews are not a main factor in whether or not a student gets in. Sure, they can help, but the emphasis has shifted to the application—specifically, the essays, recommendations, and accomplishments and interests. Now as I will continue to tell you, GPA and class choice are still the number one factors in the admissions decision. But, as you found out in the section on CSI (chapter 4), you can increase your chances by matching your interests to what an individual school is looking for.

In the following pages, I will coach you in how to present these interests.

Hopefully, you have completed pages 50 and 61 so you have your College Profile Sheets and your competitive advantages. If you haven't and have skipped straight to this section, I suggest you complete them now so you have a list of schools and know what they might be looking for.

One of the most important things you can do when marketing yourself is to think like an admissions person. Try to look at yourself from an overall viewpoint. In other words, your application, essays, resume, and hopefully your recommendations should center around a theme—the qualities and interests you possess that are most attractive to a given school.

Let me give you an example: You're a math goddess and a drama phenom. Two of your schools are Northwestern and Cal Tech. Your grades, classes, and test scores will give admissions officers an idea of who you are, but now you have a chance to emphasize certain aspects.

For Northwestern, which has an incredible drama department, you should definitely emphasize that drama is a passion of yours. However, you also might stress your interest in math in order to distinguish yourself from the thousands of others who are applying for drama alone.

For Cal Tech, there are an awful lot of math whizzes, but probably not too many math whizzes *and* drama studs. Therefore, you'll want to shed some light on your drama experience to set yourself apart.

Now you might be applying for a specific program (say, computer engineering), and your strength is in that one area. In this case, you should definitely discuss this strength. Otherwise, while you do not need to reinvent yourself for each school, you may emphasize one strength over another if it applies. For example, if you have a lot of experience in foreign languages, you'll definitely want to emphasize it in your resume and essays *if* you are applying to a school that wants students who will study foreign language—for example, a school that has a brand-new languages building. On the other hand, emphasize something else if the school doesn't offer foreign languages as a major.

Now here's the trick—everyone has different themes based on their interests and strengths.

If you aren't the best in a given area, don't worry. If you have spent so much time doing schoolwork that you haven't had much time for extracurriculars, that's okay. You don't have to use one big area or one big theme throughout your application. In fact, most students have two to three smaller themes they want to emphasize, and these don't have to involve how active they are. Following is a concrete example of how a student marketed herself.

Alisha was a good student at a private school in Los Angeles, except on weekends, when she would turn into a raving, psychotic werewolf. (Just making sure you were paying attention.) Actually, she had mostly Bs and a few As, took two to three APs per year, and had a 1860 SAT. She played soccer, although she was not the best player. She enjoyed drama and sang in the choruses of a few plays, but was never the star. She spent so much time doing her work for school, she really didn't have time for much else. At face value, Alisha was a very deserving student, but she didn't stand out from the many students against whom she would be competing. So how did she market herself to make herself stand out?

Well, Alisha needed to do a little self-analysis of her profile and her values. She asked her parents, her counselor, her teachers, and her coach what they thought her strengths were. She completed CSI and researched her schools. As she did these things, some interesting themes began to emerge, which she wanted to emphasize. Now, if she had gone with her original assessment of herself, her applications would have been a bit bland. But because she put in some time thinking and strategizing, she got into many more schools than she would have otherwise.

One of Alisha's themes was the strength of her character. Anyone who talked to her knew that she was honest and hard-working. But Alisha also had an amazing drive to help people. From a family of five, she put her younger brothers and sisters first in her life. Because she was the oldest, she took it upon herself to help out her parents as much as possible. She did not have a formal job, but spent countless hours driving, cooking, and teaching her siblings, not because she had to but because she wanted to.

This strength of character was mentioned by whoever talked about her. Her soccer coach said that Alisha was not the most talented player. In fact, a lot of the time she sat on the bench. But she was named team captain three years in a row because of her willingness to help younger players, because she was a constant motivator, and because she had such a strong work ethic. According to the coach's letter of recommendation, he had rarely seen any athlete in high school or in college who had Alisha's spirit. He told specific stories about Alisha's determination, which really helped paint a picture of her.

Her counselor and English teacher stated that although Alisha was not the top student in her class, she was often the most active. Because grades did not come as easy to her as they did for some students, she went out of her way to meet with her teachers, and consequently she developed strong relationships with them. She was not an A student in math, but really enjoyed history, as evidenced by several strong projects for her U.S. and European history classes. Her GPA and SAT scores were not even close to the best in her school, but her personality and persistence made an impression on many of her teachers.

While one of Alisha's themes was strength of character, it should be apparent that many other themes were also there: her love for her family, her effect on other people, her leadership, her activeness when it came to academics, her interest in history. You see, even though she may not have been a top student, she possessed a lot of traits that colleges want to see.

Alisha could have just been modest, filled out the applications, and hoped for the best given her numbers. Instead she did the following:

1. She identified schools that had programs in ancient history, and checked to see that it was not the most popular major.

2. She wrote an essay about what her family meant to her. She specifically told of how she had taken care of her brother, who had some special needs, over a long weekend when the rest of her family was away. This served not only to give the admissions people an idea of her caring attitude, but also to explain why she did not have many extracurricular activities on her application.

3. She spent time working on her resume, emphasizing her interest in history by describing her projects and the times she spent outside of school doing research. Although she did not have a big list of activities, she described in detail those things she committed herself to, like soccer and academics. If she had just listed "soccer, three years, captain," it would not have given the admissions people any idea of how committed she was. Therefore, she noted that she had started a freshmen-sophomore team and recruited younger students for it, and that her league had named her athlete of the year for two consecutive years. Alisha also stated her objectives and goals at the bottom of her resume, letting schools know she was interested in studying ancient history and literature, as well as in becoming involved with outreach programs with local high schools.

4. In addition to her English and U.S. history teacher, she obtained letters of recommendation from her coach and her European history teacher that specifically discussed her projects and her accomplishments.

5. After submitting her applications, Alisha sent a newspaper article and documentation

that one of her first-semester senior-year history projects was chosen as the best in her school. She also included a summary of the written portion of her project.

6. She sent a copy of her first-semester report card, showing she had improved her grades from her typical four Bs and an A to three As and two Bs.

7. She set up alumni interviews with the schools that offered them. In the end, Alisha got accepted to six schools, including her top choice.

Now you may not have all these things to say about yourself. Nevertheless, Alisha's example does show how making an extra effort in marketing and how continuing to strive to improve during senior year can pay off.

The next few pages include a summary of things to consider when marketing yourself, plus a sheet to fill out so you can discover your themes. You will then take that information and create your resume.

GOING TO MARKET

HOW TO MARKET YOURSELF

1. *Create a plan* to examine yourself, your interests, your traits, and your strengths to figure out how you can stand out.

2. *Use your research* about your schools and your CSI summary to determine what information each school would find the most interesting about you.

3. *Talk to anyone who knows you well*, and ask them what *you* think your strengths are and what *they* think your strengths are. This is not the easiest thing to do, but if you have established a relationship with a parent, a teacher, a counselor, or a coach, he or she will usually want to help you in any way possible. Often you will learn something about yourself from talking with people that you forgot or simply did not consider.

   This is also a good time to get a reality check. If you think you are good enough to play Division I football, but your coach strongly recommends that you apply to Division II or III schools, you might want to look at your real possibilities. (Of course, realize that everyone has his or her opinions, so go to people you respect, and in the end, trust yourself.)

4. Once you figure out your strengths, you'll want to *document them* with your awesome resume, recommendations, and essays.

5. *Contact any departments, faculty, or coaches* about any particular interests and/or questions you may have. Use the phone or e-mail to keep in touch with them if you can't visit in person. Keep them updated about any new accomplishments.

6. *Use interviews to your advantage.* Interviews cannot hurt you, and they can also *help* you. If you make a favorable impression in an interview with an alumnus or an admis-

sions officer he or she can support your application by putting in a good word about you.

7. *Send other documents to the admissions office*, such as report cards, awards, newspaper articles, and outstanding papers you have written. *Note*: Some schools may not accept additional documentation or may have specific procedures for submitting other stuff. For example, many schools have a separate Fine and Performing Arts Supplements that you must fill out and send in along with photographic slides, videocassettes, or CDs that showcase your talent. Check your application, or call the school and ask.

   Unless a school prohibits such submissions, go ahead and send them. It's not like you are sending cookies or hundred-dollar bills—which by the way you shouldn't do. Depending on what documents you have, you may want to send them to specific departments or coaches first. For example, you can send musical tapes or artwork to the specific department so they can be evaluated. You can then mention your submission in your application. If you then win some award, send proof to both the department and the admissions staff. If you're an athlete and you have made contact with a coach, perhaps send a resume of your sports accomplishments, any articles about you, tapes of your playing, and even a transcript to show that you are academically qualified. No matter what, you should show your counselor the documents you're considering sending. He or she should be able to help you identify the best place to send materials, and will also have your materials on hand if a college contacts him or her.

8. *Get extra recommendations*, but only if the person can add something specific to your application. For instance, getting a recommendation from a congressperson who doesn't know you well will not help. But obtaining an extra recommendation from a coach, an art teacher, or another teacher who can specifically write about your accomplishments and your character will add depth to your application. I'm not suggesting that every student needs to get extra recommendations. In fact, too many students send extra recs just for the sake of sending more information. Don't do this. You need to make sure your recommendations truly show another side of you. They need to be written by a person who can say more than, "Well, Johnny is very nice." If you don't have the people who can do this, keep to the one or two recommendations you've already got. You don't want admissions people to say, "Well, Johnny may not be our best choice because he sent us a bunch of useless additional information to try to make up for the fact that he's not really qualified."

Now, it's time to start writing things down. You will use the information from the worksheets on the next few pages to put together a personal resume that you will use for your applications.

Note: If you have a learning disability and want to know how to discuss this in your application, please see pages 44–45.

YOUR PROFILE SHEET

ACADEMICS

Find a copy of your report cards or your transcript. If you've lost them in the pit of darkness that is your room, get a copy from your school. You'll need your course and grade information for some applications. *Note*: When you list your classes, be sure to note whether they are honors or AP classes.

Also, ask your counselor to give you your overall GPA and your class rank (if your high school figures it out). Then get all your test scores in front of you, and fill out the following profile sheet.

GPA _____

CLASS RANK _____

TEST SCORES

SAT _____   _____   _____
     1ST TIME   2ND TIME   3RD TIME

SATII _____   _____   _____
     1ST TIME   2ND TIME   3RD TIME

ACT _____   _____   _____
     1ST TIME   2ND TIME   3RD TIME

AP _____   _____   _____
     SUBJECT/SCORE   SUBJECT/SCORE   SUBJECT/SCORE

LIST ALL OTHER CLASSES YOU'VE TAKEN OUTSIDE OF HIGH SCHOOL.

CLASS	SCHOOL	DATES TAKEN	GRADE
CLASS	SCHOOL	DATES TAKEN	GRADE
CLASS	SCHOOL	DATES TAKEN	GRADE

LIST ANY PROJECTS YOU HAVE DONE THAT YOU ARE PROUD OF.

PROJECT	CLASS	YEAR	GRADE
PROJECT	CLASS	YEAR	GRADE
PROJECT	CLASS	YEAR	GRADE

ACTIVITIES

Most students forget about all the stuff they've done until they start writing it down. Here's a list of *school* activities just to jog your memory: student government, newspaper, yearbook, music, drama, clubs, mock trial, debate.

ACTIVITY	YOUR POSITION	HOURS PER WEEK	GRADE YOU WERE IN
ACTIVITY	YOUR POSITION	HOURS PER WEEK	GRADE YOU WERE IN
ACTIVITY	YOUR POSITION	HOURS PER WEEK	GRADE YOU WERE IN
ACTIVITY	YOUR POSITION	HOURS PER WEEK	GRADE YOU WERE IN

MORE ACTIVITIES

Make a list of *outside of school* activities. Here are some to jog your memory: community service, job, internship, volunteer work, travel, church, politics, scouting, Big Brothers/Big Sisters.

ACTIVITY	YOUR POSITION	HOURS PER WEEK	GRADE YOU WERE IN
ACTIVITY	YOUR POSITION	HOURS PER WEEK	GRADE YOU WERE IN
ACTIVITY	YOUR POSITION	HOURS PER WEEK	GRADE YOU WERE IN
ACTIVITY	YOUR POSITION	HOURS PER WEEK	GRADE YOU WERE IN

SPORTS

SPORT	HOURS PER WEEK	GRADE YOU WERE IN	VARSITY/CAPTAINCY AND WHICH YEARS
SPORT	HOURS PER WEEK	GRADE YOU WERE IN	VARSITY/CAPTAINCY AND WHICH YEARS
SPORT	HOURS PER WEEK	GRADE YOU WERE IN	VARSITY/CAPTAINCY AND WHICH YEARS
SPORT	HOURS PER WEEK	GRADE YOU WERE IN	VARSITY/CAPTAINCY AND WHICH YEARS

SUMMER EXPERIENCE

If you've done something over your summers that has not already been listed, write that down too.

SUMMER 1 _____

_____

SUMMER 2 _____

_____

SUMMER 3 _____

_____

SUMMER 4 (if you have any plans) _____

_____

FAMILY EXPERIENCE

Write down anything you think is important about your family and how you have been involved. (For example: moved a lot; parents separated; death in the family; lots of brothers and sisters; lived on a farm; anything that can show who you are.)

_____

_____

_____

SKILLS/TALENTS

Do you do anything unique? Do you juggle, water-ski, sew, teach yoga, meditate?

_____

_____

_____

AWARDS

Did you place in a competition? Did you get an award like the Harvard Book or the Yale Book? Have you received some sort of recognition outside high school, like "Most Inspirational Player" on your basketball team? Speech awards? National Merit semifinalist or finalist? Boys or Girls State? Were you nominated to go on a special field trip? Dean's list or honor roll? Essay competition? That time you won the county fair mud-wrestling championship?

_____

_____

_____

NOW PICK ONE ACTIVITY (OR MORE IF YOU'D LIKE) AND ANSWER THE FOLLOWING QUESTIONS.

ACTIVITY: _____

_____

DESCRIBE IT: _____

_____

_____

_____

_____

_____

WHAT HAVE YOU LEARNED AS A RESULT OF THE EXPERIENCE?

_____

_____

_____

_____

_____

_____

_____

_____

HAVE YOU HAD AN OPPORTUNITY TO LEAD OTHERS? IF SO, DESCRIBE IT.

_____

_____

_____

_____

_____

_____

_____

YOUR RESUME

Why did I make you do all the work in the last section? First, so you'd write down all the stuff you'll have to put on your applications. And second, to get you to create content for your resume and essays.

What's a resume? Well, some people call it a brag sheet. Essentially it is a list of things you did in high school. Figure 8-1 is a sample resume for someone most of you will recognize. Figure 8-2 and 8-3 are real student resumes, one general and one sports-specific. The sports resume is targeted to potential college coaches. Don't be intimidated if you do not have as much information as these resumes. I am giving extreme examples that include as many sample activities as possible. (By the way, these sample resumes can be found on the Resource CD, if you want to use their formats.)

FIGURE 8-1 SAMPLE RESUME

TOBEY McGUIRE
Social Security no. 123-45-6789

SUMMARY OF ACCOMPLISHMENTS AND ACTIVITIES

2002 **Saved the World from the Green Goblin.** After finding out that a crazy guy developed some potion to make him, like, a hundred times stronger, and after he stole this flying skateboard-looking thing, I ended up offing him, saved my girlfriend M.J., kept my secret identity unknown to the rest of the world, and won the science award from my school.

2002 **Had photographs published in newspaper showcasing crime in the city.**

2002 **Developed super "spidey" powers.** While in my senior year, developed ability to scale walls with my bare hands, increased my reaction time a hundred-fold to be able to avoid flying razor things, and got my body to produce a sticky web-type substance that I can shoot out of my wrists.

2002 **Won science award from local high school.**

2001 **Interned with local doctor resulting in my acquisition of complete medical degree and complete knowledge of *The Cider House Rules*.** Also got to hang out with Charlize Theron.

2001 **Published first novel while working as the *Wonder Boys* protégé of Michael Douglas.**

2000 **Added color to the local town of *Pleasantville* through over a thousand hours of community service.** Also, knew Reese Witherspoon before she was making $20 million per movie.

FIGURE 8-2 EXAMPLE RESUME 1

ESTER GONZALES
Social Security no. 987-65-4321
Wilson High School
SUMMARY OF ACCOMPLISHMENTS AND ACTIVITIES

ACTIVITIES	SCHOOL YEARS	HOURS/WEEK, WEEKS/YEAR	DESCRIPTION/HONORS/ RESPONSIBILITIES
Swim Team	9, 10, 11, 12	10, 24	Captain 11, 12 / Varsity 10–12
Synchronized Swimming	10, 11, 12	5, 28	Founded the Wilson High Synchro Club, which puts on a performance each year.
USC Twin Study	12	5, 24	Currently spending 8 hours per week working with USC professor in the Department of Psychology researching behavioral genetics.
NCCJ Student Youth	11, 12	5, 36	Completed the yearlong youth Leader leadership training and was selected to participate as a youth facilitator/peer counselor at the Brotherhood-Sisterhood Camp. The camp is for students ages 15–18 and addresses social issues such as racism, sexism, and homophobia. Led groups of students in roundtable discussions surrounding these issues and acted as mentor to students throughout the year via e-mail and telephone.
Student Body Visual Arts Representative	12	5, 36	A member of the Wilson High School Student Body Council responsible for organizing art shows including the Invitational Art Show, publicizing the arts in L.A., and coordinating school-wide art projects.
Photographic Exhibition Partipant	11, 12		11th grade—Presented personal exhibition of black-and-white double-exposure photography. 12th grade—Participated in group exhibition that included both black-and-white and color photography. Won regional Silver Key Scholastic Art Award for black-and-white photos.

AWARDS	SCHOOL YEARS		DESCRIPTION/HONORS/ RESPONSIBILITIES
Yale Book Award	11		Awarded to the student who, in the opinion of the faculty and administration, is the outstanding member of the junior class in terms of effort, character, leadership, and academic achievement.

Sunshine League Outstanding Sportsmanship Award	12		Presented to the athlete from each of the schools in the Sunshine League who exhibit outstanding sportsmanship both to their teammates and competitors, demonstrating the ideals and philosophies set forth by the League.
Cum Laude Society Member	11, 12		Eight members of the junior class are selected to be part of this distinguished society, which honors academic excellence as well as dignity and justice. Members are selected based on their academic achievement (top 10% of their class) and their strength of character.
California Scholarship Federation Member	10, 11, 12		The Wilson High School Chapter focuses on service as a key aspect of this national organization for academic achievement. Participated in tutoring program.

WORK EXPERIENCE	SCHOOL YEARS	HOURS/WEEK, WEEKS/YEAR	DESCRIPTION/HONORS/ RESPONSIBILITIES
Swim Instructor	10, 11, 12 Summers	30, 12	Swim instructor and lifeguard for two summers for children 2–12. Started own swim lesson company in 11th grade.

COMMUNITY SERVICE	SCHOOL YEARS	HOURS/WEEK, WEEKS/YEAR	DESCRIPTION/HONORS/ RESPONSIBILITIES
UCLA Medical Center Volunteer	10, 11 Summers	15, 12	Worked as an administrative assistant in the Department of Nursing Education. Instructed staff on computer usage.

SUMMER EXPERIENCES	SUMMER	NO. WEEKS/ MONTHS	DESCRIPTION
NYU Affiliated Photography Program in United Kingdom	Between 9th–10th grades	4 weeks	Traveled to London, Scotland, and Ireland to learn different photographic techniques. Resulted in show in a London art museum.

HOBBIES AND INTERESTS	SCHOOL YEARS	HOURS/WEEK, WEEKS/YEAR	DESCRIPTION
Reading with my brothers and sister	9, 10, 11, 12	3/52	My family and I have reading times each week where I either read to my little brother and sister, or my 7th grade brother and I read the same book and then talk about it.
Learning about pregnancy	11, 12	1/52	I do some reading or research on pregnancy to fuel my interest in becoming an obstetrician or pediatrician. Recently I had the opportunity to videotape a cesarean section.

COMMENTS ON THE FIRST EXAMPLE RESUME

If you read through the resume, you should get an idea who Ester Gonzales is and what she is emphasizing. She obviously has been an active swimmer, both as a team captain and as the founder of a synchronized swimming team. She also started her own business teaching summer swimming lessons.

She enjoys working with children, having been a mentor, a tutor, a swim instructor, and a researcher on a study of twins at USC. She also has an artistic side, not only showing her own photography, but organizing events for other student photographers.

So would you be surprised to learn in the rest of her application that she wants to find a school with a developing art program for photography, and eventually wants to be a pediatrician?

Here are the main factors that make this a strong resume:

- She is honest and shows commitment.

- She did not pad it with every single thing she did, but chose to focus on areas that were important to her.

- She gave details about her awards, her activities, and her jobs to paint a clear picture of who she is and what she is made of.

- She put down the years and the time commitments to show she did not join clubs just for the fun of it, but because she felt passionate about her interests.

- She used action words to describe what she did:

  participated

  founded

  acted as

  responsible for

  planned

  organized

  won

  completed

  volunteered

  worked

  and so on . . .

But what if you don't have as many activities as Ester? What if you are a student athlete and spend most of your time participating in sports? Well, check out the example resume in Figure 8-3.

FIGURE 8-3 **EXAMPLE RESUME 2**

THOMAS RICHIE
Social Security no. 555-55-5555
Junipero Serra High School

WATER POLO RESUME
PERSONAL DATA

Height	6'3
Weight	180 lbs

COACH RECOMMENDATION

High School Coach
Dave Black

Thomas has a great competitive spirit. He is one of the best goalies in the Southern California region and has tremendous potential for growth. He has been a consistent team leader both in and out of the pool and possesses an exceptional can-do attitude. His work ethic is excellent, and I feel he will really come into his own with a few more years of experience and weight training.

HIGH SCHOOL TEAM HIGHLIGHTS

9th–12th Grade

Four years as a goalie; 3 years varsity; 2 years captain Varsity coach—Dave Black

12th Grade

Averaged 23 blocked shots per game.
Allowed average 2.5 goals per game.
CIF (California Interscholastic Federation) 2nd Team.
Sunshine Belt League 1st Team.
Team reached CIF (California Interscholastic Federation) semifinals.

11th Grade

Averaged 19 blocked shots per game.

Allowed average 3 goals per game.

Sunshine Belt League 1st Team.

Team reached CIF (California Interscholastic Federation) semifinals junior year

CLUB TEAM HIGHLIGHTS

9th–12th Grade

Four years as a goalie in Southern California League.

12th Grade

Voted goalie of the year in division; voted player of the year on my team.

11th Grade

Voted most inspirational player on my team.

10th Grade

Traveled with team to New York to play in exhibition tournament with European teams.

JUNIOR NATIONAL TEAM

12th Grade

Traveled with team as backup goalie. Played in 5 games across U.S. Averaged 10 blocked shots.

ACADEMIC QUALIFICATIONS

GPA	3.6
SAT Scores	1820 SAT I—680 Math, 600 Critical Reading, 540 Writing 670 Math IIC, 600 Literature, 530 Chemistry.
AP Tests	4 AP U.S. History, 3 AP English Writing and Composition. AP Calculus AB exam planned for May of 12th grade.

COMMENTS ON SECOND EXAMPLE RESUME

Thomas Richie not only listed his sports accomplishments in a clear, easy-to-read format, but he also included information about his academic qualifications and some comments from his coach. Such information gives a prospective college coach a full picture of Thomas's abilities. A coach may like that Thomas has a strong academic profile because it will impress the admissions office. He may also like the fact that Thomas has the potential to improve with more playing time and more conditioning. Thomas's growth from his junior to senior year also shows the coach that he may be a player worth looking at. And the fact that Thomas seems to be a team player and good communicator may also be to his benefit.

If you are an athlete, a musician, an artist, or someone with a particular talent, it is important for you to make contact with a coach, a professor, or the dean of the appropriate department. In addition to a resume, you can send a videotape of your performance, some examples of your work, or both. Make sure you get recommendations from your high school coach or teacher to support your work. If possible, meet with the college contact in person and maintain correspondence about any new successes during your senior year. Include any newspaper write-ups or awards you have received. You might even send a copy of your transcript to the college contact as evidence that you are academically qualified, if this applies to you.

Taking a proactive approach to contacting people, while acting mature and professional, will allow you to stand out from those students who only fill out an application and send it in. Even if you have unbelievable talent, a school will be impressed with how you handle yourself and how you have created an organized approach to keeping them informed. *You* should do these things, *not* your parents. Since you are the one going to college, you should write the letters and make the phone calls yourself—even if it isn't easy for you. It's not easy for many students, which is exactly why you will stand out if you do it.

IT'S YOUR TURN

Now it's your turn. It's time for you to take your activities and make your own resume. Take the information from your profile sheet (page 117–120), and use the sample resumes on the Resource CD to type in your own info. The resumes were done in Microsoft Word, and you can fill in your own information by highlighting each section and replacing it by typing in your activities. Remember, you might write more about a certain activity for a given school or add/subtract an activity, depending on what you want to emphasize. Be sure to follow the guidelines in the comments following the sample resumes to make your stuff stand out (see pages 125 and this page, above).

CHAPTER NINE
BIG ESSAY FUN TIME, PART 1

FIREWRITING

Okay, here's your assignment: You're about to "firewrite." Write for 7.5 minutes on the lines below and answer the question that I am about to ask you. Here's the deal, though. Once you start writing, you can't stop your pen from moving. In other words, you can't stop to think. Even if you have to write, "I hate this dumb assignment. I can't believe Danny is making me do this, blah-blah-blah . . ." and then start with a new idea—fine. But you can't stop, agreed? Most students are not enthusiastic about this, but believe me, it's important or I wouldn't ask you to do it. So ya ready? Get a watch out. 7.5 minutes. Have some extra paper handy if you need it.

I want you to answer the following question: Who are you?

_____

_____

_____

_____

_____

_____

_____

_____

_____

_____

_____

_____

_____

Finished? Great job. Although many students start writing about nothing, they find that they actually end up writing down some interesting things about themselves. In fact, you may want to put it aside for a few hours and then come back and look at it. Does anything you wrote surprise you?

More often than not, students write what they think they are *supposed* to write. Most students are used to writing papers about books, answering questions like, Describe the use of symbols in *Lord of the Flies*. Sound familiar? The problem is that most high schools don't encourage personal writing, and unless you love keeping a daily journal, you probably don't have a lot of experience writing about yourself. Consequently, when something as important as the college essay comes along, students get frustrated about what the "right" way to do it is. How can you make yourself seem smart, witty, well-rounded, passionate, and basically someone a college wants to admit? Well, here's the good news—you don't need to do all these things.

What you do need to do is *tell a story that shows something about you that only you could tell*.

Don't worry, this is not as difficult as you might think. In fact, I am willing to bet that your first draft will be a breeze. But, you have to realize that this essay is not some b.s. you make up because you think you know what admissions people want to hear. The essay must be real, honest, and direct. This was why I had you firewrite. When asked to tell about themselves, many teenagers paint a beautiful picture of good little students. This is boring! But when they firewrite, there is usually something juicy, even if it's just one sentence, that makes me want to know more about them. Firewriting is simply an exercise that frees up your subconscious and allows you to write without fear of what other people will think. Keep this in mind as you go through this chapter. Whether or not you use something specific that came out from this assignment, it will serve as part of the process for getting a compelling story out of you. If you want, you can do this assignment again and just write from the heart. Don't hold back. No one's going to read it but you.

KEYS TO ALL ESSAYS

STEP 1: THE PLAN
Here's how it's going to work. I am going to walk you through your essays over the course of the next several chapters. (*Note*: I will ask you to write a lot. Feel free to type if that is more comfortable.)

Chapter 9 (this chapter) goes over the key things you need to do to succeed on all your essays. I then walk you through some exercises to help you come up with the meat for your main essay in Chapter 10.

Chapter 10 focuses on the "Big Essay," the general essay you can use for most of the main essay questions on your applications (including the Common App). I will then walk you through examples of essays so you can see exactly what I am talking about. Next you will write your first draft, find out how to get it revised, and find out how to improve it through multiple drafts. I will also show you how to "recycle" an essay by taking one you have already written and making it work for a variety of questions.

Chapter 11 focuses on one of the more popular smaller essays schools ask for. Here you will learn the keys to writing this type of essay and then be guided through how to write your draft. We will again look at some examples, and we will make sure you don't put off writing until the last minute.

Chapter 12 focuses on another popular essay schools ask for. It comes in two forms depending on the school—another longer essay or a short answer essay. You will find out how to write both.

Chapter 13 focuses on other questions lurking out there in application land. Here you will learn some tips to attack each question.

Note: If you are working on the 30-day program discussed on page xi, there are average times that students spend on writing drafts of their essays. These estimates vary widely and generally do not include making corrections and proofreading. Rather, they represent the time it takes some students to crank out a completed quality draft that will most likely need to be revised. Therefore, what I'm going to say next is *very* important.

Writing essays is a process. Do not expect to write a perfect essay in one try. It takes time! The more you write, the better your essays will be. Trust yourself. If you believe in your essay, keep working to improve it. Get a couple of opinions from people you respect, but remember it's ultimately *your* essay. Do not scrap it because someone doesn't care for your writing.

STEP 2: KEYS TO AN EFFECTIVE ESSAY

REVEAL SOMETHING ABOUT YOURSELF.
Think about it. You are an admissions reader sitting in an office with a huge stack of folders to read through and evaluate. You pick up one of the folders and look through the application. It holds lots of what you have seen a thousand times before—grades, SATs, recommendations, student council, and so on. Now you turn to the essay. What would you like to read? A report on what an eighteen-year-old thinks about hunger in the United States? An essay that talks about how great a student's dad is? *I don't think so.* You'd be looking for something unique, something to make the application come alive. You might ask yourself the following questions:

- Who is this kid?

- Is he going to come to campus and be active and make a difference?

- What is he interested in? Is there passion there?

- Is he fired up about going to our school's marine biology center to study how dolphins use language? Or is he a student who simply likes chemistry and maybe wants to take more science classes at our school?

- What values does he have?

- Does he say, "I'm a good person"? Or does he tell a story of how he handled an argument with his teacher and what he learned from it?

- Can I get a picture of what this student looks like, how he acts, and what he will be like on our campus?

- Do I have reasons for wanting to admit him because of what I learn about him from his essay?

I know what you're thinking: "How the hell do I do all this? I don't know if I want to work with dolphins. I don't even know what I am going to wear to school tomorrow or how I'm going to pass the math test on Friday."

As always, don't worry. You don't have to know exactly what you want to do with your life. The point is to tell a story about something that happend to you. Instead of just rambling on about a subject or talking about how great your mom is, discuss how an event affected *you*. How *you* felt about it. What actions *you* took. What *you* learned. If you're still freaking out, I'm about to show you *how* to do this.

SHOW, DON'T TELL.

Okay, every book on college essays says this, but what does it mean? I'll illustrate it with four examples. See if you can tell which one "shows" the most about the person's experience:

1. I inched my way down the hole by wriggling my hips and shoulders forward. My chest and body were flat along the dirt while my arms lay along the sides of my body. Suddenly, I couldn't go any further. The walls blocked my shoulders from fitting through. I could see the narrow passageway opened up in about ten feet, so I dug my toes into the ground and tried to push my way through. Oh oh. Now I was officially stuck. I couldn't move my arms and I couldn't back up. The ceiling of the cave I was trying to navigate was about six inches from my head. I imagined this was probably as close as I would ever get to being buried alive. As I stared forward, the light from my headlamp illuminated the pitch black ahead. I suddenly saw a shape floating toward me. About a foot from my nose, a baseball-sized bat flew into the side of the wall. It sort of bounced off the side and flew up to grab ahold of a rock at the top of the cave where it hung upside down. I could see its little tiny fangs as I swallowed hard and meekly tried to whisper, "Mike . . . Mike . . . Mike! Pull me out! Pull me *out!*"

2. I remember this one time when I was caving with a bunch of friends and I agreed to go on "point"—caving speak for taking the lead. I soon found myself stuck in a tiny cave because I tried to crawl through too small an opening. What I didn't know is that caves have nasty bats. Suddenly I found myself face-to-face with one of the small

guys and knew that I wanted the heck out of there. I had to call for my friend Mike to pull me out by my feet.

3. One example of a time my adventurousness got me in trouble was when I went caving. I got stuck in a cave and saw a bat land right in front of my face. I felt really scared because I was stuck and had to get pulled out.

4. With guts comes fear. I feel that fear can serve two purposes: either paralyze a person into doing nothing or motivate him to take action to overcome it. I have had many experiences where I overcame fear and thus become the person I am today.

Get the picture? Which example would you most likely hear around a campfire? In which one can you better get a picture in your head of what happened? Which one would you want to read more about? Now, I'm not suggesting that every essay has to be some drama-filled adventure. I am also not suggesting that you know how to write like paragraph one naturally—especially when most of your papers have probably had titles like, "The Symbol of the Whale in *Moby-Dick*." The key is to keep writing. You sit down, write something about yourself, and then come back to it later to revise. Following are some ways you can make your writing become more alive.

Replace "describing" words like "tiny," "nasty" (paragraph 2), and "scared" (paragraph 3) by using one of the following:

- Better description "The ceiling of the cave I was trying to navigate was about six inches from my head." (Replaces "tiny.")

- More action. Write in the *active voice,* meaning something does the action: "I bought the bread" instead of "The bread was bought by me." (This is *passive voice.*)
  "I could see its little tiny fangs as I swallowed hard and meekly tried to whisper." This is a good sentence written in Active Voice.
  "The *walls blocked* my shoulders from fitting through." (Not "My shoulders were blocked . . ."—This is a weaker sentence written in passive voice.)

- Paint a visual picture. "I imagined this was probably as close as I would ever get to being buried alive."
  If the writer can get the reader to visualize being buried alive, the reader can better relate to the feelings the writer had. This is stronger than just writing, "I was scared," or "I felt trapped," or even "I felt like I could die."

And by the way, this incident really did take place—in West Virginia in 1994. I wasn't really scared though. Yeah. Okay. Sure.

Now if you follow the guidelines I have just discussed, you will:

1. Write the kinds of essays admissions people are looking for.

2. Find it easier to write because you will be telling a story about yourself.

Most books on college essays have about forty pages of instructions. But in this book, I don't want to bog you down with a ton of rules. The important thing is to get you to tell a story about yourself in the *first person* ("I" rather than "he") that gives me an idea about who you are.

The bottom line is to just start writing—forget about grammar and whether your writing is good. Too many students stay in their heads, thinking over all the options of what they could/couldn't or should/shouldn't do. The beautiful thing about writing is that once a thought comes out of your head and goes onto the paper, you make room for another idea to come in. Just write! We'll worry about making it stand out later.

One final note. Many students are afraid that writing about themselves will produce an essay that doesn't have any point to it. Yes, it's true that you do want to eventually go beyond just the story to illustrate options such as: who you are, what you learned, how you will apply the lesson in future life, or why you want to pursue something in college. Don't worry about this in the beginning. Most students start out trying to make themselves look good and end up sounding forced or not genuine. Instead, we are going to start with a story and discover how simple events can reveal who you are.

THE PERFECT STORM, PART 1

Whenever I hear the word "brainstorm," I think, "Yeah yeah, brainstorm . . . whatever." Although things like brainstorming and concept mapping (where you make little linked boxes about your ideas) work real well, I, for one, never got into them. (I'm not suggesting you shouldn't concept map, but I have found that it is good for essays and reports, but not necessarily for getting a story to flow.)

In this section I'm going to walk you through some exercises to get you to tell some stories, one of which may become the backbone of your first big essay. So get out of your head any particular question from your applications or the expectation that your essay needs to make the admissions people cry.

First, just write down activities you enjoy (examples: surfing, reading, learning biology, competing in speech competitions, watching *Lost,* hanging at the Coffee Bean, tutoring little kids, playing soccer, playing violin, acting). Remember, the list doesn't have to involve just academics or school extracurriculars.

_____   _____   _____

_____   _____   _____

_____   _____   _____

_____   _____   _____

Don't worry if you didn't fill in all the blanks or have more things to say. It's all good. However, if you wrote, "I don't like to do anything," I suggest you think about it some more. And then think about it some more after you put down the PlayStation controller.

Pick one of the things from your list. Now, pretend I am sitting there with you. Tell me a story about something that happened to you regarding the activity you chose.

For *example,* I had a student tell me she had nothing to write about for her essay. Patty said she didn't do anything exciting—all she did was study and occasionally hang out with her friends. She made her list. Playing softball was on it. "Tell me a story about playing softball," I requested. "Well, it's not like I'm a superstar or anything," she replied. "That's okay," I retorted. "Just tell me something that happened to you once." Here's what she said:

PATTY: "Well, when I first started, I really sucked. I fell on a ball."

DANNY: "Excuse me, you fell on a ball?"

PATTY: "Yeah, well, I didn't really have a glove. I was ten years old and my dad bought me one of those Fisher-Price plastic gloves, so of course I was sent into the outfield during our first game. I remember it was the first game because my shoes were brand new and shiny black, while everyone else's had scuffs on them. Anyway, so I'm standing out there hoping no one will hit the ball and I'm staring off into space, when some kid hits the ball in my direction. 'Oh, no,' I think, as the ball came bouncing right to me. Well, I knew I had to stop it, so I just sort of fell on it."

And folks we have a story. Was it that hard? Will Patty's essay come out of this? Maybe not, but we don't care about that right now. If I tell you this high school senior weighs all of eighty pounds and is about five-three, can't you see her as a little girl falling on a ball?

Okay, it's your turn.

Tell me a story:

_____

_____

_____

_____

_____

_____

_____

_____

_____

_____

_____

_____

_____

_____

_____

_____

Now that you have written one story, think of another one, involving either the same activity or a different one. Write it down.

_____

_____

_____

_____

_____

_____

_____

_____

_____

_____

_____

_____

_____

_____

Use a separate sheet of paper, if you've got some more juicy stuff to write down. If you don't have more, try to use the following lines to make notes about possible stories you *could* write. Here are some questions to jog your thoughts:

- Has something funny happened to you recently?

- Did you accomplish something recently that you are proud of?

- Tell me about your last sports game.

- Tell me about the last test you took. Did you do well?

- Do you procrastinate? Do you have one of those "once I didn't start writing my paper until 3 a.m." stories?

- Have you been in a recital or performance recently? Did you have fun?

- Have you gotten bad news in the last year? What was it? How did it make you feel? How do you feel about it now?

- Have you traveled recently? Where did you go? What did you do there? Was it cold?

- Have you ever been in a fight? If you had to do it again, would you fight again? What was it over?

- What's the most enjoyable time you had with your friends or on a date?

- Just write down ideas of what you could tell a story about, or if you're feeling saucy, go ahead and write out a story or two.

_____

_____

_____

_____

_____

_____

_____

_____

THE ULTIMATE COLLEGE ACCEPTANCE SYSTEM

Remember, you want to tell me stories that *you* took part in, not the time your friends dropped a bowling ball through some guy's windshield.

Are you getting the feeling yet that you actually have some stories to tell? Do you think anyone other than you could tell those exact same stories? Do you see that the essay is a way to show your uniqueness? If you are having a hard time telling a story, just keep at it for another day or so. If you're watching Ryan and Marissa argue about something again on *The OC* reruns and this triggers a story, pause the Tivo and jot a note to yourself to write about it later.

THE PERFECT STORM, PART 2

Write down some traits that you look for in others. Let me put it another way: write down things you look for in someone you'd want to go out with. (Examples: sense of humor, trustworthy, outdoorsy, popular, athletic, sincere, a good listener, friendly, kind, adventurous, confident, having a "can do it no matter what" attitude, caring about their family, religious, spiritually aware, calm, persistent, sexy, smart)

_____   _____   _____

_____   _____   _____

_____   _____   _____

_____   _____   _____

_____   _____   _____

_____   _____   _____

Do you know people who have these qualities? Great! List their names and the qualities they possess.

NAME   **TRAITS**

_____   _____

                            _____

_____   _____

                            _____

                            _____

_____   _____

                            _____

_____   _____

Now, it's your turn!

I had two reasons for making you write down other people's traits. First, it's often easier to come up with good qualities in others than in yourself. Second, I wanted you to identify people you like or respect because they may come into play in an essay or two later on. Now, it's your turn to make a list of qualities that *you* possess. Remember, be honest with yourself. No one else is going to read this. If you think you're good-looking, write it down. And if, for example, you value trust in someone else, I would guess that you try to be trustworthy as well, and that you value this in yourself. Now start writing.

_____	_____	_____
_____	_____	_____
_____	_____	_____
_____	_____	_____
_____	_____	_____

The next thing I want you to do is take a look at your list. Are there some things that you value more than others? For me, it'd be determination, sense of humor, and a real caring for other people. For you it might be totally different. Just think about it.

Now think of your best friend. How would he or she describe you? Write down a trait that your friend would say you had. Then jot down something that happened to you that might explain why your friend would choose that trait to describe you. By the way, it could be a story you have already written or made note of in a previous exercise.

Note: You don't have to list three traits. As always, you can do as few or as many as you want—it's your choice.

EXAMPLES:

Sense of humor

Time when I walked onstage in front of the entire school, tripped on my pant leg and did a face plant, stood up, took a bow, and announced to everyone, "Please tip your waitresses."

Determination

Time during hell week for swimming, when I had to hold a kickboard between my legs off the ground for five minutes to get the coach to let everyone go home early. (Note: I would probably just write "kickboard holding—swimming" to refresh my memory.)

TRAIT	INCIDENT
_____	_____
	_____
	_____
_____	_____
	_____
_____	_____
	_____

Now think of an adult whom you respect and have a good relationship with.

This could be a parent, a teacher, a coach, a sibling, an older friend. Write down a trait he or she would say you have, as well as an incident that would explain why the person would pick that trait.

TRAIT	INCIDENT
_____	_____
	_____
	_____
_____	_____
	_____
_____	_____
	_____

ONE MORE EXERCISE

Write down two to three "failures." Jot down something you tried but did not achieve, or something you expected to happen but that did not come about the way you thought. This can be something simple: you studied for a test that you bombed, or you blanked out during a debate competition. Or it can be something more serious: you thought your parents were getting back together, but instead they got divorced, or you thought you would enjoy hunting but then had a different experience.

Try to choose situations that meant something to you, even if they are a bit painful to think about. Did you learn something from the experience? It doesn't have to be good or bad, big or small. For example, you might have learned that you play better football when you are trying to have fun and not trying to go for statistics. You might have learned that not all adults are right just because they are older.

Remember, no one is going to see this list, and you may not base your essays on it. However, you may get an idea of what you *could* write about in an essay by simply getting the words on a page. More likely, you may use different parts of these exercises in your essays. Either way, the exercises are forcing you to take a look at your life to help you answer the question, "Just who am I anyway?"

EXPERIENCE   **ANYTHING YOU HAVE LEARNED AS A RESULT**

1. _____   _____

   _____   _____

                                 _____

2. _____   _____

   _____   _____

                                 _____

3. _____   _____

   _____   _____

                                 _____

By now you should have some interesting stuff written down about yourself. If you have or if you can think of more stories you can write about, make notes to remind yourself of the possibilities. In the next chapter, you will discover how to expand one of your stories and make it into a college application essay.

Keep the following items in mind as you begin your applications:

1. When you start writing any essay, put your full name and social security number in the upper right-hand corner. That way, in case somebody accidentally loses your essay because it was stuck to the Krispy Kreme donut box in the admissions office, he or she will be able to put it in the right file when it's found.

2. Look through all of your applications, and make a list of the essay questions they ask. This will help you see what you've got ahead of you, as well as which sections of this

book you can skip. Start thinking about how you can "recycle" — that is, use one story or one essay for multiple questions.

Now write the questions in the following spaces.

SCHOOL   **ESSAY QUESTION**

_____   _____

                                    _____

                                    _____

_____   _____

                                    _____

                                    _____

_____   _____

                                    _____

                                    _____

_____   _____

                                    _____

                                    _____

_____   _____

                                    _____

                                    _____

_____   _____

                                    _____

                                    _____

If you need more space, photocopy this page or take a piece of blank paper, list the remaining schools, and staple the sheet to the back of this one so you know where it is.

CHAPTER **TEN**
BIG ESSAY FUN TIME, PART 2

YOUR BIG OL' ESSAY

Just about every college and university has a main essay, or a "big" essay. Some schools require only one big essay, others require two big essays, and still others require one main essay and a few short-answer questions. Among these, there is a variety of questions that can be asked. Right now, however, we don't care about any of them. While I will help you answer the "Why do you want to go to our beloved institution?" type of question, that's for later. For now, you'll concentrate on using your stories and traits from the last section to put together an essay of 500 to 750 words, an essay that makes admissions officers say, "I'd like to meet this person. This person seems like a great fit here."

Remember, all the questions designed by colleges are simply meant to get to know you. You *do* have to answer the question, but your particular answer or style is not as important as what they learn about you as a result.

If you look at the Common App, for example, you will see there are six essay choices. This gives you a lot of flexibility, especially since choice 6 is Choose the "topic of your choice." Therefore, I'm gonna walk you through creating a general personal statement that can be used as is for the Common App, may fit certain questions automatically (depending on your personal story), or can be easily tailored to fit different application questions.

First, you have to determine how you want to use a personal story. Successful essays come in many shapes and sizes, but they generally fit into two categories:

1. Where a single personal story sets up a "theme" of your essay. That is, you take a story—say, the girl falling on the softball (page 135)—and a few other little stories that relate to it to give an overall view of who you are. These other little stories can be about the same subject, like playing softball, or they can be about other events demonstrating the same value as illustrated in the first story.

2. Where a single personal story is the main body of the essay. Your experience itself—what you did, what you said, how you responded, and what you learned—will "show" the admissions people who you are. Confused? Well, I have included two essays (one for each type) to show you what I mean.

Be careful, however. Many students think they have to write in the same style as the examples. Not true! There are many different ways to write these essays. Also, your own writing is probably better than you think it is. And you're going to edit, rewrite, edit, rewrite, and rewrite, so it will get even better.

I have included only a few examples for each step of the essay-writing process so as not to overwhelm you. If you do want more examples, check out *100 Successful College Application Essays* by the Harvard Independent. But just as I believe you should not let too many people critique your essays (because everyone has an opinion and you need to trust your own work), I also believe you don't need to read too many other student essays. If you follow my guidelines and get good editors, your unique voice, style, and creativity will come out.

Do not feel frustrated because you don't think you can write an essay like the examples. I like the movie *Gladiator*. I also like *Ferris Bueller's Day Off*. Some will say that the first is a better movie. Others will say that they can't be compared, because they are totally different. I'd still watch both of them again because I like them for what they are. Get my drift?

SAMPLE ESSAYS

FIRST ESSAY EXAMPLE

Mud squished between my toes with every step I took upon the unfamiliar surface. I cocked my arm back and threw the algae-covered oyster back into the water.

"All right, fine, no pearls!" I yelled back to him in disappointment, as he leaned gazing, eating grapes on the balcony.

I stood exploring the murky waters of the Hudson River with my feet, as the seaweed surrounded me, and the barge blared in the distance. I grasped two foreign objects with my toes from the mushy river floor and lifted them out of the water. Two purple marbles covered in mud, one slightly larger and chipped. The corners of my mouth turned up, and I spun toward him, bounding out the water.

"Dad! Dad! I found two marbles! They're so beautiful."

I ran and reached up to place them in his big hand.

"These are your pearls," he said with a warm smile.

It was almost two years later and was nearing nine o'clock. The car lights shone down on the curves as we traveled down Mulholland Canyon. My face was sticky from the tears, and I could feel them gather at my chin. I had just finished telling my father that I had been diagnosed with Attention Deficit Disorder. I was scared and confused. I asked him to help me. He told me to breathe deep and wipe my tears; everything was going to be all right. I wiped my puffy eyes and clenched my arms through my sweatshirt, burying my cheek into my shoulder. I could feel the pressure swelling in my head; I was stupid and nothing but a disappointment. The car turned out of the bends and onto its first main street. We passed some familiar intersections and were close to my school when we came to a stop.

"What are we doing?" I asked, slightly annoyed.

He said nothing as he walked around the car to get me. He picked me up and carried me like a child through the park, where the only sounds were his footsteps crunching in the grass. Not more than ten feet from the car, he held me up high and put me in a tree. He began to walk away.

"What are you doing? It's dark! I can't get down from this tree by myself!"

He stopped, slowly turned to me, and said, "Right now you're in an uncomfortable place, by yourself. You didn't ask to be put there, but there you are. And now you have to get out of this on your own. I can't help you."

I was infuriated, but he turned and walked away, and waited patiently in the car. My heart beat faster. Realizing what I had to do, I gripped the bark with both hands and pushed myself out of the tree, fleeing to the car. I opened the door and sat down. He looked at me with pacifying eyes and smiled as he leaned over, brushing my hair back to kiss my forehead. The entire way home, we didn't speak a word.

I remember just last year, kneeling down behind the white line. I felt my right knee scuff against the orange clay track as I kicked my spikes into the blocks. I carefully placed my fingers on the chalky powder, and I spread my thumbs wide. Staring into the open space above, I heard my father's words. "If you don't get nervous before a race, it either means you'll do amazingly or you won't do well at all." I felt nothing as the gunshot broke my stare. I could feel the lightness of my feet as they came out of the blocks and onto the track, finally feeling as if I had perfected the start I'd been practicing for years. I felt only a little pressure on my torn left quadricep as I turned into the curve of my first hundred meters. The first straightaway seemed smooth, but pushed me into my second curve with a fatigue throughout my body. The end was near, and I could hear the breath of an opponent behind me as she advanced to my shoulder to take the lead. I had come to the end of the last curve, leading me to my final straightaway. My heavy legs felt like they couldn't push me any further, but somehow carried me the smallest bit faster. Out of the corner of my eye, I could see her struggle, and as I crossed the finish line, I realized she had fallen on the ground. I had taken the win. My teammates cheered and gathered around to hug me. I began to cry as the loudspeaker echoed, "A new league record for the girls' Delphic League 400 meters!" It was then that I wished I hadn't been so stubborn. I never let my father come to my track meets, for fear of not performing to the best of my ability, and now I couldn't wait to tell him. I broke away from the crowd, and the pain throughout my body seemed to vanish as I ran up to get my medal. As I scaled the bleachers with anxiety and pride, my eyes paused upon a red paper taped to the side of the highest row. I stopped and bent down to read the small writing. "I was here."

My father passed away suddenly during the end of my sophomore year of high school. I try to remember the many things that he taught me through his unique methods. He made me understand the substantial need for pride and self-reliance throughout all of my life. And like the day at my track meet, though it may not seem as if he is with me, I know he always is. Last night I had a dream that I saw him, and he took his hand alongside my face and stroked me in comfort. As I sat up and stared, I could swear that he was standing right beside me, or so it appeared through my cloudy eyes. My vision suddenly became clear, and with a jolting heartbeat I realized that it was in fact my own hand that was brushing the side of my cheek. He now lives within me. The little lessons he taught me throughout his life have molded me into the person I am today. Greater still, every day of my life he teaches me strength. I am thankful for the little tokens he has shown me and know that I will now teach myself these lessons. I will carry them close with me as I walk along the unknown road to my future.

COMMENTS

Not bad, huh? Believe me, it took a lot to get this essay to this point. As you will see in the editing section, the final draft often looks a heck of a lot better than the original. There are some important things, however, to point out about this essay that can help you with your own writing.

You'll notice that each little section illustrates a lot about the student named Cathy, even though each paragraph just tells a simple story about something that happened between her and her father. She doesn't try to tell the admissions people, "My father was a great teacher," or "My father was caring," or "My father inspired me." Instead she showed those things through the stories.

By picking stories about herself and not just saying what her father did, Cathy also shows a lot about herself without directly stating it. We learn in the first part when she is looking for pearls that she is inquisitive and curious by nature. Cathy is also a bit stubborn: "All right, fine, no pearls!" We learn that she has ADD and how it made her feel when she was diagnosed. We also see that she learned something about herself when she had to get down from that tree. Do you think she applied it to her ADD? She doesn't have to say—not only is it implied, but her improving grades in grades 10 to 12 illustrate this. One activity she is obviously passionate about is track: she writes that she was "finally feeling as if I had perfected the start I'd been practicing for years." We learn that she has drive and a competitive spirit. Cathy also exposes herself by admitting she was scared of not "performing to the best of her ability." Now the last paragraph was the hardest to write, and obviously not everyone will have the experience of losing their father. But don't worry, I will help you sum up *your* stories to show how they support *your* values. Finally, it's important for you to know that the writer did not plan all these things. They came out naturally as she told the stories.

SECOND ESSAY EXAMPLE

"Kay-tee . . . you hungry?"

My own grandmother couldn't pronounce my name properly. I looked at her in the far corner of the kitchen, her black hair streaked with white and pulled back with a scrunchie, the same checkered scrunchie I had seen her wear for the past seventeen years. She always smelled the same too—like her old apartment back in Korea. Her smell overwhelmed me.

"Yeah, I am. Do you have Oreos?"

She looked at me, still smiling. After waiting a few awkward moments for a response, I looked under the smile and saw her confusion. I realized she didn't know what an Oreo was.

"I changed my mind. Can I have an apple?"

"*Apple?*" Finally her eyes crinkled at the sides with understanding, and I knew that we were finally speaking the same language.

Communication between my grandmother and me didn't happen very often. I've always wanted to know so much about her, about her past, about her opinions, about her problems, all of which seemed to be sealed up behind the folds of her wrinkled skin. Yet even if I became bold enough to inquire about the Korean War and the lost children that she never speaks of, or ask how the small scar on her left arm came to be, I would never hear it straight from her. I always needed someone to translate from Korean to English and back, to bridge the gap between our two languages and worlds of apples and Oreos.

Throughout the years, the frustration has overwhelmed me more than her smell. It hurts that I am not able to carry on a conversation with my own grandmother that does not consist of three phrases: "Are you hungry?" "I love you," and "Merry Christmas." It is embarrassing that I dread Korean dinners at home, because it means that if I want a second helping, I have to request the food by its name—a Korean name that my mouth cannot form the sounds to say. I have been told by a few of my younger Korean relatives that I have become a "banana"—white on the inside and yellow on the outside. Despite my fond memories of spending the last six years in a predominantly white upper-class girls' school, I have come to develop an internal conflict between two ideal images I hold for myself. Throughout most of junior high and high school, I have seen myself as a driven American teenager, special only in my academic voracity and in my goal to attend an excellent university. In the last two years, however, I have begun to see outside the ethnocentric bounds of my local and national environment and to long to fill the cultural hole that is the Korean part of me.

I want to explore my heritage—specifically, learn the Korean language in order that I can learn about the culture firsthand. I innately feel that through this journey, I can on some level tap into my coding and remember my history, embrace it, and be proud of it. Up until this point, I have been scared that the more I opened up to this unknown part of me, the more I would lose the identity I have built in my first seventeen years. Even now, I don't know how it will change me. With this next step "out of the nest" and onto college, however, I am ready to face my fears. I somehow know that any connection I make to Korea, the language, or my relatives will make me a more complete person, for I will no longer be denying the deep call of my soul.

COMMENTS

The second essay does not just tell of one incident, but I have included it because the details for the essay came out of the telling of the incident. This student did a firewriting exercise in which she wrote that she felt an internal cultural conflict. When asked to elaborate, she had a hard time putting into words the frustration she had come to feel about being Korean while being raised predominantly American. It wasn't until she came up with the incident with her grandmother that she was able to get at the root of her issue.

The first part of writing her story was easy. The second part, explaining her feelings, was much more difficult and took several drafts. She could have chosen to either continue the story with her grandmother or write about other incidents, but she wanted to delve into how she felt.

Note, however, how she describes her grandmother—the scrunchie, her smell—these make the story more realistic. Also note that the writer is honest about her fear of losing her identity, and she does not specifically state how she is going to fill the void inside her. The fact that she is still working it out and says so makes the essay believable. Admissions officers don't expect that you have your life all worked out at eighteen. However, this student shows her maturity by describing coming to grips with a personal issue that she had not even realized was inside her until her senior year.

This student was concerned that the ending was "cheesy" because it talked about facing her fears. But as you will see in the discussion of conclusions (page 158), a conclusion should sum up what you have learned and show admissions officers how this will affect your future interactions and choices.

TIME TO WRITE!

Okay, do you know which of the two types of essays you want to write? Look back at your firewriting exercise. Look at your stories and your traits. Are there one or two stories that stand out for you? They do not have to be major life events. In fact, rarely does a single event change someone's life forever. More often, it is a simple event that taught you something that then changed your future experiences.

Look at your list of traits or ideals again. What are the two or three strongest ones? Does one of your stories *show* this trait like we've discussed?

Can you put together several of the stories around a theme? A theme could be something like the girl's relationship with her father, it could be about a time you faced a fear, or it could even be about several activities that made you feel joyous or excited.

Can you take one story of an activity and come up with a story or two about the same activity that shows your growth in some way? Here's part of the essay by the girl who sat on the softball in which she discussed two other incidents around the theme of playing softball.

We would go to the park whenever we had free time. My dad would carry all the equipment we owned, and I would follow, cradling my new leather glove. We would spend hours working on every aspect of the game: running, throwing, catching, batting. On good days only a couple of balls would go through my legs. On bad days the ball would hit me in the head, punch me in the gut, and bruise my shins. I would get frustrated at myself and want to scream. But when my dad started to take off his glove and head toward the car, I insisted on playing more. It was not because I wanted to impress anybody or shatter any stereotypical perceptions of myself, but for a sincere love of everything about the game: the competition, the team spirit, and the challenge I took upon myself because I wanted to do it for me.

A walk isn't as good as a hit. You have to hit that run in. You have to be the out-standing player who wins this game.

Bases loaded. Three balls and only one strike against me. With my mind spinning, I looked down at my dirt-caked cleats and clenched my jaw and sank into my batting stance. But no matter how calm I looked as I stood awaiting the pitch, I felt burdened with the pressure to succeed. Determined to impress my coaches with a solid hit, I took a hopeless golf swing at a ball that was almost in the dirt even though I knew better.

Stupid stupid stupid stupid. Play like you deserve to captain this team. League officials are sitting right there. Get a great hit and wow them. You have to win a league award to show the colleges.

I heard strike three whiz by me.

YOUR POSSIBLE STORIES
Make a list of stories you could tell in one of two categories below (you don't have to fill in every blank):

ONE OVERALL STORY OR EVENT THAT YOU CAN DESCRIBE IN DETAIL.
Example: The time I got yelled at by my water polo coach.

1. _____

2. _____

3. _____

A SERIES OF STORIES SURROUNDING A THEME.
You may have several little stories that support one theme.

Story 1 _____

Story 2 _____   Theme or central idea _____

Story 3 _____

Story 1 _____

Story 2 _____   Theme or central idea _____

Story 3 _____

NOW PICK ONE OF THE OPTIONS, AND WRITE THE STORY OR STORIES HERE.
Don't worry about linking them together or making them perfect—just get them down using as much "showing" as possible by employing the strategies discussed previously.

_____

_____

_____

_____

_____

_____

_____

_____

_____

Use these lines if you need some more space or if you want to write another story.

_____

_____

_____

_____

_____

_____

_____

_____

_____

_____

_____

_____

_____

_____

_____

_____

_____

_____

_____

_____

Once you've got something down on paper, you might want to let it sit for a while—a few minutes to a few hours. Your subconscious mind will still work on it, and when you come back to your story you will discover a way to make it better or something you want to add. Even if this doesn't happen, congratulations; you have done what is the hardest part for many students—you've started writing. Whether you expand this section to a full essay or decide to write about a new experience, you are on your way.

Now reread what you have written. Pretend you don't know you and you're an admissions officer. What have you discovered? Who is this student? Could you visualize the student as a real person? Can you identify with the incident? Does it make sense? Does it give you a clue into the writer's values? Is he or she upbeat? Is she determined? Does he possess a strong sense of character? Look back at the values you listed as important. Do these come through in the story?

Can you add anything to the story that would *show* more?

HERE'S AN EXAMPLE:

Draft 1. "I picked up the phone, and it was a girl I had been tutoring in geometry. She seemed stressed. I calmed her down and made her feel better."

Draft 2. "I rolled over at 1:00 a.m. to grab the seemingly louder than normal ringing phone. It was Jenny, the girl I had been tutoring every other day in geometry for two hours after school. I wanted to tell her to get a clue and calm down, but I could hear the strain in her voice. She seemed to have a hard time getting enough air between pauses.

"Ta—Tammy?"

"Hi, Jenny."

"I—I don't know if I can do this."

"Hey, Jenny, who wrote *Billy Budd, Foretopman?*"

"What?"

"I asked, who wrote *Billy Budd?*"

"Herman Melville . . . why?"

"Remember when we had that big test on *Billy Budd* and you thought it was Wednesday, not Tuesday?"

"Yeah."

"What did you do?"

"Well, you know what I did. I looked over the key points of the notes right before the test and ended up getting an A."

"Jenny, what's SOH CAH TOA stand for?"

"Sine equals opposite over hypotenuse, cosine equals adjacent over hypotenuse, and tangent equals opposite over adjacent."

"You've reviewed the notes tonight, huh?"

"Yeah, and I guess I really shouldn't be worried, huh?"

"Why not?"

"Because when I study, I always end up okay?"

"I believe in you."

"Thanks, you're the best."

Does the second draft give you more insight into the writer's values? Would you be surprised to learn that her three stories all speak to her passion for teaching? Now her stories might have been based around her proficiency in geometry. But you still would have understood that she obviously is patient, caring, and pretty quick on her feet.

What do your story or stories say about you? Do you want to expand on anything to bring out a trait or value? If you wrote more than one story, do your other stories support the person you created? Does each add to a theme by revealing more about a value or by establishing new ones?

Spend some time now jotting down ideas about how to improve your story or stories or about what else you could add. If you want, use a separate piece of paper so you can write and still refer to your first effort. Or tear out your first story—hey, there are no rules here.

At this point you may have a good paragraph, several paragraphs about the same idea, or several paragraphs with different stories. Wherever you are, it's okay. If you look back at your work and absolutely detest it, don't throw it away or light it on fire just yet. Instead, whip out a fresh piece of paper, and when you are ready, go through the steps again and write a brand new story. Some students have done this several times with different ideas, just to see what comes out of their heads. Often, what you end up writing down is much better than your original idea.

If you can't stand this process and want to go ahead and write the whole thing, fine. I encourage you to. Or if you have your own method of brainstorming, by all means try it. The only thing I want you to avoid is doing nothing. I know for some of you writing means pain. Unfortunately, you have to write sometime. So even if you're tired or hungry or depressed or anxious, I encourage you to force yourself to write a few sentences. And then force yourself to write some more. If you start now, even if the essay is due tomorrow, your final product will be better than if you put it off. Okay, enough said.

Now, for those of you who have written a story or two that you think has some potential, look back on the incident or time you discussed and see if you can answer the following questions:

- How did the experience(s) make you feel at the time? How did you feel about it a week later? How do you feel about it now? How do you think you will feel about it in the future?

- What new perspectives do you have as a result of your experience?

- What do you know now that you didn't know then?

- How have you acted differently in similar situations since then? (These situations may or may not be related to the initial experience.)

- If you could meet yourself right before the event, what, if anything, would you say to yourself?

- Can you tell another story that shows any of the answers to the questions above? Please write it out.

_____

_____

_____

_____

_____

_____

_____

_____

_____

_____

_____

_____

_____

_____

_____

_____

_____

_____

_____

_____

_____

_____

Guess what? Whether you know it or not, you now have the substantial makings of a first draft. Now might be a good time either to take a break or, if you are satisfied that you have the start of a draft, to type it up on a computer (if you haven't already been using one). If you're not there yet, don't worry. Just keep working on the past exercises and playing around with different stories. If you're frustrated, take a step back and do something else, or go talk to someone about what you have been rolling over in your head. Just hearing *yourself* talk may help.

INTRODUCTIONS AND RECYCLING

At this point, you should have a general body to your essay. Depending on how your story begins, you may or may not want to write an introductory sentence or two. I find that starting right in with the story itself often serves as a "hook" to capture the reader's attention. If, however, the story needs some background to help the reader understand what you're talking about, then you can lead in with a few sentences.

Examples:

And as the bear stood up on his hind legs and looked down at me, I wished I was back in Mrs. O'Connell's European history class.

This sounds like an interesting beginning, doesn't it? I don't necessarily want to know all the details of why the writer was faced with this situation. I would like to find out as the story unfolds. Therefore, I'd keep it the way it is.

My mouth was agape. I thought someone was playing a cruel joke.

Now, you could use this as your intro—it still makes me to want to read on. But it might be more powerful if the writer had provided a setting or some background details. Something like this:

Just when I thought I was feeling as bad as I had ever felt after making the final out in the Little League World Series, I came home to find half my school waiting for me on my front lawn. My mouth was agape. I thought someone was playing a cruel joke . . .

You will also want to write a few intro sentences if you have to answer a specific question on an application. This is when you might recycle, or take one essay and make it fit many questions. Let's say you have written a solid essay that gives a good picture of who you are. You use this essay for question 6 on the Common App. Then you open another application and find this question: "Take a picture of something that has importance to you and explain its significance." Will you have to write another essay to answer this question? Heck, no.

Remember, most of the time, college essay questions are simply devices to get you to write about yourself. While you should not ignore the question, there are a variety of ways to answer it. What you have learned about thesis statements and topic sentences in high school does not necessarily apply here.

Let's take the first sample essay, the one about the girl and her father, as an example (you might want to relook at pages 145–47). She did not start writing with the "take a picture" question in mind. However, she could easily adapt it to address that question. How? Well, she could use a picture of her father, the tree he left her in, or the "pearls" she found on the beach. She could take a snapshot of the bleachers where she found the sign. The possibilities are numerous with a little creativity.

She should, however, address the picture in her essay to show that she can follow directions and that she cared enough to write an entire essay just for this school. She could do this several ways:

- Write a standard first-sentence intro before her first story.

  The picture I have chosen is of my father. He was caring, encouraging, and patient not only through his words, but through his actions.

- Write a more subtle intro before her first story.

  This is the beach where it all began.

- Write about the picture at the end of her essay, making the reader wait to find out about it.

  I carry this picture of my father with me, although I know now that he lives within me.

CONCLUSIONS

Aren't conclusions the worst little buggers to write? How do you sum up everything you have said in the rest of the essay? Students often feel enormous pressure to make a huge impact statement that somehow will make the admissions people weep and automatically let them in.

While your stories should have a point, admissions people are not looking for students who have saved the world. They don't expect that because of one single event, you became a completely new person who is now going to be the greatest college student who ever lived. Rarely does one event change someone so completely. As I have stressed, admissions officers want real. They want honest. They want you. They *don't* want your opinion on how to end world hunger, unless they specifically ask. They also don't want a student to be overly dramatic: "And when my turtle Binny died, a large part of me died with him. I have never been the same since and will dedicate my life to the preservation of small box turtles as pets."

The questions asked on page 155 are designed to get you to reflect on each of your stories and to write down why you chose to tell that story. What does your story show about you? It may not be a huge event; in fact, if you've followed my guidance, it probably isn't. But I want you to expand on what your experience means for you.

The story itself paints a picture of who you are. Just wrap it up with your reflections on the situation as you see it today. The girl in the softball essay learned over time that doing something with passion—for the sheer enjoyment of it—helped her grow and become a stronger person, much more than did working for external awards. But even though she ended up writing this in her conclusion, the stories had already illustrated it. Remember, the girl would spend hours practicing simply because she wanted to improve. She would throw with her dad simply because it was fun for her. This contrasts with her striking out when she had to do well while her coaches were watching.

Remember, you might include your conclusions at the end of each story or wait until the end of the essay. Heck, you can even start the paper with your conclusions and then tell stories to give them some support. Go ahead and write out or type up your stories and any introduction, along with the answers to the questions from page 155. Be as creative as you want and try moving parts of your essay around to see how it changes. Soon you should have a draft you can show to others and begin to edit.

YOU ARE NOT ALONE: THE SEARCH FOR INTELLIGENT EDITING

You've got a draft. That's got to feel good. Now you've got to make it shine. But I've got some good news for you: you have already been editing. When you wrote your stories and when you answered questions and then wrote up the latest draft with intros and conclusions, you were editing. Each time you reread your essay, make a change, try something new, add a sentence, or rewrite another, you are editing. In fact, you may think you have a pretty decent draft already, or you may still need some time. Either way, once you have an essay that contains a story, or a couple of stories and your reflections, you have a draft. You may have way over five hundred words (or whatever the number of words your colleges limit you to), or you may have only the meat of the essay and still need a little work in certain areas. If you have some solid ideas typed up, it's time to give them to someone who can help you.

You think John Grisham, Shakespeare, or the author of the screenplay for *Shrek* just cranked out their work as is? Hell, no, they had editors—kind people who look at your work objectively and both catch your grammar errors and make suggestions on style and content. Isn't it nice to know that you don't have to do it all? The trick is to get the right editors. Who is "right" for you? It depends. Here are some options:

- Parents. Some students can work with their parents and take their criticism. Some parents can be objective and not try to rewrite the entire essay for their offspring. Some students and parents couldn't do either of these things if they were forced at gunpoint. You know which category you fit in.

- Teachers. English teachers usually get the brunt of editing work for obvious reasons. However, do not assume that just because they taught you about stories like *To Kill a Mockingbird* that they know how to edit or how college essays should be written.

- Counselors may have a good idea about what colleges are looking for, but then again, they may not.

- Friends. Recruiting a friend can be a good idea if you have a trusted friend who is willing to give you real feedback. Unfortunately, most friends don't like to criticize or do not have the grammar skills necessary to edit effectively.

After reading these options, you might want to get a couple of different people to give you feedback. Notice I said, a couple, not a boatload. You ask five people to look at your stuff, you're going to get five different opinions, which most likely will cause you to question just about everything you wrote in the first place. If you have a good grammar person (like an English teacher) look at your work, you can be pretty sure that your punctuation and syntax will be okay. Therefore, with no more than two or three editors, you can weigh what each one says and then make your own decision. And it's very important that you make your own decision. If you choose people you respect and who know you well, you'll naturally want to trust their opinions. Just stick to your gut instinct. It is your essay after all, not theirs.

Examples:

- You write an essay about an argument you had with your parents. Your mom thinks you need a new essay, but your English teacher thinks it's great. What do you do?

- You write an essay on your last football game that you feel strongly about. Both your counselor and your English teacher suggest picking a new topic. What do you do?

- You write an essay about your three-week meditation in a Buddhist temple in Japan. One English teacher loves it; one hates it. What do you do?

See, there's no easy answer. Most of the time, however, you won't have to deal with this. Most experienced editors will help you make your essay better, not tell you to scrap it. Just know that you owe nothing to anyone but yourself and that you have to be the one happy with the essay you send with your application. If everyone tells you that your *Star Wars* parody is funny but not appropriate for a college essay, you ought to listen. But if you are writing about a sensitive subject that upsets someone, this is not necessarily a reason to redo it.

The bottom line is that you are going to have to play around with your essay for a while after you get the editors' comments back to produce a second, third, or final draft.

IMPROVE YOUR ESSAY THROUGH EDITING

I've already gone over some ways to make your writing "show" rather than "tell" (Chapter 9). Now, instead of presenting a kajillion rules, I will simply suggest six primary issues to look for when editing, as well as a few ways of finding out where you need to make corrections. (If you want the kajillion rules of grammar, check out *Writing a Successful College Application Essay* by George Ehrenhaft, or pick up *The Write Source*, by Patrick Sebranek et al.)

Here are the six things you should look for when you start editing:

1. Make sure you have answered the question.

2. Figure out what you want the reader to come away with and to know about you. Does your essay accomplish this, or do you have to add something?

3. Is your subject specific enough? If you were an admissions officer reading the essay, would you get an accurate picture? Do you need to add more details or more explanation?

4. Do the ideas flow together to make a point, or do they jump around?

5. When you start reading your essay, are you hooked pretty quickly? Do you want to read more after the first few sentences? Does your conclusion add anything about you?

6. Does each section or paragraph add something new? Does each one contribute to the overall essay? Do you need to add something, take out something, or replace something?

Here are some ways to find out what your essay needs:

1. Let it sit for a while without reading it. Then read it out loud. Then read it again with a pen in hand. Make notes about anything that is unclear or wordy or just not right. You don't have to know how to change it, just that it perhaps needs revision.

2. Have someone read your essay to you out loud. Listen to hear if anything doesn't work. Watch the reader's face and listen to the reader's voice to see if he or she gets it or not.

3. Cut things and move things around to see if it makes any difference. Ask yourself, Could I add something to this sentence or paragraph to make it clearer or better? Try writing something else just for the heck of it and see if it improves the essay. If you are stuck on a section that's not quite right, rewrite it without looking at the original essay and then compare the two to see if you prefer the new version.

FIRST DRAFT

When I play baseball, I think of it as a game of chess, not <u>chekers.</u> I think about the
checkers
next pitch, the next batter, even the next time through the lineup. I couldn't do it

any other way. When I face a hitter that <u>I tell</u> thinks he's better than me, <u>I feel angry,</u>
can tell   **no comma**
and determined. A teammate may want me to put a fastball right in his ear, but

I remain determined to send him back to the bench with a changed mind.

Once I begin to pitch, my mind clears, and all that I think of is <u>the catcher's</u> glove
space
and the pitch I'm about to throw. After the final out of a <u>win I</u> am filled with joy and
comma
pride. I feel it with my whole body, because my mind is clear of all other thoughts,

and I can just enjoy that moment.

Can you make this paragraph more into a first-person story, as if you are telling it from the pitcher's mound and a fierce batter comes up to the plate?

Moments of triumph are the ones that I remember best throughout my life. I can re- **rewrite for clarity**

member when I could not seem to grasp the function of the salt bridge in an electrolytic cell in my chemistry class. There came a point when there was nothing more **Describe this in more detail if you can. What were you doing—a lab? What was there to "grasp"**

my teacher could say or do to help me, which made the revelation even more enjoyable.

why was it more enjoyable?

Finally in class one day, while thinking of a totally unrelated topic, it hit me, like it

make into 2 sentences.

fell out of the sky and into my head. These are the moments that I treasure most, **Can you add more about what came into your head—specifically, what you figured out about the salt bridge?**

which is why I enjoy subjects involving the understanding of concepts, rather than

the memorization of facts.

Can you tie this into the 1st paragraph about baseball? Can you include another incident or time that is related to these examples, but that may show another trait or ideal you feel is important? Maybe another sports story?

These moments of understanding are what drive my curiosity which I expect will re-

comma

main with me for the rest of my life. I cannot help but look at a mechanical object

and wonder how it works, or look down a road and wonder what is at the end of it, and most of all, look at a problem and seek out the solution. I can dismiss nothing **Such as? If you can, give me a specific example or two of something you'd like to learn about, even though you may not know what you want for a major.**

as impossible and am incapable of quitting. I believe that this curiosity and tenacity

will drive me to excel in my next level of education. I am excited about the new chal-

lenges that I am about to face. I'm sure that I will enjoy working with professors and

classmates to understand complex concepts.

You should now add a concluding sentence or two that discuss a goal for the future or what you bring with you as a student to their college.

LATER DRAFT

He was big, I'll give them that. This six-four, probably 220-pound senior stepped up to the plate, swinging his arms in wide circles to get warmed up. All the while, he fixed his gaze on me. Intimidation. Bravado. Fear. These are just a few of the psychological battles that go on between a pitcher and a batter. Many hitters come up to the plate with an "I'm better than you" attitude. While many believe that a good way to break a cocky batter's concentration is to put a fastball right in his ear, I instead want to send him back to the bench with a changed attitude knowing that he can't hit me. This is why I play baseball like chess, not like checkers, as my coach likes to say. When I am standing on the mound I am analyzing my opponent—his body movements, his eyes, his stance. I am thinking about my options—the location, the speed, the "quadrants" on the catcher where I can throw the ball. Yet when I begin to pitch, my mind clears, and all I think about is the catcher's glove. I am totally focused on the moment. *First two pitches fouled off. One more to go. A changeup toward the outside. Strike three and my moment of triumph. Their big hitter doesn't look at me while he walks off with his shoulders slumped.*

The way I approach baseball is no different really than the way I approach the rest of my life. I can remember when I could not seem to grasp the function of the salt bridge in an electrolytic cell in my chemistry class. Because I did not understand what was making the electricity pass through the cell, I did not understand the purpose of having a salt bridge. There was nothing more my teacher could say or do to help me, which made me more determined to figure it out. Only when my mind relaxed, however, and I was engaged in a completely different activity, did the answer hit me. It was as if a whole world of knowledge had just been dropped in through the top of my head. Sitting in English class two days after the lab, I suddenly understood that the oxidation-reduction reactions occurring on either side of the cell were causing the buildup of ions inhibiting the ability for the reactions to continue. Consequently, the salt bridge was required to react with the ions to neutralize the solutions. I have always enjoyed trying to figure out concepts rather than simply memorizing facts. Therefore, whether it is analyzing a batter or a complex science problem, I treasure the opportunities when I have to come up with solutions.

Additionally, I hold myself to high standards, especially when it comes to supporting those around me. If, for example, I feel I have let my teammates down in any way, I have a sick feeling in my stomach until I believe deep down that I have made up for it. Last football season, my team had only two wins on the season, and all our players seemingly took a beating in every game. Yet what hurt the most for me was not the losing, but when I failed to make a block that my teammate was depending on. It was during one of the final games of the season, and I walked back to the huddle untouched, having to watch my teammate be pulled off the muddy field and assisted over to the sidelines. I have found that although my individual victories have been sweet and my individual failures difficult, I possess a quality that enjoys working with others toward a common goal. Whether it is football or academics, I believe no individual can achieve more than a cohesive team can. Thus, when I have been the weak link in a group, I have pushed myself to improve to allow the group to better succeed.

My striving to understand and to achieve drives my curiosity, which I expect will remain with me for the rest of my life. I cannot help but look at a mechanical object and wonder how it works, or look down a road and wonder what is at the end of it. I dismiss nothing as impossible and like to think of myself as incapable of quitting. I believe that this curiosity and tenacity will drive me to excel in my next level of education. I am excited about the new challenges that I am about to face. I am sure that I will enjoy working with professors and classmates to understand complex concepts, even though at this time, I am unsure of exactly what I want to study in college. My main goal is to find a field where I can explore complex ideas and bring my own unique insights to them. I have interests in various fields of study, including architecture, chemistry, and mathematics. I therefore look forward to bringing an intellectual curiosity, along with a drive to accomplish, to a school where I can make a real impact.

CHAPTER ELEVEN
SMALLER ESSAY FUN TIME, PART 1

SMALLER ESSAY 1: WHY YOU WANT TO ATTEND . . .

One of the most popular questions asked by colleges is, Why do you want to attend our school? Actually, this question is asked many different ways, but each way wants the same kind of answer. You may see the following questions:

Why do you want to attend this particular college?

Tell us about the academic areas that interest you most and your reasons for applying to our college.

What opportunities do you see yourself taking advantage of at our college?

And on and on.

The key to answering this question is to be specific. You have to know about the school and have definite reasons for wanting to attend. The more admissions people see that you've done your homework and seem to really want to go to their school, the more they will like your essay. They want to know that if they admit you, they will have an excited, motivated student who will be active on campus—and who hopefully will become an active alumnus who will donate money down the road.

SAMPLES

FIRST EXAMPLE ANSWER

Stanford University is a place I would like to attend because of many opportunities available for undergraduates. Obviously, the reputation of such high-quality academics appeals to me because I believe that I can grow by meeting people of such diverse backgrounds. The size of Stanford is a perfect number for me at 6,500 undergraduate students. There seems to be plenty of opportunities for contacts with professors, yet it seems that there is also a lot of diversity among the students. I have always envisioned myself going to a university with quality sports teams, so that I can get a traditional "college experience." When I went on a tour of your institution, the students I met, the architecture, and the surrounding area all appealed to me. I like the fact that Stanford is a somewhat isolated campus, but has access to San Francisco, forty-five minutes away. I want to take advantage of the many research opportunities available, as well as the study-abroad programs. Overall, the mixture of world-class academics, sports, and opportunities for community service make Stanford one of my first choices.

Not bad, huh? Well, it's not bad, but it's also like fourteen thousand other answers. Remember, being specific is key. Following is an example of a more detailed answer in which a student understood how to get a school's attention. (This was originally part of an appeal letter that will be discussed later in the book.)

SECOND EXAMPLE ANSWER

I recently met a Stanford graduate from the class of 1994. He was very enthusiastic about the school and, after hearing about my interests, recommended that I look into the human biology major. This program turns out to be exactly what I am looking for as an undergraduate. Biology is the subject that I am most passionate about, and my ultimate goal is to go to medical school and become a pediatrician. The human biology major would enable me to fulfill the premed requirements without limiting me to the confines of a basic biology major. Through this program, I would be able to combine my interest in biology with my interest in human development, psychology, and art.

The amazing research opportunities are yet another reason why Stanford is my first choice. I have recently begun conducting advanced research at USC that seeks to examine the inheritance of biological and social risk factors for antisocial behavior. I am currently developing a new observational test for nine-year-old twins, which utilizes physical manipulatives to elicit aggressive behavior. I am including a brief summary of my work for your review. At Stanford, I hope to continue my research in this general field. I am particularly interested in the research of Dr. Allan Reiss that explores behavioral neurogenics, a topic that I have not been able to investigate due to the limitations of my current laboratory.

I am not only interested in Stanford because of its academic and research opportunities. I am passionate about art, especially photography. This year, I am the visual arts representative on the student body council. It is my job to organize and promote the art exhibits we have in our gallery. I am currently organizing an invitational art show, which features the work of high school students from over twenty schools around Los Angeles. I have also submitted a portfolio to the regional Scholastic Art Contest, and I will be photographing children with developmental disabilities at a local physical therapy clinic in the upcoming months. Two weeks ago, I had the unique opportunity to videotape a cesarean section from the surgeon's vantage point, and I am currently in the process of editing this piece. The Cantor Center for the Visual Arts is an incredible resource that I will definitely take advantage of at Stanford. I am impressed by the permanent collection of photography, which includes work by two of my favorite photographers, Berenice Abbott and Ansel Adams.

As I mentioned in my application, my work at the National Conference for Community and Justice has inspired me to organize a series of open-forum discussions on social issues. This semester, I am working with the other members of the Student Diversity Organization on additional discussions surrounding homophobia and religious tolerance. At Stanford, I plan on joining Amnesty International and Kids with Dreams in order to continue my involvement in social justice and community service.

Do you see the difference? I'm not suggesting that you be as focused as this student; I know this second example freaks out many students who think they could never write like this or write so much. Don't worry; whatever you write will show who you are. This is an extreme example. But note that this student obviously knows Stanford well and knows just how she will excel once she is there. Also notice how she worked in her experiences and then related them to specific programs. This just backs up her statements. If she suddenly wrote, "Oh, and I want to come to Stanford because I just love basket weaving," but she showed no prior experiences with basket weaving on her application, an admissions person might think, "Hmmmm . . . b.s. perhaps?" Therefore, open the viewbook, get online, look at your visitation notes, and answer some of the questions below.

THE PERFECT STORM: THE SEQUEL

1. Which of the college's programs are interesting to you? Majors, extracurriculars, volunteer possibilities, sports? Look them up, and use their names in your answer.

2. Even if you don't know what you want to be when you grow up and have no idea of your major, look through the school's information (especially if it has an online course book, which lists all the classes it offers, along with descriptions and the names of professors). Try to find some classes (and professors) that interest you. Write 'em down.

3. Does the school have new programs or departments it is "selling" that may interest you? For example, if a school has a brand-new forty-million-dollar physics lab and you are interested in physics, make sure you mention your interest, especially if the school is not known for its sciences. Each year, schools try to improve their reputation, often by strengthening their less popular areas to attract new students. Imagine then how happy a school would be to find a student who was not only interested in its developing program, but who also mentioned it in the application.

Guess what? Yes, it's your turn. First, take some time to do research on your schools that require this essay question. Then fill in the spaces below.

SCHOOL

CLASSES, PROGRAMS, SPECIFIC REASONS FOR
WANTING TO ATTEND

_____

_____

_____

_____

_____

_____

_____

_____

TIME TO WRITE!

Once again, it's your turn. If you're the type who likes to write things down before you type them, use the following lines. Otherwise, take your research, and type up your answer to the smaller essay question. *Do not think that the short answer essay question does not mean as much as the big essay!* Take your time with this question, just as you did with the big essay. Get it proofread and edited before you even think about sending it with the application. If you intend to print out an answer and paste it onto the application, I suggest making a copy of the application and sending that in rather than an application with pieces of paper glued to it. Or simply attach a separate sheet with the essay on it, and write on the application, "Please see attached page." If you do this, be sure to put your name and social security number on each attached page.

_____

_____

_____

_____

_____

_____

_____

_____

_____

_____

_____

_____

_____

_____

_____

_____

_____

CHAPTER TWELVE
SMALLER ESSAY FUN TIME, PART 2

SMALLER ESSAY 2: DESCRIBE AN EXTRATERRESTRIAL ACTIVITY

Another popular short-answer essay question is, Please describe an extracurricular activity that is meaningful for you and state why. And still another is, What is an academic area that interests you the most?

In fact, the Common App includes the first question in the Work Experience section. Note, however, that some schools make one of these questions a secondary big essay or include it as one of the choices for the main essay. Large or small, you should know what the admissions officers are looking for. You also should know how to craft another eye-catching essay that shows a little bit more about you and what your interests and values are.

In the following pages, we'll discuss how to succeed at both varieties of questions. But first, here is a question for you: Which of the following do you enjoy reading most?

1. I really like being involved in community service.
2. Because I am really well rounded, I want to discuss my involvement in Student Council, Mock Trial, and Tennis.
3. When I stepped on the stage for the first time, I felt electric. My heart, which had been thumping like a bass drum, slowed way down, and I no longer thought about my lines. Instead, I just became Conrad Birdie, musical superstar.

Okay, maybe you wouldn't want to read any of these. And, yes, the last one is a bit cheesy. But even so, these examples illustrate a point about what the majority of students do and don't do. Most students don't take short-answer essay questions seriously. Either they just list their activities, or they talk too generally about an activity they participate in. They don't show any passion or offer any concrete stories showing *why* the activity is meaningful for them.

Here are the key points for responding to short-answer essay questions.

1. *Pick a subject that is supported by your application.* You do not have to choose the activity or subject that you are best in, or the activity or subject that you have spent the most time at. But if you say you love playing baseball and you have played all of a half an inning—well, this is a problem. Ask yourself, What activity haven't I talked about in the rest of the application that could show a different side of me? If you

wrote an entire essay on soccer, for example, then pick some other activity you enjoy and are passionate about. In discussing an academic area that interests you, think about "positioning" yourself if it is appropriate. See page 112 for more details on this.

2. *Write about something you know about and truly enjoy.* I had a student who was trying to impress the admissions people with an essay about how he liked to do community service. Unfortunately, it came off sounding forced. After getting him to tell me some stories, however, it became clear that he really enjoyed acting. However, his parents weren't very supportive, and he kept trying to downplay his enjoyment by saying things like, "Yeah, but I stink . . . that wouldn't be a good thing to write about." Yet, when he talked about the plays he had been in, his whole body changed. He sat up. His eyes got bigger. He smiled. He used gestures. It was obvious what he should write about. No, he never had a lead part. In fact, he had been in only two performances. But when really pushed, he admitted that he would enjoy doing more acting in college, even though he didn't feel he was good enough. His essay reflected his desire to act and the minibattle he had to fight with his parents and with himself. He admitted that something besides getting good grades could be important to him.

Now this strategy also applies to discussing academic subjects. You don't want to say you hate every school-related subject, but don't fake it and say you love algebra if you don't. Pick a project or a paper that you learned something from, or discuss how a teacher motivated you in a specific area. Again, the more personal you make it (perhaps through a story), the more your answer will stand out from other applicants.

3. *Answer the questions, Why? and How?* If you write that you enjoy European history or student government, the reader should not have to ask why or how. For example, if you are interested in continuing with an activity or a subject in college, say why.

In the next section, I have included two drafts of the same essay. The first version is much too generic. Note that the second version, which answers the *why* and *how* questions, is much improved.

SAMPLES

FIRST VERSION

William Shakespeare is one of my favorite literary figures. (Why?) As a young boy, I was well informed of his gift for words through my grandfather. (How?) I sought to share my grandfather's appreciation of Shakespeare. (Why?) It had always been a goal of mine to read one of Shakespeare's plays, but learning issues hindered me from reading him earlier. It appeared to be an unreachable goal, particularly to my elementary teachers. The day came when I was placed in a special school designed for kids with learning issues. Fortunately, I was able to progress as a student through different learning techniques and at a faster rate than most other children. (How?) This is when I was given my first opportunity to read Shakespeare.

Life, unfortunately, took a cruel turn for my grandfather and his loss of vision prevented him from reading books. I became his eyes and began to read Shakespeare to him. It was at these moments I felt the most connected with him (Why?), and I was able to let him continue to pursue a passion he no longer thought he could.

After his death, I was compelled to continue my Shakespearean studies. Every week during high school, I read and studied many of Shakespeare's plays and sonnets with an independent tutor, my favorite being *The Merchant of Venice*. (How?) Till this day, I am in awe of the material he was able to produce and the language he used. (Why?) Shakespeare's literary works have not only inspired me in my own writing, but his poetic and creative words also became a bond in the loving relationship that I had with my grandfather. (How?)

SECOND VERSION

The last time that my grandfather came over, I read the newspaper to him. Since he had lost his vision, I had been reading a variety of books and magazines to him, his favorite being Shakespearean plays. On this day, however, the United States had put a rover on the surface of Mars. This, however, did not seem to interest my grandfather. He told me that it would not be the accomplishment that he would remember about the day; what he would remember was that his grandson had read to him.

My grandfather was the first person to introduce me to Shakespeare. It was during the times that I read to him that I felt the most connected to him. Perhaps this is one of the reasons I began to feel connected to the characters in Shakespeare's plays.

At first, in junior high, I would read plays like *Othello* or *The Tempest* without an appreciation for what the words meant. After my grandfather's death, however, I felt compelled to continue my Shakespeare studies. The day came when I was placed in a special school designed for kids with learning issues. Fortunately, I had the opportunity to study with a tutor who not only taught me to understand the language, but also to appreciate the rhyme, the meter, and the motivations behind Shakespeare's characters. She would teach me by walking me through one scene at a time. At first, I would stare at my watch, hoping she wouldn't make me keep going. But as I kept reading, the iambic pentameter began to naturally flow in my head. The words I had once thought were a different language began making sense. We would stop after every few stanzas and discuss what I thought they meant. I learned to trust my interpretations, and I soon began to feel a sense of accomplishment when I realized I was understanding and enjoying text that my friends wouldn't even think about reading. I then began to find myself thinking about the stories when I wasn't reading, as well as challenging my initial beliefs about the characters.

By the time I reached high school, for example, I picked up *The Merchant of Venice* because I wanted to see how Shakespeare would treat a Jewish character. At first I was angry that he had made the one Jewish character, Shylock, the antagonist. Yet, as I broke down Shylock's soliloquies, I began to see him as a truly sympathetic character representing very human tendencies that I have found myself to possess. As I began to identify with each of the characters in different ways, I began to appreciate Shakespeare's ability to capture the similarities in all humans and make certain traits universal through his characters. I no longer regarded Lady Macbeth as the "crazy character." Instead, I came to recognize how her subconscious worked against her. It is these realizations that encourage me to continue my studies, not just of Shakespeare, but of other writers in other times. I hope to possibly pursue an English degree in college so that I can one day pass along the gift of literature to someone, as my grandfather and tutor passed it along to me.

Can you see that by answering the why and how questions through details, the second version is much more alive than the first?

A PERFECT STORM, PART 3: FREDDY RETURNS FROM THE GRAVE

Okay, it's your turn. If you've got a short-essay question on one of your applications, let's get you writing.

You're probably tired of making lists, and you don't *have* to do this one, especially if you already have an activity or subject in mind. But if you need to write down some ideas, try this: list activities you not only enjoy, but that you also think will be supported by the rest of your application. Think about something you would like admissions officers to know about you.

ACTIVITY OR SUBJECT

_____

_____

_____

_____

Why do you enjoy it? Why is it meaningful? Is there a specific time you can write about to illustrate it? Did anyone work with you or help in making this activity or subject rewarding? How has it contributed to the person you now are? Would you like to continue it in college? Why? How? Is there a specific program at a college that will allow you to continue with this activity?

Is there another activity or subject that you want to compare to the first to see which one is better?

ACTIVITY OR SUBJECT

_____

_____

_____

_____

YES, MORE WORK

Use the preceding guidelines and examples to write a draft. You can either write your draft here or type it out. Make sure you put your name and social security number on each page. Then absolutely, positively, get it edited, and proofread lik fifty-seven times fro errerz.

_____

_____

_____

_____

_____

_____

_____

_____

_____

_____

_____

_____

_____

_____

_____

_____

_____

_____

_____

_____

THE ULTIMATE COLLEGE ACCEPTANCE SYSTEM

CHAPTER THIRTEEN
ADDITIONAL ESSAY: NO MORE FUN TIME

EXAMPLE QUESTIONS: WHAT IS LURKING OUT THERE?

Schools like to ask many types of questions, both short-answer questions (100 to 250 words) and those that require longer essays (500 to 700 words). As discussed on page 157, you can often recycle an essay and use it to answer several different questions. However, colleges never make your life easy, so some questions will require specific answers. Most of these questions come in short-answer form. Following is a list of questions you might see, along with some hints for answering each one. By now, you should have a handle on telling stories and being specific in your answers. Many of the strategies you have learned thus far should help you with whatever comes your way. Just be sure that someone else reads and proofs everything you write, even if it's only a few sentences. Nothing spoils an appliicaton lke a few mispeled wrds.

POSSIBLE QUESTIONS
Since most schools allow you to choose one question from among several, there's a good chance that one of them will be from this list.

1. *What was your most significant leadership experience?* Telling a story will help you here, but be careful. This question looks a lot like, Describe one of your most significant experiences or achievements. Note this question has the word "leadership" in it, so you will have to discuss the process of overseeing or managing other people instead of just telling what happened to you. You should pick an experience where you can write about what methods you used to get people to follow you or to do what you wanted them to do. Maybe it just happened naturally. You'll still have to discuss what you said and did to foster their cooperation and then write how you led them to some kind of result. You'll also want to discuss what you learned and if your methods have changed since then. You want to come off as mature, so pick a story where you either successfully led others or tried and failed to lead others. Don't tell of a time you simply babysat someone. You might want to include some of your values into the essay, such as sensitivity, communication, cooperation, persistence, caring, honesty, and trust.

2. *Tell us about a person who had a strong influence on your life*: For this one, it's all about the story or series of little stories. Remember to always answer the questions Why? and How? like I have discussed in previous sections. Also, make sure the story relates to what you learned. And discuss how you developed as a result of this person's influence rather than just talk about how great or crappy they were.

3. *Discuss an issue of local, national, or international concern that is important to you*: Pick something you do know about. Don't try to impress, but at the same time go into some depth to show your understanding. Pick a topic that supports your interests. If, for example, you have had a lot of experience with children and want to continue to work with kids in college, an issue concerning education or a question concerning children's health care makes sense. I suggest asking a question and then answering it by doing the following: discuss what has been done, what is currently being done, what alternatives are out there, what challenges exist for the solutions, and what your opinion is on how to improve the situation. Try to be as specific as possible. Find out what other people are saying by going to the library and asking the librarian to help you run a subject search for magazines on your topic.

4. *Write a note to your future college roommate that reveals something about you*: This is a fun one, huh? How do you *not* come off sounding like a cheesy dweeb? The key here is to talk about one of your values—but not by saying, "And I am a real trustworthy person who can't wait to hang with you for hours and hours and hours." You could talk about your family, a friend, your school—basically, tell your roommate a little about yourself and in the process tell the admissions people as well.

   Following is a real student answer. Note that she wrote the note as if she and the roommate already knew each other.

   Hey, Roommate!

   Just wanted to let you know I will be out of town for the weekend. I'm going to LA to see the latest Harry Potter movie with my brother.

   You might wonder why I would spend twelve hours in the car just to see a movie, so let me explain. As you know, I am very connected to my siblings. Back when I was in high school, my brother and I would always see the latest kid flick on opening weekend and stuff ourselves with candy and popcorn. Now that I'm here, we can't really keep up this tradition, but Harry Potter is special. He and I read the books together, and went to see the last movie at 8 on opening day. Needless to say, he is very excited about the latest movie, and I am hoping to surprise him at school on Friday and take him to see it.

   I hope you have a good weekend! Let's meet up at our normal time at the Coffee House on Sunday night.

5. *Tell us who your best teacher has been and why*: Once again, it's all about the story! The key here is to tell an anecdote or two that shows why a teacher has been so great. Discuss how the teacher's style affected you. If you have learned things from this

teacher about life outside of school, discuss this. Sometimes a student's best teacher is not the one who the student liked the most, but the one who helped the student in the long term. I had an English teacher who once took a paper I had written and threw it back at me with a D on it. She said she knew I had probably written it the night before (actually, it was the class before) and it was not a good example of the work I could produce. She eventually taught me how to write, as well as to demand more from myself. You get the idea.

6. *What did you do last summer?* Use a story to illustrate how you grew, how you learned something, or how you developed an interest. Don't just tell about your trip to Europe. Make it meaningful. Did you work? Did you learn anything from it? Did you stay at home and play video games? If this last one was exactly what you did, pick an event other than playing Grand Theft Auto, and discuss how that event affected you. Remember, you don't have to write about your entire summer. You can say you traveled to New Zealand, but then pick a simple event or two to show what you learned.

7. *Describe an ethical dilemma you had to deal with, and explain how you resolved it.*: This is a tricky one. First, you have to come up with an actual dilemma, a situation that involved a difficult decision. Following are two types of dilemmas that may help jog your memory.

   1. *A time when you could have taken advantage of someone.* Remember when that nerdy kid wanted to hang out with you because he didn't have a lot of friends, and he started offering you his homework because he knew you were having trouble in AP physics? Things like this.

   2. *A time when you had to choose between being loyal to a friend and being honest.* Remember when your friends pulled a "prank" by cutting down the main tree in the center of your school and they just barely escaped from the school's security? Then the vice principal questioned you to see if you knew who had done it. Something like this.

   No matter what you choose, you should discuss real situations that caused you to think about your options. You probably shouldn't talk about the time you had a major meltdown worrying about whether you should return the forty-five extra cents a grocery checker mistakenly gave you. Nor should you make blanket statements like, "And so I learned it's never okay to lie." True dilemmas encountered are not this clear-cut, so you'll want to discuss the *conflicts* you encountered in making a decision. You also don't want to tell about the time when you beat up some kid to get his history notes because you needed to get an A. People have to make decisions all the time, and we all make mistakes. Look at your answer from an admissions person's point of view, and make sure it is real and thoughtful, not just an opportunity to show what a good person you are.

8. *Describe a book that has had an impact on you. Please discuss how it changed your understanding of the world, other people, or yourself*: Don't try too hard to be cute or

overly academic. That is, don't use *Green Eggs and Ham* as the book that altered your life, but also don't try to write about the existential nature of Camus unless you know what you're talking about. Honesty is always a nice idea. Pick a book that made you think or challenged a belief you had. Explain *how* the author accomplished this. Give examples from the book, but don't give a plot summary, like in a book report. The important thing is *how* you changed or expanded your views about yourself, another person, or the world. Note that the question states "or," not "and." You don't have to discuss all three.

You might also want to use this opportunity to strengthen your positioning in the rest of your application. For example, if you have emphasized your math and science skills in your application, an analysis of a work by Einstein might be a good idea. On the other hand, you might want to choose something quite different to show you are interested in more than math and science.

9. *Write your own application question and answer it*: This is a good opportunity to recycle an essay you have written for another school. Be sure, however, of two things: First, choose a topic that is general enough to not make it look like you just grabbed an essay from another application. Second, pick a question that allows you to show something about yourself that has not been specifically mentioned in the rest of your application and that supports how you have positioned yourself. You might change the wording of the previous question you answered to make it your own: "Please choose an ethical dilemma you had to deal with and explain how you resolved it" could become, "Tell us about an instance where you had to make a tough choice." You could then explain the choice, and indicate whether you would make the same choice if you had to do it again.

10. *You have just completed your autobiography. Please submit page 203*: Here's another chance to recycle a previous essay or write a completely new one. This question really allows you to be creative. You can write about something that happened in the past, or make up a story of something that will happen to you. Once again, you'll want to show who you are, how you handle situations, what you are interested in, or what your values are. You can start the story part way in (remember, an autobiography starting on page 203 may not have a real beginning and may even start in the middle of a sentence). If you want to recycle another essay, you might have to tweak it a little to fit in your autobiographical profile. Remember, an autobiography is your life story, so you should pick an essay that tells a story or reflects back on one. One student used this question to present a series of flashbacks to events that had to do with swimming. She worked in multiple stories and told them as if she had reached the point in her autobiography where she was reflecting on her high school experience.

Think outside the box, but don't force an answer from another application if it doesn't work. You don't want the admissions people to think that you simply didn't want to write another essay.

11. *Describe a time when you took a risk. Tell us why you would or would not do it again*: The important thing is to show that you gave the risk some thought before you did or did not take it. Jumping off a 500-foot cliff because someone dared you to shows fearlessness, but it does not show your maturity. Again, try to see your essay from the viewpoint of an admissions person. Fearlessness is a good quality to discuss, but you don't want the admissions staff to think you would do something just because you were dared. Write about what went through your head as you decided to jump. Talk about the consequences of your decision and what you learned from it, especially if you think you made the wrong choice.

CHAPTER FOURTEEN
LETTERS OF RECOMMENDATION

WHY YOU SHOULD REALLY, REALLY, REALLY CARE

Many people think recommendations (or recs) are things you get automatically. Whether you're applying for a job or applying to colleges, you just ask someone for a recommendation, the person says some good stuff about you, and that's it, right? Wrong.

First, don't assume that every person who recommends you knows how to write recommendations. Of the thousands of applications that will be sitting next to yours, do you know how many will say something like, "Johnny is a very good student. He has received solid As in my class, and the quality of his work is at the top of his class"? Gee, thanks. Not that this is bad, but admissions freaks already know your grades. A recommendation should work like the essay. It should paint a picture of you as a human that goes beyond the rest of your application. Admissions officers have been known to read recs with a highlighter, scanning over them and highlighting only the information that speaks about the student as an individual. Something like, "The time Jamie gave her presentation on the Civil War and brought in costumes to stage a reenactment is just one of the many ways she threw herself into my class and injected creativity whenever she could." Now we're talkin'!

Second, many students treat recommendations as one of the least important parts of their application. They don't give their teachers or their counselors (counselors have a separate rec to fill out) enough information or enough time to do a good job. They therefore pretty much ensure that their letters will be *generic*. Put yourself in a teacher's shoes. You have, say, twenty to one hundred students who want recommendations, and some of them are applying to several schools. You get a bunch of forms thrown at you and a limited time to complete them. Then you have to deal with the students who constantly bug you about whether the rec has been completed. Do you know how long it takes to write a letter for someone, especially if you want it to be good? Do you know how much time a good teacher spends in order to prep lessons and grade papers? More time than your homework takes you, I guarantee. Therefore, can you see why a teacher would write one letter and then just change parts of it to fit each student? How then can you ensure that you get individualized recommendations that will really help you?

YOU JUST CAN'T PICK YOUR TEACHER'S NOSE

You know what they say: You can pick your friends and you can pick your nose, but you just can't pick your friend's nose. What the heck does this have to do with getting awesome recommendations? Absolutely nothing. Well, almost nothing.

HOW TO GET GOOD RECOMMENDATIONS

1. *Pick your teachers wisely. Don't choose a teacher just because you got an A in the class.* You typically need to get two different teachers from two different subjects. So, ask yourself the following questions:

   - Which teacher really knows me well as a student?

   - Which teacher do I have (or have I had) the best relationship with?

   - Which teacher could write the best recommendation?

   - Which subjects would best support my application? (For example, if you are applying to an engineering program, you should probably get a math or science rec.)

   - In which class did I do well? Or in which class did I write an outstanding paper or create a great project that the teacher could write about?

2. *Use my patented system for determining which teacher is best by talking with them individually.* (I'll go into this in the next section.)

3. *Ask the teachers to give your recommendations back to you to send, rather than have the teachers send them out.* Then you can ask more than two teachers for recs and compare the letters to pick the best ones. (This will not always work, but I'll show you how to ask.)

4. *Create packets for your teachers* that will make their lives easier and ensure that you get more than just a form letter. Of course, you are going to give these packets to your teachers ASAP, right? (Packets are discussed on page 185.)

5. *Send thank-you notes.* Okay, writing a thank-you note won't ensure you'll get great recs because they will already be done. But if you knew how much time it took your teachers to do these damn things, you'd get off your butt and write the thank-yous. (I have included sample thank-you notes on the Resource CD.) If you really want to say thanks, a small gift or flowers might be a nice gesture as well.

HOW TO APPROACH (AND EVEN TALK TO) YOUR TEACHERS

Here's a superpatented way to talk to your teachers that will help you get dazzling recommendations.

1. Go up to your teacher and say, "I would like to meet you for ten minutes to get your advice on some things. When would be a good time for you to meet?" Or say something to this effect. The point is don't go up to a teacher during or right after class and say, "Hey, can you write my college recommendations for me?" Teachers generally appreciate students who want to meet with them rather than bug them right before the next class is coming in.

2. Meet with the teacher and do the following:

   • Tell the teacher what schools you are thinking about applying to and how many of them require recommendations.

   • Ask, "Do you think you would be a good person to write me a letter of recommendation?" This question allows you to see the teacher's reaction. If he or she seems enthusiastic, great. But if it looks like the teacher would rather have a root canal, you may want to evaluate a few more teachers. You might want to approach four or five teachers to get their reactions, but remember, *you have not yet given them the forms*. If you decide not to ask a teacher to write a rec, you can honestly say, "I'm going to be asking several teachers, so I appreciate your time and I will get back to you if I need you." Teachers will understand this; you are not wasting their time. This question also lets them get out of writing your rec if they don't think they should. It is possible that they might say critical things about you that you may not be aware of.

   • If you decide you want to have certain teachers write a rec, tell them you are going to give them a package containing a resume; copies of papers, assignments, or projects you did for them; and the deadlines when the recommendations are due. Then say this: "I am not sure what your procedures are. Can I make it easier for you and handle all of the mailing to the schools?"

The teachers may appreciate this, in which case you will get to read their letters before you send them. However, they may say they need to keep the recommendations confidential, in which case you should include in the packet addressed *and stamped* envelopes for each of the schools you are applying to.

Note: Although a high school's policy may be that teachers should not give you back your recommendations, they may do it anyway if you ask. Now I am not suggesting you do something dishonest. You should not doctor your recommendations in any way. However, you do want to be sure to send your best recommendations, especially when you have multiple recs to choose from.

Final note: Sometimes college applications ask if you want to waive the Buckley amendment. This amendment allows you to see your college files, including your recommendations. It's a good idea to waive this right because admissions people will then feel more confident about the honesty of your recommendations. However, just because you waive your right to see your college files does not mean that you can't see your recommendations *before* they are sent, if your teacher allows it.

- When you drop off your packets to your teachers and to your counselor (who gets a separate recommendation form often called "The Secondary School Report Form"), you might want to go over all the parts of your packet and ask if they have any questions. As you will see in the next section, you will be giving teachers a lot of information to help them write a good rec. Therefore, when you go over your materials, you can simply explain, "Your recommendation is really important to me, and I wanted to make your job as easy as possible. I've included all this information because I want to help myself stand out from the other applicants. Therefore, I have put in my resume, and some stories to refresh your memory." While you don't want to make them feel like they don't know how to write a recommendation, you do want to make sure they talk specifically about your traits. You'll also want to indicate whether you are positioning yourself for certain schools, so they can emphasize specific work in that school's recommendation. I know it's not easy to talk to teachers about this, but most teachers will be impressed, not offended, if you present your packet in a nice, helpful way.

CREATING THE MASTERPIECE PACKET

Here's what you should include in the packet to your teachers and to your counselor after they have agreed to write your recommendations (samples can be found on the Resource CD):

1. *A cover letter* thanking them for writing your recommendations and summarizing what is in the packet. Be sure to include the dates when each recommendation is due to each school. Also, for each school indicate whether their form requires additional boxes or information to be filled in. Finally, mention why you are applying to each school, so they can get an idea of how to position you as a student. (See page 195.)

2. *The recommendation forms* from each of the individual applications. (Examples of teacher recommendation forms, secondary school report, and mid-year school report, are included in figures 9-1 through 9-3.) Make sure you fill in your personal information on each form *before* you give them to your teachers.

3. If your teacher is not going to give you back your letter, then include *legal-sized or nine-by-twelve-inch stamped envelopes addressed to the schools*. They should also have a return address with your teacher's name, the name of your high school, and the school's address. (You might have to give counselors two envelopes for each school if the school requires a Mid-year Report, a form that states your first-semester senior grades.)

   Important: Some schools do not require or accept recommendations, so don't be alarmed if you can't find a recommendation form. Make sure this is their policy, however, because some schools don't have a form, but still want recommendations. For example, instead of providing a form, USC has in the past used bar codes that students had to give to teachers to stick on their letters.

If you're using the Common App for multiple schools, give teachers one copy of the recommendation form and multiple envelopes for the schools it needs to be sent to. Teachers can make copies rather than fill out the form multiple times.

4. *A copy of your resume and copies of your college essays* (if you have completed them) to give the teachers a better idea of who you are.

5. *Any papers, assignments, or projects you have done in their classes* that the teacher can refer to in the letter. If you can't include the project, write up a brief summary of it to refresh their memory. For example, create a page titled "Project Summary," and then write a paragraph describing the time you presented *Macbeth* by dressing up as several of the characters and standing on the desks acting out a scene. This may seem to be a pain as well as pointless, but it's important to help your teachers write specifically about you. You are not telling them how to write; you are just giving them something to write about. For counselors, you might include a list of your most important activities in and out of school, along with an explanation of how they have benefited you. Remember, a bad or even lukewarm recommendation can ruin the rest of your application because it's the only outside feedback admissions people get on you.

6. Include *a story or example or two about an experience* you had that your recommender could use in your favor. While you don't want to use the same stories you used in the essay, telling an English teacher about how you taught a homeless child to read is a great way of getting more info in your application to show who you are. Remember that time you did science experiments for the local neighborhood kids? Great. Write it under "Additional Information" on a separate page, and give it to your science teacher. (See page 196.)

7. *A list of your strengths and areas for improvement.* Virtually no students include this, so you will blow your teachers and counselor away by providing this information. Again, it's a good idea to talk to your teachers about your materials. That way, you can discuss the kinds of things they can write about you, and you can make sure that even your weaknesses are portrayed in a good light. (See page 197.)

If you are a senior and it is already December, run, don't walk, to get your recs written. Otherwise, begin talking to your teachers at the end of your junior year or the beginning of your senior year. You can also wait until after you begin to get your applications in the mail—sometime between mid-August and early October. Just know that the sooner you get your teachers your packets, the more time they will have to write a quality recommendation for you. Finally, remember to use your MOAC in chapter 7 to check off each step as you complete it.

FIGURE 9-1

 **Penn**

FORM 3A TEACHER RECOMMENDATION I

ADMISSIONS STATUS AND DEADLINES (*Please check one*)

1 ☐ **Regular Decision Freshman**
Postmark by January 1

2 ☐ **Early Decision Freshman**
Postmark by November 1

3 ☐ **Transfer for September 2006**
Postmark by March 15

4 ☐ **Transfer to Degree Standing**

APPLICANT'S LAST NAME   FIRST NAME   DATE OF BIRTH (MMDDYY)   U.S. OR CANADIAN SOCIAL SECURITY NO. *Non-citizens will be assigned an ID number.*

ADDRESS   CITY   STATE   ZIP CODE

SCHOOL   CITY   STATE   ZIP CODE

TO THE APPLICANT:

After you have filled in the section above, give this form to a teacher or faculty member who has taught you an academic subject within the last two years. Transfer applicants should have a college faculty member fill out this form. **It is most helpful to us if this teacher is from a course that relates to your intended major or lies in an area of continuing interest for you.** If you wish to waive your right of access to this document, please sign the following release:

I request that this report be sent to the University of Pennsylvania Office of Admissions with the understanding that it will be used in support of my application. I understand that I may not read this evaluation, and I will not seek to do so, either while I am enrolled at Penn, or subsequently.

APPLICANT'S SIGNATURE   DATE

TO THE TEACHER/FACULTY MEMBER:

The student whose name appears above is applying for admission to the University of Pennsylvania. Because so many of our applicants present strong credentials for admission, a detailed recommendation from you offering specific information about the accomplishments and qualifications of the applicant is an essential and invaluable tool for the Admissions Committee.

Your candid appraisal of the candidate's academic performance, intellectual promise, and personal qualities will be seriously considered. If necessary, feel free to use additional sheets. You may simply attach this form to a letter, but we urge you to make sure that each of our questions has been amply addressed. Specific illustrative examples are especially helpful.

The University of Pennsylvania is committed to equal access and education for students with disabilities. Penn makes reasonable accommodations and otherwise complies with the Rehabilitation Act.

Confidentiality: Under the provisions of the Family Education Rights and Privacy Act of 1974, the student named above, if enrolled at Penn, has the right to review his/her educational records. The student may waive his/her rights of access to this specific recommendation by signing the statement above.

TEACHER'S NAME   LENGTH OF ACQUAINTANCE   # YEARS TEACHING

SUBJECT OR COURSE   DATES TAUGHT   GRADES EARNED

1. What do you know of this student's intellectual qualities? What are your impressions of the student's academic priorities? We are especially interested in any evidence you can give about the nature of his/her motivation for academic work — the breadth and depth of intellectual interests — the originality, independence and sensitivity he/she displays in course work — the quality of performance as compared to that of his/her classmates.

FIGURE 9-1

FORM 3A – TEACHER RECOMMENDATION 1 *(Continued)*

2. Which personal qualities stand out in the applicant? Are there any features in the applicant's background that will help us better understand his/her academic or extracurricular performance? Are there any personal strengths, weaknesses, or problems about which you feel we should be aware?

_____
_____
_____
_____
_____

3. In your best estimate, how will the applicant respond to the academically competitive environment at Penn?

_____
_____
_____
_____
_____

4. Please use this space for any additional comments about the applicant and his/her candidacy.

_____
_____
_____
_____

5. Do you have any reason to doubt this student's academic integrity? ☐ Yes ☐ No
If yes, please be specific in your explanation.

_____
_____
_____
_____

6. How would you compare this applicant to his/her entire class? *(Please mark as appropriate on the continuum.)*

	AVERAGE OR BELOW	GOOD (above average)	EXCELLENT (top 10% this year)	OUTSTANDING (top 5% this year)	ONE OF THE TOP FEW I HAVE EVER ENCOUNTERED IN MY CAREER OF ____ YEARS
Academic Achievement					
Academic Potential					
Character/Personal Qualities					
Overall Rating					

MAILING INSTRUCTIONS

Please return completed form to:
Office of Admissions
University of Pennsylvania
1 College Hall
Philadelphia, PA
19104-6376

Thank you for taking the time and effort to complete this form. Your comments are very important to the selection committee at Penn.

SIGNATURE _____ DATE _____

E-MAIL ADDRESS _____

FIGURE 9-2

 **Penn**

FORM 2 SECONDARY SCHOOL REPORT

┌

ADMISSIONS STATUS AND DEADLINES (*Please check one*)

1 ☐ **Regular Decision Freshman**
  Postmark by January 1

2 ☐ **Early Decision Freshman**
  Postmark by November 1

3 ☐ **Transfer for September 2006**
  Postmark by March 15

4 ☐ **Transfer to Degree Standing**

APPLICANT'S LAST NAME   FIRST NAME   DATE OF BIRTH (MMDDYY)   U.S. OR CANADIAN SOCIAL SECURITY NO. *Non-citizens will be assigned an ID number.*

ADDRESS   CITY   STATE   ZIP CODE

SCHOOL   CITY   STATE   ZIP CODE

TO THE APPLICANT:

After you have filled in the section above, please give this form to your college advisor, headmaster, or principal. Transfer students should forward this form to the high school from which you graduated or have your high school send us your final transcript. If you wish to waive your right of access to this document, please sign the following release.

I request that this report be sent to the University of Pennsylvania Office of Admissions with the understanding that it will be used in support of my application. I understand that I may not read this evaluation, and I will not seek to do so, either while I am enrolled at Penn, or subsequently.

_____   _____
APPLICANT'S SIGNATURE   DATE

TO THE COLLEGE ADVISOR, HEADMASTER, OR PRINCIPAL:
This student is applying for admission to the University of Pennsylvania. A full and candid report from his/her school is essential if he/she is to be given fairest consideration. We therefore ask for careful ratings of and comments about talents, motivations, and character. **Please keep comments to one page.**
  Please enclose your school profile with this form.
  The University of Pennsylvania is committed to equal access and education for students with disabilities. Penn makes reasonable accommodations and otherwise complies with the Rehabilitation Act.
  Confidentiality: Under the provisions of the Family Educational Rights and Privacy Act of 1974, the student named above, if he/she enrolls at Penn, has the right to review his/her educational records. The student may waive his/her right of access to this specific recommendation by signing the statement above.

ACADEMIC PERFORMANCE

1. Does your school rank? ☐ Yes ☐ No

1a. This applicant ranks _____ in a ☐ college prep group of _____ ☐ entire class of _____

1b. How many others share this rank? _____ This rank is: ☐ weighted ☐ unweighted

1c. Is this rank cumulative? ☐ Yes ☐ No

1d. If the rank is cumulative which years does it include? ☐ 9th ☐ 10th ☐ 11th

1e. Applicant's unweighted cumulative GPA _____

1f. Of this applicant's graduating class, approximately _____ % plan to attend a four-year college.

1g. Compared to other college-bound students in your school, the applicant's program can be described best as:
  ☐ above average ☐ rigorous ☐ most rigorous in many areas ☐ most rigorous in all areas

TRANSCRIPT

2. An official copy of the candidate's transcript must accompany this form in order to complete the application. The transcript should indicate which courses have been at the honors, accelerated, Advanced Placement or International Baccalaureate levels. *Please include with the transcript a school profile or brief explanation of your school's grading system.*

FIGURE 9-2

FORM 2 – SECONDARY SCHOOL REPORT *(Continued)*

CURRICULUM

Please complete the following information if it is not included on your school profile:

3a. Does your school offer Advanced Placement or International Baccalaureate courses? ☐ Yes ☐ No
If yes, in which subjects?

_____

_____

3b. Does your school offer honors or accelerated courses? ☐ Yes ☐ No
If yes, in which subjects?

_____

_____

3c. Does your school offer a block scheduling program? ☐ Yes ☐ No

TEST SCORES

4. We require the SAT I with writing and two SAT II: Subject Tests of the College Board or the ACT with writing. The applicant must have an official report sent to the Office of Admissions by the appropriate testing service, but it is helpful to have the scores entered below.

SAT I

Critical Reading/Verbal	Math	Writing	Date

SAT II: Subject Tests

Subject	Score	Date

A.P./I.B. examinations

Subject	Score	Date

ACT

Subject	ACT Standard Scores (01-36)	ACT Norms (Percentiles)	
		Local	National
ENGLISH			
MATHEMATICS			
READING			
SCIENCE REASONING			
COMPOSITE SCORE			
WRITING SCORE			

TOEFL

Composite Score	Sec.1	Sec. 2	Sec. 3	TWE	Date

FIGURE 9-2

FORM 2 – SECONDARY SCHOOL REPORT *(Continued)*

GENERAL RATINGS

5a. Has this applicant ever been suspended, placed on probation, or dismissed from school for academic or disciplinary reasons or incurred other formal disciplinary action?

☐ Yes ☐ No *If yes, please explain on a separate sheet of paper.*

5b. Has this applicant had to leave school for medical or personal reasons?

☐ Yes ☐ No *If yes, please explain on a separate sheet of paper.*

5c. Do you have any reason to doubt this candidate's academic integrity?

☐ Yes ☐ No *If yes, please explain on a separate sheet of paper.*

5d. Does your school have a community service requirement?

☐ Yes ☐ No *If yes, what is the requirement and has this student met or surpassed it?*

_____

_____

5e. Do you believe that this candidate will embrace the diversity of Penn's student body?

_____

_____

5f. Does this applicant have the respect of the faculty and students?

☐ Yes ☐ No

If so, what are the main factors contributing to the respect accorded to the applicant?

☐ superiority in studies ☐ accomplishment in activities ☐ success in athletics ☐ interest in other students
☐ leadership in activities ☐ personality

5g. Is the applicant's record a true index of her/his ability?

_____

_____

_____

_____

SUMMARY REPORT

6. Critical assessment from counselors is extremely helpful to us in evaluating candidates for admission to Penn. Particularly useful are specific comments on and examples of the candidate's potential for rigorous study, his/her contributions to the school or local community, and such qualities as personal maturity, sensitivity, concern for others, leadership, and sense of humor. Please avoid the mere listing of a student's activities, as this information will be presented elsewhere on the application form. If appropriate, please include an explanation of unusual circumstances that may shed further light on the applicant's qualification for admission. *Please attach to this form a letter or photocopied report.*

_____

_____

_____

_____

_____

_____

_____

_____

FIGURE 9-2

FORM 2 – SECONDARY SCHOOL REPORT *(Continued)*

7. Are there any additional comments you would like to add?

_____

_____

_____

_____

8. How would you compare this applicant to his/her entire class? *(Please mark as appropriate on the continuum.)*

	AVERAGE OR BELOW	GOOD (above average)	EXCELLENT (top 10% this year)	OUTSTANDING (top 5% this year)	ONE OF THE TOP FEW I HAVE EVER ENCOUNTERED IN MY CAREER OF _____ YEARS
Academic Achievement					
Academic Potential					
Extracurricular/ Community Contributions					
Character/Personal Qualities					
Overall Rating					

How long have you known the applicant? _____
In what capacity other than counselor? _____

This report is based upon *(check more than one if appropriate)*:
☐ Personal observation and contact with student   ☐ Other counselors' observations
☐ Teacher comments   ☐ Records   ☐ Other (specify) _____

TO BE COMPLETED FOR EARLY DECISION CANDIDATES ONLY

9. I have discussed the request for Early Decision with this applicant and endorse him/her as a first choice for Penn. If the student is offered admission in December, I will remind the student of the conditions of the Early Decision commitment.

_____   _____   _____
SIGNATURE   POSITION   DATE

MAILING INSTRUCTIONS

Please return completed form to:
Office of Admissions
University of Pennsylvania
1 College Hall
Philadelphia, PA
19104-6376

Thank you for taking the time and effort to complete this form. Your comments are very important to the selection process at Penn.

_____   _____   _____
SIGNATURE   TITLE   DATE

_____   _____   _____
NAME *(please print)*   PHONE   E-MAIL

FIGURE 9-3

FORM 7 Mid-Year School Report

ADMISSIONS STATUS AND DEADLINES (*Please check one*)

1 ☐ **Regular Decision Freshman**   2 ☐ **Early Decision Freshman**

APPLICANT'S LAST NAME   FIRST NAME   DATE OF BIRTH (MMDDYY)   U.S. OR CANADIAN SOCIAL SECURITY NO. *Non-citizens will be assigned an ID number.*

ADDRESS   CITY   STATE   ZIP CODE

SCHOOL

ADDRESS   CITY   STATE   ZIP CODE

TO THE APPLICANT:

After you have completed the section above, give this form to your college advisor, headmaster, or principal. If you wish to waive your right of access to this document, please sign the following release:

I request that this report be sent to the University of Pennsylvania Office of Admissions with the understanding that it will be used in support of my application. It is understood that I may not read this evaluation and that I will not seek to do so, either while I am enrolled at Penn, or subsequently.

APPLICANT'S SIGNATURE   DATE

TO THE COLLEGE ADVISOR, HEADMASTER, OR PRINCIPAL:

This Mid-Year School Report is to be used to report the applicant's grades for the first term of the current school year and any significant additions to or changes in his/her academic, extracurricular, or character record. Please complete and **return it no later than February 15** to the Office of Admissions. *If you use your own transcript form, please attach this form to insure quick identification and filing in our office.* Please add any significant comments since your previous report and ratings on the reverse side.

    Confidentiality: Under the provisions of the Family Education Rights and Privacy Act of 1974, the student named above, if he/she enrolls at Penn, has the right to review his/her educational records. The student may waive this right to access specific recommendations by signing the statement above.

CLASS RANK

1a. This applicant ranks _____ in a ☐ college prep group of _____ ☐ entire class of _____

1b. Is this rank cumulative? ☐ Yes ☐ No

1c. If the rank is cumulative which years does it include? ☐ 9th ☐ 10th ☐ 11th ☐ 12th–1st semster/trimester

CURRENT COURSES

2. Please list candidate's current course titles (*please indicate any honors/advanced level*). Has candidate dropped any classes? (*If yes, please be specific in your explanation.*)

MID-YEAR GRADE

_____   _____

_____   _____

_____   _____

_____   _____

_____   _____

_____   _____

FIGURE 9-3

FORM 7 – MID-YEAR SCHOOL REPORT *(Continued)*

TEST SCORES

3. We require the SAT I with writing and two SAT II: Subject Tests of the College Board or the ACT with writing. The applicant must have an official report sent to the Office of Admissions by the appropriate testing service, but it is helpful to have the scores entered below.

SAT I *(highest only)*

Critical Reading/Verbal	Math	Writing	Date

SAT II: Subject tests

Subject	Score	Date

ACT

Subject	ACT Standard Scores (01-36)	ACT Norms (Percentiles)	
		Local	National
ENGLISH			
MATHEMATICS			
READING			
SCIENCE REASONING			
COMPOSITE SCORE			
WRITING SCORE			

TOEFL

Composite Score	Sec.1	Sec. 2	Sec. 3	TWE	Date

ASSESSMENT

4. How would you compare this applicant to his/her entire class? *(Please mark as appropriate on the continuum.)*

	AVERAGE OR BELOW	GOOD *(above average)*	EXCELLENT *(top 10% this year)*	OUTSTANDING *(top 5% this year)*	ONE OF THE TOP FEW I HAVE EVER ENCOUNTERED IN MY CAREER OF ____ YEARS
Academic Achievement					
Academic Potential					
Extracurricular/ Community Contributions					
Character/Personal Qualities					
Overall Rating					

5. Has your impression of this student changed since your original recommendation? If so, please explain.

_____

_____

_____

_____

_____

MAILING INSTRUCTIONS

Please attach this student's most recent transcript to this document and return both by February 15 to the following address:
Office of Admissions
University of Pennsylvania
1 College Hall
Philadelphia, PA
19104-6376

SIGNATURE   TITLE   DATE   LENGTH OF TIME ACQUAINTED WITH APPLICANT

SAMPLE COVER LETTER

Dear Mr. Thompson:

Thank you for agreeing to write my letters of recommendation. As I mentioned, I have created a packet of information to make this job easier. I understand how much time these letters must take, so please let me know if you need additional details or have any questions.

The packet is organized as follows:

1. This cover letter with a list of schools, their requirements, their deadlines, and an explanation of why I am applying.

2. A copy of my resume.

3. A copy of my college essays for your use if you want to get a better sense of who I am.

4. Two papers I have written in your class. [*Do not include these for a counselor recommendation letter.*]

5. A few stories and examples of my activities and values outside your (or outside school).

6. A list of my strengths and areas for improvement to give you insight into how I see my work.

7. The application forms from each of the schools with stamped return envelopes. Because some of the schools require the Common App, I have included one form along with the envelopes for each of the schools. This form can be copied, so you only have to fill it out once.

[*Even though you may not be able to be as specific as the examples below about your reasons for applying, if you want to market a particular strength of yours, or if you want to apply to a certain program, let your recommenders know so they can tailor their letters accordingly. If you don't have any specific angle, just list the school, the due date, and the requirements. Most of your schools will get the same letter from your recommenders, and this is fine.*]

[*Do not include envelopes if your teacher is willing to give you back your recommendation to mail.*]

SCHOOLS	DUE DATES	REQUIREMENTS
1. Yale University	Applying early, due Nov 1	Common App form

This is my first choice of schools. I am emphasizing my writing and drama experience because I would like to possibly study in Yale's comparative literature and drama program. Yale offers several classes in Hemingway that I would like to take and for which I could build on the work I did in your class.

SCHOOLS	DUE DATES	REQUIREMENTS
2. Lewis and Clark	February 1	Common App Form

I am applying to Lewis and Clark because I am interested in their East Asian Studies program and want to study abroad in China.

3. Columbia University	January 2	Has its own form

I am applying to Columbia because I am interested in their core curriculum, as well as studying in their African American program.

SAMPLE ADDITIONAL INFORMATION SHEET

For your reference, here are some anecdotes and stories of things I did in your class and outside class.

1. For a presentation on *Brave New World*, I brought in different colored masks and passed out one to each member of the class so I could then label them in groups, like Aldous Huxley did in his novel. I then gave an oral presentation on Huxley's view on utopia and how society somewhat mirrors what he predicted in the story.

2. I feel a real desire to help kids. I helped teach my brother to read before he started school at four using some phonic skills I picked up when I volunteered at a kindergarten last year. Seeing my brother "get it" has been one of the most rewarding experiences of my life thus far.

3. I tend to do things I feel passionate about rather than just joining things to join them. Last summer, I started my own business giving swimming lessons to children aged 5 to 10. Although I mentioned this in my application, I didn't mention that I donated a quarter of my earnings to the Make-A-Wish Foundation, which I might want to work for later in life.

I have painted the picture of a super student here, and I do not expect you to necessarily have stories like this. However, do use any opportunity you have to help your teacher talk about you in a positive, specific light. You'll notice that the student has given this teacher plenty of info: a specific project; the desire to work with kids; the idea that she does things because she is truly interested; and her donating to charity. These things should be supported in the rest of the application, especially if she is trying to emphasize a love for children and the desire to help others less fortunate. (Remember the themes from Chapter 8, Marketing Your Strength?) The stories that you give your teachers, however, should be new. You don't want them telling the same stories you have written about in your application or your essays.)

Note: For your guidance counselor, you might add some specifics about your extracurricular activities and why and how they have affected you. This will help the counselor write a recommendation without having had you in a class.

SAMPLE STRENGTHS AND AREAS OF IMPROVEMENT SHEET

On this page, I am including my strengths and areas in which I need improvement because I am trying to stand out at each school I apply to. Therefore, I want to position my strengths throughout my application, essays, resume, and hopefully recommendations, so the admissions people get a good sense of who I am and why I would be a strong student at their school.

STRENGTHS:

- Am a good communicator, both in class and with other students.

- Am enthusiastic about English.

- Able to think independently.

- Possess creativity in approaching assignments.

- Have good analytical ability.

- Have strong ability to explain my reasoning in arriving at a solution.

- Very capable of analyzing literature critically.

- Good at making connections between results and conclusions.

- Self-confident.

- Organized.

- Open-minded.

- Able to persevere when I don't understand something.

- Willing to seek assistance from teacher when I need it.

- Insightful.

- Interested in helping others.

AREAS FOR IMPROVEMENT:

- Improve grammatical structure in essay writing.

- Discipline myself to start early and write multiple drafts.

- Develop presentation skills, especially speaking in front of class.

- Improve ability to complete geometric proofs.

- Speak up more in class, including asking more questions.

- Improve ability to take the insights I have from reading and to write them in an organized, clear way so that others understand my points.

WHY EVEN THE PRESIDENT OF THE UNITED STATES CAN'T HELP YOU

As discussed in Chapter 8, Marketing Your Strengths, you may want to include additional recommendations with your application. While some schools provide forms for optional recs, others do not, and it is your call if you want to include them. Again, extra recommendations can be beneficial, but only if you get them from someone who knows you well and can discuss a quality you possess or an experience you have had that is *not* mentioned in the rest of your application.

Too many students think a recommendation from another English teacher or from some influential person will help them get in, when in fact the opposite may be true. If admissions people see extra recommendations that say the same things as the other recs or add nothing substantial about the student, they think, "This student obviously isn't confident with the rest of the application and is sending in this stuff to try to make up for it." **Whatever you do, if you are thinking about submitting extra recommendations, talk to your counselor about why you think doing so will benefit you.**

Here are some reasons to submit extra letters of recommendation:

1. You have overcome a hardship that has not been addressed in your application. For example, an educational therapist you have been working with writes about how you have persevered through a disability and substantially improved over the course of several years. Or a coach writes about how you broke your leg, but still managed to play in the league championship after six months of strenuous rehabilitation.

2. You spend significant time participating in an activity outside school that a supervisor, church official, scout leader, etc., can discuss in detail. It is not enough that you volunteer at a nursing home or are an Eagle Scout. Consider this option only if you have made a *significant* impact and this person can really explain how.

3. You have gone through a traumatic event that has affected you severely. Have a therapist, a friend, or someone who knows your situation explain what happened, how it affected you, and how you dealt with it.

4. You know someone connected with the school, like a professor or trustee, who can discuss why you're such a good match for the school.

CHAPTER FIFTEEN
INTERVIEWING

WHY YOU CAN'T FAIL, NOT EVEN WITH THOSE NASTY CLOTHES OF YOURS

No, really, it's true! The interview cannot ruin your chances of getting into a school.

Over the years, the importance of the interview has been decreasing, and more emphasis is now placed on the essays. While some schools still require interviews, many either do not offer interviews or make them optional.

Interviews are either conducted on campus or with a local alumnus in your area. Some schools offer one or the other, while some offer both. If you have the choice and can swing it, try to interview on campus. There is a greater possibility that you will interview with an actual admissions person. However, make sure you call a school early and make an appointment. Some schools conduct interviews before the application deadline, while others wait until after. Either way, the spaces often fill up quickly. Interviewing when you go on a visit is a good idea, but I recommend you tour the campus before you interview. This will allow you to gain more knowledge about the school that you can discuss.

But if an interview can't hurt you, why should you care? Well, there is a chance that an interview can *help* you. Even though it is probably one of the least important factors in your application, it's possible that the interviewer will make a strong recommendation to admit you based on your interview. Although the interview won't have a lot of weight, every little bit counts. An interview is also valuable because you can ask questions, and the answers may help you decide if the school is for you. You can also get an idea from the interviewer of what your chances of getting in are.

THE UNDERGROUND, BLACK BOOK OF LITTLE SECRETS TO SUCCESS

INTERVIEW DOS

- *Arrive early.*

- *Dress decently.* This does not mean a tuxedo or suit, but not ripped T-shirt either. Be yourself, but make an impression. Wear khakis, a dress, a nice shirt, perhaps a tie, dress shoes, possibly a sport coat, clean underwear—you get the picture.

- *Shake your interviewer's hand firmly, and look him or her directly in the eye.* You have no idea what a good idea this is. In fact, when you ask or answer a question, make sure you look the interviewer in the eye. Of course, you shouldn't stare at the interviewer without looking away. Practice with Mom or Dad or a friend. Heck, talk to yourself in the mirror if you have to.

- *Sit up straight.* You might scoot toward the end of the chair, seat, couch, etc., to help you keep upright. On the other hand, try to stay relaxed—you *can* lean back and be comfortable, just don't lay your head on the headrest and pick up the remote to see what's on HBO.

- *Be honest and straightforward.* Answer the questions honestly. Try to stay on the topic, unless the interviewer goes off it.

- *If you're nervous, remember to breathe, and it's OK to tell the interviewer you are a bit nervous.*

- *Don't over rehearse.* (Look, I have had more interviews than the next twenty people put together [twenty-seven jobs, remember?], and I have almost always been successful. I don't rehearse every single answer, but I run through a few questions so I know what my general answers will be. I keep my statements positive. I make eye contact. I ask intelligent questions. And bam! I'm done.)

- *Research the school before you go.* A popular interview question is, "Why do you want to go to this school?" Like the essay question, it's nice if you can give the interviewer specific reasons for wanting to attend, like a certain class or program. By being specific, you show that you are serious and the school is high on your list.

- *Thank the interviewer at the end and send a thank-you note.* (There is a sample thank-you note on the Resource CD.)

THINGS THE INTERVIEWER MIGHT ASK

Possible Interview Questions (Note: These are some of the most popular, but obviously, he or she may ask you other questions.)

- Tell me about yourself. (Or here's a fun one: Describe yourself in 150 words.)

- How would your friends describe you?

- What is your favorite subject? Why?

- What is your favorite book? Why?

- Why are you interested in attending our school?

- What do you want to get out of college?

- What goals do you have?

- Tell me what you did last summer.

- What other schools are you considering? (It's okay to answer.)

- Which is your first choice? Most interviewers won't ask this, but just in case they do, say something like "I am still considering several schools and want to visit them once I get accepted." If you have applied someplace for Early Decision, you can still use the same answer because you haven't gotten in yet. If asked if you've applied anywhere early, answer honestly. It's not like an interviewer thinks his or her school is everyone's first choice, and it won't be held against you.) Of course if the school is your first choice, definitely say so!

- Where do you see yourself in five, ten, or twenty years? (Just be positive and give possibilities. Saying you have no idea is not the best answer, however.)

- Do you want to ask any questions?

THINGS YOU CAN ASK THE INTERVIEWER

Again, these are just possibilities. While you don't have to ask all of these, you should come up with a list of questions beforehand.

- I am interested in———. Can you tell me more about your school's program?

- In your opinion, what makes this school distinctive?

- Has the school changed over the last few years, and if so, how?

- How would you describe the students?

- What is the relationship between the school and the surrounding town?

- If the interviewer attended the school, ask, What was your experience as a student like? (It's usually good to get an interviewer talking about himself or herself—the interviewer will end up liking you more. However, don't go overboard, be genuine.)

- Ask questions that apply to you specifically, especially about things you want to know more about. Try to explain what you do know, and follow it up with a question. For example: "I have researched your program for learning disabilities, and I know there are tutors available. Can you tell me about what other resources they offer?"

The interviewer may indirectly indicate what your chances of admission are by saying things like "We look forward to receiving your application," "You should apply to other schools in addition to ours," or "You do not look like a strong candidate." Some people suggest asking what your chances are, while others discourage it. I say, feel it out. If the interviewer does not offer the information or give you some clue, but you feel you have a good rapport, ask what he or she thinks your chances are. Most will answer frankly. If it is really awkward, don't ask. But either way, it's all good.

Beware: Some interviewers will sneak in a question while they are walking you out. Don't think the interview is over and tell some off-color joke. Maintain your cool until you are driving away. Friendly is fine, but telling your interviewer that you're going to go party may not be the best idea.

CHAPTER SIXTEEN
FINANCIAL AID

THE OVERALL SKINNY

You've got to keep one thing in mind when you are trying to figure out how you're going to pay for college: **if you want to go to a school badly enough, you can find the money to pay for it. Period.**

Now, having said that, this chapter on financial aid

1. Briefly discusses how the process works.

2. Teaches you how to use each school's aid policies to your advantage.

3. Shows you how to appeal a financial aid offer.

4. Walks you step-by-step through the FAFSA form.

5. Discusses what you need to know for the PROFILE form and provides sample worksheets for reference.

6. Talks about scholarships and if and how you should go after them.

7. Discusses other ways to pay for school.

There is so much stuff written about how to pay for college that students find it overwhelming. Thus I have tried to make this chapter as simple and straightforward as possible. See, I have found that applying for financial aid is the one part of the application that many students blow off. First, they are tired after filling out the rest of the applications. Second, they think their parents will handle it. Unfortunately, this isn't the way it works.

Now, you should know about financial aid because you're an adult and you need to be responsible for knowing what's up, even if your parents are footing the tuition bill. But there is an even better reason: you really do need to know what's going on.

Most of the time, you'll be the one at school who has to pick up the loan or the grant checks, you'll have to budget your expenses, and you'll be the one paying off the student loans after you graduate. If this is the case, there is paperwork and things you must do *while you are at school*. By being familiar with how things work now, you will keep ahead of the game once you get to school. Therefore, I recommend that you read this chapter yourself and fill out your part of the financial aid forms. Then give this info to your parents and let them complete the forms.

HOW FINANCIAL AID WORKS

Here's a few important points right off the bat:

1. Only certain schools are still need-blind—that is, your ability to pay has no influence on whether you get admitted. Years ago, most schools had this policy, but it has changed over time.

2. Many schools now give aid for academic achievement in high school.

3. Some schools have readjusted packages to benefit middle-income families.

These trends are not necessarily good or bad news. They are just things you need to keep in mind; I will explain them later in more detail. What you must keep in mind, however, is this: **Don't rule out applying to a college because you think you can't afford it.** Investigate the policies at different schools so you can maximize your chances of getting in and getting the best financial aid package. But don't cut out a school until you actually apply and get its package. Too many students and their parents limit their choices before they know all the information. Other families don't think they are eligible for financial aid and so don't even apply. In most cases, I suggest applying for aid if your family can use it (unless your parents are multimillionaires, for example). You don't *have to* accept every part of your package (for example, your parents don't want to take out student loans, but would cover the tuition themselves). Keep in mind that many schools cost as much as $45,000 per year, so every little bit helps.

Financial aid packages can consist of several parts:

1. *Scholarships or grants*: Money given by a school that does not have to be repaid.

2. *Loans*: Money that has to be repaid, usually at low interest rates. To get specific information as to what kinds of loans are available, see page 213 and go to www.finaid.org.

3. *Student job:* The amount a school expects you to earn from an on-campus job while you are going to school.

4. *Parental contribution*: The amount a school wants your parents to come up with to fill the gap between the total cost of a year of school and the amount of aid you receive. There are several ways your parents can pay for this. See page 210.

5. *Student contribution*: The amount a school expects you to pay from your savings or from earnings from summer jobs. There are ways to decrease this amount, which will be covered beginning on page 210.

Now, you may get a "full-ride" scholarship, which means that your family will not have to come up with any money or may not qualify for any grants or scholarships. If you do not qualify, it does not mean that you can't get aid. You can get student loans, your parents can get loans and tuition payment plans, and you can work on campus. In fact, most aid packages are made up of a combination of grants, loans, work-study, and an expected family contribution.

To find a calculator that helps families approximate potential financial aid, go to www.finaid.org.

How do colleges determine a student's financial aid package? While each school can produce very different packages, most schools use one or two forms and methods of determining aid:

- *Institutional methodology*: This is the system used to determine aid by the College Board, the organization that evaluates the CSS PROFILE; a financial aid form utilized by many private schools.

- *Federal methodology:* This is the system used to determine aid by the federal government, who evaluates the FAFSA or Free Application for Federal Student Aid. Some schools use only this form, while others use this one and the CSS PROFILE.

Typically, a family fills out one or both of these forms and sends each directly to the respective evaluating agency. They in turn determine a family's eligibility for aid based on a number of factors too complicated to detail here. An eligibility index is then passed on to the individual schools a family designates on each of the forms. Each school then uses this information to determine how to put together its package for the family. The size of the school's resources will depend on how much and what kind of aid it will offer.

JUDGING A SCHOOL BY ITS PACKAGE

Not all schools are created equal. As mentioned, there has been a trend among colleges to move away from need-blind admissions, in which a student's chance of getting accepted was not based at all on his or her ability to pay tuition. While many of the "richer" schools (such as the Ivies and schools like Amherst, Wesleyan, Williams, and Stanford) still generally stick to this policy, other schools now give preferential offers to certain students to lure them away from competitors, while giving less aid to "less desirable" students.

In the past, all schools generally looked at your family's financial need, used the same formulas, and provided very similar aid packages. Now, although many schools still base their aid packages on financial need, they play around with the amount of loans versus grants. Consequently, they give more grants to certain groups or certain students to try to get them to attend.

Knowing these facts, you can find out the policies for each of your desired schools and then use your particular situation to your advantage. You'll need to do two things:

1. Find out how each of your schools determines its aid packages by asking the right questions.

2. Maximize your aid package by applying to schools where you are at the top of the ap-

plicant pool; by appealing aid packages and allowing schools to compete; by having your parents increase the amount they are entitled to receive by adjusting their finances at the right time; and by knowing all the different options that exist for paying for college.

If you are saying, Huh? right about now, don't worry. Just stick with me, and I will break everything down for you and your parents.

- Find out how each of your schools determine its aid packages by asking the right questions. There are two basic ways of getting the answers:

  1. Look at the following resources available about schools:

     Fiske Guide to Colleges—at the end of each school summary is information about whether or not the school guarantees to meet all financial need.

     And a college's website or viewbook—these will often state the average amount of aid awarded to admitted students.

  2. Call the financial aid office at each school, tell them you have questions about its aid policies, and ask who would be the best person to talk to. If you have to call back or make a "telephone appointment," do it. Financial aid officers are there to help you, and talking to a live person can often save you a lot of time searching around different websites.

Here are the questions. You should ask each school:

Does the school guarantee to meet demonstrated need? In other words, does it provide aid to every admitted student who has financial need? Some schools, such as Duke, Stanford, Cal Tech, MIT, the Ivies, and many selective small private colleges, still do this. Other schools underfund their students—that is, they don't provide enough aid to cover the students' full need. In the past, Vanderbilt, Pepperdine, and Hampshire College have been just a few schools that have fallen in this category. Determining whether a college will meet demonstrated need lets you know what to expect from the school. Don't be afraid to apply to a school that won't cover have fallen need, especially if you are eligible for a merit scholarship (see page 207). But if finances are an issue, make sure that some of the schools you apply to meet all demonstrated need. Then you can compare packages when the time comes.

Is the school need-blind in its admissions? If a school is need-blind, it will accept you without any knowledge of your financial situation. Therefore, when a school is not need-blind, it primarily affects the admitted students who have the lower GPA/SAT scores. Schools want to keep the top students to make themselves look good and keep those numbers in *U.S. News and World Report* high. Top students, therefore, will get in no matter what their financial situation is.

Compared to the other accepted students, you may get a different aid package depending on where your CSI profile placed you. Let's say you have a 3.3 GPA with a solid honors/AP curriculum, a 1860 SAT, you are varsity-lettered in a sport, and went to a private high school. While you could be accepted to, say, Amherst, you would not be in the top of the applicant class. At a school like Puget Sound or Emerson, on the other hand, you would be toward the top of the applicant pool. (And if you have a 3.0 and a 1560 SAT or even something else, remember, there are many schools out there for you, too.) The bottom line is that if you are at the top of a college's applicant pool, you may receive a bigger aid package because the school will really want you.

Does the school offer merit-based financial aid? Merit aid is scholarship money that is not based on need, but on things like academic performance in high school. While Ivy League schools do not give merit aid, many other schools offer scholarships to try to lure the best students away from their competition. These can be National Merit Scholarships for those who excelled on the PSATs or just big fat checks to students they want to tempt to attend. Many schools give merit aid, including Cal Tech, the University of Chicago, Duke, Johns Hopkins, Rice, Swarthmore, and Vanderbilt. Knowing your schools' policies, you can compare financial aid packages. You can then even appeal, using a higher package at one school to get more money from another school.

How does the school consider "outside aid"? Outside aid refers to scholarships that you receive independent of the college aid package. You see, most of the time you can't hide outside money from schools. Many colleges will reduce their aid package by the amount you get from outside scholarships. While some schools allow you to keep all or most of this money by reducing the amount of *loans* they give you, other schools use part of your outside scholarship money to reduce **loans** and take the rest to reduce the **grants** they give you. Seems unfair, doesn't it? You can win a $10,000 scholarship, but it may not reduce your loans or your parents' contribution as much as you would expect.

Therefore, if you don't expect to receive any financial aid, scholarships are great because they put money into your pocket. *But if you are going to get financial aid, you need to see what the school's policies are and determine if it's even worth applying for scholarships.*

In past years, schools like Bryn Mawr, Harvard, Oberlin, University of Virginia, and Williams have all used outside scholarships to replace loans until there are no loans left. Schools like Amherst or Bowdoin have used the first $1,000 in outside scholarships to reduce loans, and then anything over $1,000 is split to reduce loans and school grants.

What is the school's policy regarding changes in financial aid after freshman year? Some schools start upping the amount of loans and/or work-study and decreasing grant or free money as a student gets older. Sometimes it is not a lot of money, but you need to find out. (Note: Some schools, like the University of Virginia, go the other way. Because they don't want freshmen to work their first year, the loans are generally bigger the first year and smaller in later years.)

What is the school's policy on financial aid appeals? Most schools say they will not increase a student's aid package to compete with other schools. Their official statement is that they don't negotiate. However, if you have new or additional information, most schools will reexamine your aid package, especially if your other schools gave you more aid. In fact, in the past, schools such as Carnegie Mellon, Harvard, and Swarthmore have suggested that students fax in their best offers of financial aid from other schools. Depending on how bad a school wants you, it may make you a better offer, with more grants or reduced loans. (I'll talk about how to appeal on page 211.)

Remember back on page 205 I said there were two things you need to do to? Well, the second is:

- Maximize your aid package by applying to schools where you are at the top of the applicant pool; by appealing aid packages and allowing schools to compete; by having your parents increase the amount they are entitled to receive by adjusting their finances at the right time; by knowing if it will benefit you to look for outside scholarships; and by knowing all the different options that exist for paying for college.

Now that you know what questions to ask, the following are things you and your parents can do to make sure you get as much aid as possible:

1. Decide if Early Decision is a good idea. Ah, you didn't think financial aid and Early Decision had anything to do with each another, did you? Well, unfortunately they do. If you have a lot of financial need, you might consider not applying for ED to schools that do not guarantee to meet the financial need of all students or that do not award Merit Scholarships. Because you are willing to commit if you get in early, colleges that don't have these policies may give you less aid because they know you have to attend if they let you in. Now this doesn't apply to all schools, so it doesn't mean you shouldn't apply for ED overall. However, if you do apply for ED and are accepted by a school that doesn't give you enough financial aid, you have a legitimate reason to ask to be released from your commitment and to apply to another school.

2. Apply to schools that give Merit Scholarships if your GPA and test scores place you in the top quarter of the applicants. Not only will you have a better chance of receiving more aid, but you will have more negotiating power if you appeal.

3. Apply to schools that give good aid. Many schools with a lot of money have started changing their policies to benefit middle-income families.

4. Apply to schools where your CSI (see Chapter 4) makes you a good candidate. If you are interested in a program a school is trying to build or have a talent that the school is interested in, you may get extra aid.

5. Apply to schools that are similar. If Pomona knows Amherst and Swarthmore have given you more aid, for example, it'll be more inclined to up its package; it would hate to lose you to a direct competitor because of money.

6. Appeal the aid package offered by the school you want to attend if it does not meet your needs or if another school has substantially beat the aid offer. (How to do this is discussed on page 211.)

7. Apply for outside scholarships. As discussed, this may or may not be a great idea depending on the school's policy, the amount of time you have, and the amount of money you want to apply for. (These issues are discussed on page 207.)

   Check whether a school offers additional scholarships that you have to apply for separately. State schools are known for this. The University of California system, for example, has a list of scholarships in the back of its application booklet.

8. Consider state schools. If your home state has state schools that interest you, by all means apply. However, if you apply to a state school outside your home state, you won't see nearly as much savings in tuition because these schools charge out-of-state students more. Typical state schools run about $8,000 to $18,000 per year as opposed to $30,000 to $40,000 for private. But because private schools often have more money and thus often offer more aid, the cost of attending a private school may not be much different from the cost of going to a public school. For example, with financial aid it cost me about $4,000 more to go to Stanford for four years than it would if I had attended UCLA.

9. Remember the military.

   - *Academies.* If you are considering going into the Air Force, Army, Navy, Marines, or Coast Guard, you might apply for an appointment to the appropriate military academy. (You have to get the appointment, or recommendation, from a senator or congressperson.) By attending a military academy such as West Point, you can get four years of education for free as long as you agree to serve as an officer in the armed forces, generally for four to five years after you graduate.

   - *ROTC (Reserve Officer Training Corps)* programs. Members of ROTC attend a regular university and are paid to take part in exercises and training while in school. They have to agree to join one of the services after they graduate. Usually a four-year active-duty commitment, but the amount of service time can vary. Scholarship amounts and requirements vary and not all schools offer ROTC programs, so make sure you check it out if you are interested.

   - *Scholarships.* If one of your parents is a veteran, you may be eligible for certain scholarships. You may also be able to get instant residency in a different state and be able to benefit from its state schools.

10. Get athletic scholarships. If you are a good athlete or are being recruited by coaches, ask schools what kind of scholarships are available, especially if you are considering playing NCAA Division I sports. If you are not being actively recruited, write letters to coaches and go meet them to talk about the possibility of your playing and getting scholarships in the future.

11. Study in overseas programs. While studying abroad for a semester or a year can sometimes save a bit of money depending on the program, attending an international school can save a lot of money and still provide you with an excellent education.

12. Take AP tests and additional courses at a local college during the school year or during summers. Often students will use credits from AP tests or from classes taken at less expensive schools to reduce their total tuition. They get a degree from their primary college, but sometimes pull off graduating in three years, thus saving a significant amount of money.

13. Consider public service. Consider programs like AmeriCorps, where you do community service and receive financial aid to pay for upcoming school tuition or to pay off past loans. Check out www.cns.gov.

    For parents: Following are things you can do to increase the amount of aid your child receives by making adjustments to your finances before the base year, or the year in which your child applies to college.

14. Consider leaving off a minor piece of information on the FAFSA, the PROFILE, or an individual school's financial aid form. This will give you a legitimate reason for appealing an aid package. Many schools will not consider reevaluating aid without an overlooked or new piece of information—for example, unexpected medical bills or extra childcare expenses. I am not suggesting being dishonest or lying about figures to try to increase aid. I recommend, however, that you leverage your finances and your reporting to ensure that the calculations made on the financial aid forms adequately assess the amount of need you have.

15. Pay down debt. Debt is not calculated into the need for financial aid. Your aid is based on your income and your assets during the year in which your son or daughter applies to college. Therefore, if you owe $100,000 on credit cards, the financial aid people don't care. They will, however, look at your assets of $50,000 in a savings account. Thus, one option is to pay off debt with your savings to decrease the assets you show you have.

16. Avoid capital gains. If you are going to sell assets that will result in capital gains, this will be counted as income and will thus decrease the amount of aid. Therefore, sell *after* college has started (although the gains may be taken into account for the next year).

17. Transfer money from your child's accounts to your accounts. Student savings and parent savings are treated differently. Schools want approximately 35 percent of student savings but only approximately 6 percent of parent savings.

18. Consider your mortgage. First, you must find out which schools use the FAFSA, the PROFILE, or both to determine aid. Home equity is not considered in the FAFSA, but it is in the PROFILE.

19. Look into payment programs. Many schools offer financing programs where, for a minimum fee, you can spread your yearly tuition costs over ten months. Check with each school to find out what they offer. Private companies also offer this option. One program is USA Group Tuition Payment Plans at www.usagroup.com.

20. PLUS loans (Federal Parent Loans for Undergraduate Study). PLUS loans are available to parents who have dependent students and to independent undergraduate students. They typically provide money above what is offered by a school and have interest rates of up to 9 percent. Each school's financial aid office will have more info about these loans. (To determine dependency status go to www.finaid.org/calculator/dependency.phtm.)

21. State savings plans. State savings plans allow parents to put investment money toward their child's future college education. Initial contributions can be as much as $50,000, with earnings on the account tax-deferred until the student uses the money. The tax is then based on the student's, not the parent's, tax rate. Some programs allow parents to put away as little as $50 per month. As these plans apply to parents whose children have some years to go before attending college, I will not go into a detailed discussion here. (For more information go to www.finaid.org.)

"I WANT MORE MONEY!": HOW TO APPEAL

If you want to appeal an aid package, do the following:

1. Find out the policy of the school. If it has procedures for appealing, go ahead and follow them. These procedures may be published on its website or in its viewbook. Of course, you can always call the financial aid office.

2. Write a letter explaining your case.

   • State any new information. Make sure to send any supporting data like bills, tax forms, and receipts.

   • If you do not have any new information, consider discussing a piece of information you might have left off the application.

   • Mention any upcoming expense, such as a new child on the way. Additional information can include health-care expense, child-care expense, death in the family, job change, unemployment, parental separation, or divorce, and insurance fees.

   • Use better aid packages from other schools (preferably schools that are similar or have a better academic reputation) to negotiate more aid. If you can point out why another school came up with more money, you may persuade the school to reevaluate its position.

3. Be persistent, but as always, be courteous and nonthreatening. Instead of complaining about a school's package, point out information for the school to reevaluate its offer, and then negotiate using other offers.

COMPLETING THE FORMS

FAFSA (FREE APPLICATION FOR FEDERAL STUDENT AID)
Here's what you need to know:

1. The FAFSA is the form you and your parents or guardians will fill out to apply for Federal financial aid. The application is free, and you can fill it out in one of two ways.

   • Get a blank paper copy from your high school after January 1, fill it out using the sample FAFSA in this book as an example, and send it in.

   • Apply online at www.fafsa.ed.gov. If you apply online, the instructions will still be the same. But either you'll have to sign up for a Personal Identification Number (PIN), which will allow you to complete the whole nine yards online, or you'll have to print out the signature page, sign it with your parents, and send it in. (Note: Your parents will have to get their own PIN when it comes time for them to fill out their information online.)

   Even though there's a paper-copy example in this book, I suggest doing everything online with a PIN. Filling out the FAFSA is easier and quicker online. However, if your parents balk at submitting information online, or if you don't have access to a computer, then use paper forms. The address to mail the paper version to follows:

   Federal Student Aid Programs
   P.O. Box 4691
   Mountain Vernon, IL 62864-0059

   Here's the phone number if you have any questions. 1-800-433-3243.
   You don't have to send in a FAFSA to each school, just to the address above or online.

2. You have to submit the FAFSA form **between January 2 and June 30** of the year you apply to college. (Different schools have different deadlines, with the majority falling sometime in March.) However, to increase your chances of receiving aid, apply as early as possible.

3. After you turn in the form, a central agency will process your information and send you the SAR, or Student Aid Report. Basically all of your financial info is put into a formula so that the government can figure out your EFC, or Expected Family Contribution—the amount your family will have to pay before you receive any outside awards. Remember, the FAFSA form is just for federal funds. You will also receive an aid statement from each school, which will be based partly on the FAFSA.

4. If you or your family has a change of circumstances—a parent lost a job, there was a

death in the family, or something else that you couldn't list on the FAFSA but will affect your need—make sure you call the financial aid office at each of your schools and let them know what's going on.

5. Here's a list from the FAFSA website of ways the government can help you pay for school, depending on your eligibility. You might want to show this to your parents.

- Federal Pell grants are available to undergraduate students. Grants do not have to be repaid. Federal Pell grants have ranged in past years from $400 to $3,800.

- Federal Stafford loans are student loans that must be repaid. They are available to both undergraduate and graduate students. If your school participates in the William D. Ford Federal Direct Loan (Direct Loan) Program, the federal government provides the funds for your Stafford loan. If your school participates in the Federal Family Education Loan (FFEL) Program, a private lender provides the funds for your Stafford loan, although the federal government guarantees the loan funds. First-year undergraduates are eligible for loans up to $2,625. Amounts increase for subsequent years of study, with higher amounts for graduate students. The interest rate is variable, but in the past, has not exceeded 8.25 percent. There are two types of Stafford direct loans: (1)*a subsidized* loan, for which the government pays the interest while you are in school, during grace periods, and during any deferment periods, and (2) an *unsubsidized* loan, for which you are responsible for paying all the interest that accrues at any point in time.

- Federal PLUS loans are unsubsidized loans made to parents. If you are independent or your parents cannot get a PLUS loan, you are eligible to borrow additional unsubsidized Stafford loan funds. The interest rate is variable, but in the past, has not exceeded 9 percent.

- Campus-based programs are administered by participating schools. These include:

  - Federal Supplemental Educational Opportunity Grants are grants available for undergraduates only; awards range from $100 to $4,000.

  - Federal Work-Study Program provides jobs to undergraduate and graduate students, allowing them to earn money to pay for education expenses.

  - Perkins loans are low-interest (5 percent) loans that must be repaid; the maximum annual loan is $4,000 for undergraduate students and $6,000 for graduate students.

Here's some other info for parents: Two educational income tax credits can reduce your federal taxes. They are based on the college tuition and fee charges. The Hope Scholarship tax credit can be claimed during the first two years of college, up to a maximum of $1,500 per year. The Lifetime Learning tax credit is available for any level of postsecondary study, up to a current maximum of $1,000 per year. Note that only one type of credit (Hope or Lifetime

Learning) may be claimed for a student in any given year. For more information about tax credits, visit the IRS website at www.irs.gov.

Now let's get to the form.

THE FORM INSTRUCTIONS

As on the school applications, the sample FAFSA form shown in Figure 16-1 includes circled numbers that look like this: ③. They correspond to numbers in the text that answer commonly asked questions about that part of the form. Sometimes I will quote directly from the FAFSA instructions. I have done this so you don't have to have a bunch of different papers all over your desk.

Before we get to the form, however, remember that completing the FAFSA and the PRO-FILE will involve your parents. I find that it's best if you put in all your information, and then just pass the book over to your parents to let them fill out their part, either online or on paper.

Note: The FAFSA in Figure 16-1 was the latest available when this book went to press. The form rarely changes from year to year, so all the information should still apply. However, if you discover minor differences and you have questions, consult your counselor or call the FAFSA people directly.

Also, you and your parents are going to need some documents before you can answer all the questions. Here's what you'll need:

1. Social Security number (student, parents).

2. Driver's license (student, parents).

3. W-2 forms, if employed (student, parents).

4. Federal tax return, if you have worked (student).

5. Federal tax return (parents) (unless the student is independent—the parents no longer claim the student on their taxes and the student is making his or her own money). See www.finaid.org/calculator/dependency.phtm for independent status criteria.

6. Untaxed income records—that is, Social Security benefits, veteran's benefits, or welfare benefits (parents).

7. Bank statements (student, parents)

8. Business and investment mortgage information, business and farm statements, and other investment records (student, parents).

Note: Students and parents will need some or all of the preceding information, including financial records or estimates. You do not need to have filed a tax return for the year in which you are filling out the FAFSA (the year you will begin college), although having the numbers will make it easier. You will, however, have to submit a tax return to the schools eventually.

ELIGIBILITY

Most students are eligible for federal aid. Here are the requirements for eligibility:

- You are a U.S. citizen or an eligible noncitizen with a Social Security number.

- You have a high school diploma (or will get one that year) or a GED.

- You have registered with the Selective Service System if you're a male between 18 and 25.

THREE MORE REMINDERS

- If you fill out a paper version of the FAFSA, be sure to use a black pen, skip a box between words, and print in capital letters.

- If you use a paper version, be sure you to make copies, and mail in the original of *only pages 3 to 6* to the address listed earlier.

- On the actual paper version, there are two different colored sections. One color is for the student info, and the other is for the parent info. (The form in the book is a copy and thus is in black-and-white.)

Now let's take a look at the actual form.

1. *Selective Service.* Most male students have to register with the Selective Service System upon turning 18. If you are a male under 18 at the time of filing the FAFSA, mark yes for being male (no. 21) and yes for no. 22; Selective Service will automatically register you when you turn 18.

2. *Degree or Certificate.* The form says, "See page 2," but I have included the classifications here.

   1 your first bachelor's degree (BA)

   2 your second bachelor's degree

   3 your associate degree (degree at an occupational or technical program)

   4 your associate degree (degree at a general education or transfer program)

   5 a certificate or diploma for completing an occupational, technical, or educational program of less than 2 years

   6 a certificate or diploma for completing an occupational, technical, or educational program of at least 2 years

   7 teaching credential program (nondegree program)

8 graduate or professional degree (masters', PhD, MD, JD, etc.)

9 other or undecided

3. *Grade level.* Choose one of these codes for your grade level when you begin college:

0 never attended college and first-year undergraduate

1 attended college before and first-year undergraduate

2 second-year undergraduate/sophomore

3 third-year undergraduate/junior

4 fourth-year undergraduate/senior

5 fifth-year/other undergraduate

6 first-year graduate/professional

7 continuing graduate/professional or beyond

4. *Student loans.* I suggest choosing "yes" for student loans (no. 27). Doing this will not affect your chances of getting grants, but it will potentially make you available for low-interest, flexible loans. Remember, you don't have to accept a school's financial aid package if you want to pay for it a different way, but these are about the best loans you can get, so I'd mark yes.

5. *Work-study.* Choose "yes" for work-study (no. 28).

6. *Tax return.* If you (the student) did not work during the last tax year, choose "c., I'm not going to file" (no. 32). Then skip to no. 42. If you did work, ask your parents whether you earned enough money to file a return.

7. *Tax return, continued.* Check with your parents if you worked but don't know which tax return you filed. Many people mistakenly choose IRS 1040 in item no. 33, many students file IRS 1040EZ. See page 2 of the FAFSA booklet if you have a foreign tax return.

8. *1040A or 1040EZ?* You can file a 1040A or 1040EZ if you earned less than $50,000, did not itemize deductions, did not collect money from your own business or farm, and did not receive alimony. Most students working a part-time job are eligible to file a 1040A or a 1040EZ.

9. *Income questions.* Many of these questions (nos. 35 to 39) may not apply to you. If this is the case, put 0 in the farthest right box. If they do apply, look at the line on your tax return to which each question refers, and then write the numbers in the box. For example, no. 35 tells you to look at IRS form 1040A, line 21.

10. *Student (and spouse) worksheets.* Here you have to use the first of the worksheets included with the FAFSA (see page 225). But this applies to you only if you have worked and have filed a tax return. First, you take the numbers from your tax return,

and write them in the left column under the student/spouse heading. You then add up all the entries for that section, and write the total in the white box. You then copy that number into no. 40, 41, or 42, depending on what worksheet you had numbers in. If you had numbers in worksheet A and C, for example, you would use the totals for no. 40 and no. 42 on the FAFSA and put a 0 in no. 41. Otherwise, if none apply, just put 0s in the farthest right-hand boxes.

11. Net Worth. Net worth is current value minus debt. If your family's net worth is $1 million or more, enter $999,999. If net worth is negative, enter 0.

    Investments include real estate (but not the home you live in), trust funds, money-market funds, mutual funds, certificates of deposit, stock options, bonds, other securities, education IRAs, college savings plans, installment and land sale contracts (including mortgages held), and commodities. Investment value includes the market value of these investments as of today. <u>Investment debt includes only those debts that are related to the investments.</u>

    Investments do not include the home you live in, cash, savings, checking accounts, the value of life insurance and retirement plans (pension funds, annuities, noneducation IRAs, Keogh plans, etc.), or the value of prepaid tuition plans.

    Business and/or farm value includes the market value of land, buildings, machinery, equipment, inventory, etc. <u>Business and/or investment farm debt includes only those debts for which the business or investment farm was used as collateral.</u>

12. Step Three. For Step Three (nos. 48 to 54), most students will answer no to all question. If this is the case for you, follow the directions and go to Step Four. However, if you answer yes to any question in Step Three or if you are a health-profession student, skip Step Four and complete Step Five.

13. *Parents' data.* Now you have reached the other colored section of the form, which is for your parents. You can fill in some of the information for them and then sit down with them to fill in the rest, or you can give the FAFSA to them to fill out. If your parents want to send it in for you, be sure Step Six (schools you are applying to) is completed, and sign the FAFSA in Step Seven.

14. *Identifying parents.* If you, the student, answered no to all the questions in Step Three, but you do not live with your parents, you still have to answer the questions in Step Four. Here are the possible answers.

    - If your parents are both living and married to each other, answer all the questions in the parent section (nos. 55 to 83) about both of them.

    - If your parent is widowed or single, answer all the questions in the parent section about that parent. If your parent is remarried as of today, answer all the questions in the parent section about that parent *and* the person whom your parent married (your stepparent).

    - If your parents are divorced or separated, answer all the questions in the parent section about the parent you lived with more during the past 12 months. (If you did not live with one parent more than the other, answer all the questions in the parent section about the parent who provided more financial support during the past 12 months, or during the year that you actually received support from a parent.

- If this parent is remarried today, answer all the questions in the parent section about that parent and the person whom your parent married (your stepparent).

15. *Household size.* To determine how many people are in your parents' household, include:

Your parents and yourself, even if you don't live with them.

Your parents' other children if your parents will provide more than half of their support in the year in which you are filling out this application (the year you will begin college).

Other people if they now live with your parents, if your parents provide more than half of their support, and if your parents will continue to provide more than half of their support in the year in which you are filling out this application.

Example: If your parents' household consists of your mom, dad, you, and your little sister, write "4" in no. 65.

16. *How many college students?* Always count yourself as a college student. Do not include your parents. Include others only if they will attend at least half-time a program that leads to a college degree or certificate. *Example:* You are going to college, but your sister is in junior high. Put down "1" in no. 66.

17. *Parents' tax return.* Indicate in no. 70 whether a tax return was or will be filed for the year in which you are filling out this application.

18. *Which return?* Your parents would be eligible to file a 1040A or 1040EZ if they made less than $50,000, did not itemize deductions, did not collect money from their own business or farm, and did not receive alimony.

19. *Nos. 73 to 80.* For these questions, your parents will need their tax returns or estimates for the year in which you are filling out this application. To find this information, they should look at the specified line on their tax returns, and then copy the numbers in the spaces (example: Form 1040, line 33). Or they will have to give an estimate, knowing that they will have to submit their tax return upon completion.

20. *Nos. 76 to 77.* Nos. 76 to 77 involve pulling info from either your parents' tax returns, or from their W-2s if they haven't filed yet.

21. *Parent worksheets.* Here's where your parents use the second of the worksheets included with the FAFSA (see page 225). They take figures from their tax returns as

specified in the worksheet and enter them in the appropriate column under the heading "parents." They then add up all the entries for that section and write it in the white box. Next they take that number and copy into either no. 78, 79, or 80 depending on what worksheet they had numbers in. If they had numbers for Worksheet A and C, for example, they would use the totals for no. 78 and no. 80 on the FAFSA and put a 0 in no. 79.

22. *Net worth*. Net worth is current value minus debt. If net worth is $1 million or more, enter $999,999 in no. 82. If net worth is negative, enter 0.

    For information on what constitutes investments, debts, and business/farm value, see #11 on page 217.

    Note: Nos. 24 and 25 apply only to those who answered yes to any question in Step Three.

23. *Household*. To determine how many people are in your (and your spouse's) household, include:

    - Yourself (and your spouse, if you have one).

    - Your children, if you'll provide more than half their support in the year in which you are filling out this application.

    - Other people if they now live with you, you provide more than half of their support, and you will continue to provide more than half of their support in the year in which you are filling out this application.

24. *College students?* To determine which of the individuals in no. 84 will be college students, count the person who is applying to college. Parents should not be included. Count others in the household only if they will attend, at least half-time, a program that leads to a college degree or certificate.

25. *School codes*. In Step Six, list each college you are applying to. If you are applying online, you can apply to over twenty schools at once. With the paper form, you have to call the FAFSA office to add more than six schools. To find each school's federal code, you can ask your counselor, look in your applications, get them at www.fafsa.ed.gov, or just write in the name, address, city, and state of each school. Make sure to indicate your housing plans (nos. 87, 89, 91, 93, 95, and 97) in the right column.

26. *Status*. "Full time" here means at least 12 units or credits during a college term (either quarters or semesters); "$^3/_4$" time, at least 9 units/credits; "half time," at least 6 units/credits.

27. *Signature*. Read the statement in Step Seven, and sign your name in no. 100. A parent whose financial info is included must also sign.

Finally,

- If you have any questions, ask your counselor or go to www.ed.gov/prog_info/SFA/FAFSA.

  If you are using paper versions please do the following:
  Double-check that all the info is correct and you have put os in the far right boxes where there were blanks.

- Make a copy of the completed form before you send it.

- Mail the completed form in a *stamped* envelope. Send it with a certificate of mailing (so you have a record that it was sent) to: Federal Student Aid Programs, P.O. Box 4001, Mount Vernon, IL 62864-8601. Do not include the worksheets or tax forms— send only pages 3 to 6. Also, do not send the application before January 1 of the year you will be starting college.

- If you want to be notified that your FAFSA has been received, attach a self-addressed, stamped postcard to the application.

FIGURE 16-1 SAMPLE FAFSA FORM

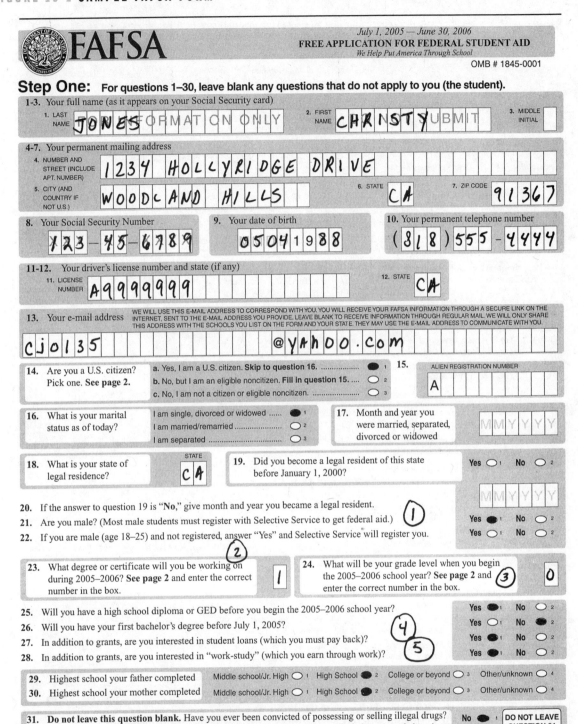

FAFSA
July 1, 2005 — June 30, 2006
FREE APPLICATION FOR FEDERAL STUDENT AID
We Help Put America Through School

OMB # 1845-0001

Step One: For questions 1–30, leave blank any questions that do not apply to you (the student).

1-3. Your full name (as it appears on your Social Security card)

1. LAST NAME: JONES (INFORMATION ONLY)
2. FIRST NAME: CHRISTY (SUBMIT)
3. MIDDLE INITIAL:

4-7. Your permanent mailing address

4. NUMBER AND STREET (INCLUDE APT. NUMBER): 1234 HOLLYRIDGE DRIVE
5. CITY (AND COUNTRY IF NOT U.S.): WOODLAND HILLS
6. STATE: CA
7. ZIP CODE: 91367

8. Your Social Security Number: 123-45-6789
9. Your date of birth: 05041988
10. Your permanent telephone number: (818) 555-4444

11-12. Your driver's license number and state (if any)

11. LICENSE NUMBER: A9999999
12. STATE: CA

13. Your e-mail address — WE WILL USE THIS E-MAIL ADDRESS TO CORRESPOND WITH YOU. YOU WILL RECEIVE YOUR FAFSA INFORMATION THROUGH A SECURE LINK ON THE INTERNET, SENT TO THE E-MAIL ADDRESS YOU PROVIDE. LEAVE BLANK TO RECEIVE INFORMATION THROUGH REGULAR MAIL. WE WILL ONLY SHARE THIS ADDRESS WITH THE SCHOOLS YOU LIST ON THE FORM AND YOUR STATE. THEY MAY USE THE E-MAIL ADDRESS TO COMMUNICATE WITH YOU.

cjo135 @yahoo.com

14. Are you a U.S. citizen? Pick one. See page 2.
   a. Yes, I am a U.S. citizen. **Skip to question 16.** ⬤ 1
   b. No, but I am an eligible noncitizen. **Fill in question 15.** ○ 2
   c. No, I am not a citizen or eligible noncitizen. ○ 3

15. ALIEN REGISTRATION NUMBER: A

16. What is your marital status as of today?
   I am single, divorced or widowed ⬤ 1
   I am married/remarried ○ 2
   I am separated ○ 3

17. Month and year you were married, separated, divorced or widowed: MMYYYY

18. What is your state of legal residence? STATE: CA

19. Did you become a legal resident of this state before January 1, 2000? Yes ○ 1   No ○ 2

20. If the answer to question 19 is "**No**," give month and year you became a legal resident. ① MMYYYY

21. Are you male? (Most male students must register with Selective Service to get federal aid.) Yes ⬤ 1   No ○ 2

22. If you are male (age 18–25) and not registered, answer "Yes" and Selective Service will register you. ② Yes ○ 1   No ○ 2

23. What degree or certificate will you be working on during 2005–2006? See page 2 and enter the correct number in the box. 1

24. What will be your grade level when you begin the 2005–2006 school year? See page 2 and enter the correct number in the box. ③ 0

25. Will you have a high school diploma or GED before you begin the 2005–2006 school year? Yes ⬤ 1   No ○ 2

26. Will you have your first bachelor's degree before July 1, 2005? ④ Yes ○ 1   No ⬤ 2

27. In addition to grants, are you interested in student loans (which you must pay back)? ⑤ Yes ⬤ 1   No ○ 2

28. In addition to grants, are you interested in "work-study" (which you earn through work)? Yes ⬤ 1   No ○ 2

29. Highest school your father completed   Middle school/Jr. High ○ 1   High School ○ 2   College or beyond ○ 3   Other/unknown ○ 4

30. Highest school your mother completed   Middle school/Jr. High ○ 1   High School ⬤ 2   College or beyond ○ 3   Other/unknown ○ 4

31. **Do not leave this question blank.** Have you ever been convicted of possessing or selling illegal drugs? If you have, answer "Yes," complete and submit this application, and we will send you a worksheet in the mail for you to determine if your conviction affects your eligibility for aid.
   No ⬤ 1   Yes ○ 3
   DO NOT LEAVE QUESTION 31 BLANK

Page 3

For Help – www.studentaid.ed.gov/completefafsa

FIGURE 16-1 **SAMPLE FAFSA FORM**

Step Two: For questions 32–45, report your (the student's) income and assets. If you are married as of today, report your and your spouse's income and assets, even if you were not married in 2004. Ignore references to "spouse" if you are currently single, separated, divorced or widowed.

32. For 2004, have you (the student) completed your IRS income tax return or another tax return listed in question 33?

a. I have already completed my return. ○ 1　　**b.** I will file, but I have not yet completed my return. ● 2 ⑥　　**c.** I'm not going to file. (Skip to question 38.) ○ 3

33. What income tax return did you file or will you file for 2004?

a. IRS 1040 .... ⊙ 1
b. IRS 1040A, 1040EZ, 1040TeleFile .... ● 2 ⑦
c. A foreign tax return. See page 2. .... ○ 3

d. A tax return with Puerto Rico, Guam, American Samoa, the U.S. Virgin Islands, the Marshall Islands, the Federated States of Micronesia, or Palau. See page 2. .... ○ 4

34. If you have filed or will file a 1040, were you eligible to file a 1040A or 1040EZ? See page 2. ⑧ Yes ● 1　No ○ 2　Don't Know ○ 3

For questions 35–47, if the answer is zero or the question does not apply to you, enter 0.

35. What was your (and spouse's) adjusted gross income for 2004? Adjusted gross income is on IRS Form 1040—line 36; 1040A—line 21; 1040EZ—line 4; or TeleFile—line I. ⑨ $ 2,100

36. Enter the total amount of your (and spouse's) income tax for 2004. Income tax amount is on IRS Form 1040—line 56; 1040A—line 36; 1040EZ—line 10; or TeleFile—line K(2). $ 368

37. Enter your (and spouse's) exemptions for 2004. Exemptions are on IRS Form 1040—line 6d or on Form 1040A—line 6d. For Form 1040EZ or TeleFile, **see page 2.** 0

38-39. How much did you (and spouse) earn from working (wages, salaries, tips, etc.) in 2004? Answer this question whether or not you filed a tax return. This information may be on your W-2 forms, or on IRS Form 1040—lines 7 + 12 + 18; 1040A—line 7; or 1040EZ—line 1. TeleFilers should use their W-2 forms.

You (38) $ 2,100
Your Spouse (39) $ X

Student (and Spouse) Worksheets (40–42)

40-42. **Go to page 8** and complete the columns on the left of Worksheets A, B, and C. Enter the student (and spouse) totals in questions 40, 41 and 42, respectively. Even though you may have few of the Worksheet items, check each line carefully. ⑩

Worksheet A (40) $ 0
Worksheet B (41) $ 0
Worksheet C (42) $ 0

43. As of today, what is your (and spouse's) total current balance of **cash, savings, and checking accounts**? Do not include student financial aid. $ 500

44. As of today, what is the net worth of your (and spouse's) **investments**, including real estate (not your home)? *Net worth* means current value minus debt. See page 2. $ 0

45. As of today, what is the net worth of your (and spouse's) current **businesses and/or investment farms**? Do not include a farm that you live on and operate. See page 2. ⑪ $ X,56X

46-47. If you receive veterans' education benefits, for how many months from July 1, 2005, through June 30, 2006, will you receive these benefits, and what amount will you receive per month? Do not include your spouse's veterans' education benefits.

Months (46) X
Monthly Amount (47) $ X

Step Three: Answer all seven questions in this step. ⑫

48. Were you born before January 1, 1982? .... Yes ○ 1　No ● 2

49. At the beginning of the 2005–2006 school year, will you be working on a master's or doctorate program (such as an MA, MBA, MD, JD, PhD, EdD, or graduate certificate, etc.)? .... Yes ○ 1　No ● 2

50. As of today, are you married? (Answer "Yes" if you are separated but not divorced.) .... Yes ○ 1　No ● 2

51. Do you have children who receive more than half of their support from you? .... Yes ○ 1　No ● 2

52. Do you have dependents (other than your children or spouse) who live with you and who receive more than half of their support from you, now and through June 30, 2006? .... Yes ○ 1　No ● 2

53. Are both of your parents deceased, or are you (or were you until age 18) a ward/dependent of the court? .... Yes ○ 1　No ● 2

54. Are you a veteran of the U.S. Armed Forces? **See page 2.** .... Yes ○ 1　No ● 2

If you (the student) answer "No" to every question in Step Three, go to Step Four.
If you answer "Yes" to any question in Step Three, skip Step Four and go to Step Five on page 6.

(Health Profession Students: Your school may require you to complete Step Four even if you answered "Yes" to any Step Three question.)

Page 4

For Help – 1-800-433-3243

FIGURE 16-1 SAMPLE FAFSA FORM

Step Four: Complete this step if you (the student) answered "No" to all questions in Step Three. Go to page 7 to determine who is a parent for this step. ⑬

55. What is your parents' marital status as of today? ⑭

Married/Remarried .... ○ 1   Divorced/Separated .... ● 3

Single .... ○ 2   Widowed .... ○ 4

56. Month and year they were married, separated, divorced or widowed

`0 6 1 9 9 4`

57-64. What are the Social Security Numbers, names and dates of birth of the parents reporting information on this form? If your parent does not have a Social Security Number, you must enter 000-00-0000.

57. FATHER'S/STEPFATHER'S SOCIAL SECURITY NUMBER
`4 4 4 - 4 4 - 4 4 4 4`

58. FATHER'S/STEPFATHER'S LAST NAME, AND
`J O N E S`

59. FIRST INITIAL
`, H`

60. FATHER'S/STEPFATHER'S DATE OF BIRTH
`1 0 1 0 1 9 5 2`

61. MOTHER'S/STEPMOTHER'S SOCIAL SECURITY NUMBER
`5 5 5 - 5 5 - 5 5 5 5`

62. MOTHER'S/STEPMOTHER'S LAST NAME, AND
`J O N E S`

63. FIRST INITIAL
`, B`

64. MOTHER'S/STEPMOTHER'S DATE OF BIRTH
`0 8 1 6 1 9 5 4`

65. Go to page 7 to determine how many people are in your parents' household. ⑮ `0 3`

66. Go to page 7 to determine how many in question 65 (exclude your parents) will be college students between July 1, 2005, and June 30, 2006. ⑯ `1`

67. What is your parents' state of legal residence? STATE `C A`

68. Did your parents become legal residents of this state before January 1, 2000?   Yes ● 1   No ○ 2

69. If the answer to question 68 is "**No**," give month and year legal residency began for the parent who has lived in the state the longest. `M M Y Y Y Y`

70. For 2004, have your parents completed their IRS income tax return or another tax return listed in question 71?

a. My parents have already completed their return. ○ 1   **b.** My parents will file, but they have not yet completed their return. ● 2 ⑰   **c.** My parents are not going to file. **(Skip to question 76.)** ○ 3

71. What income tax return did your parents file or will they file for 2004?

a. IRS 1040 .... ● 1

b. IRS 1040A, 1040EZ, 1040TeleFile .... ○ 2

c. A foreign tax return. **See page 2.** .... ○ 3 ⑱

d. A tax return with Puerto Rico, Guam, American Samoa, the U.S. Virgin Islands, the Marshall Islands, the Federated States of Micronesia, or Palau. **See page 2.** .... ○ 4

72. If your parents have filed or will file a 1040, were they eligible to file a 1040A or 1040EZ? **See page 2.**   Yes ○ 1   No ● 2   Don't Know ○ 3

For questions 73-83, if the answer is zero or the question does not apply, enter 0.   see ⑧

73. What was your parents' adjusted gross income for 2004? Adjusted gross income is on IRS Form 1040—line 36; 1040A—line 21; 1040EZ—line 4; or TeleFile—line I. ⑲ $ `5 7 , 9 0 0`

74. Enter the total amount of your parents' income tax for 2004. Income tax amount is on IRS Form 1040—line 56; 1040A—line 36; 1040EZ—line 10; or TeleFile—line K(2). $ `3 , 2 7 2`

75. Enter your parents' exemptions for 2004. Exemptions are on IRS Form 1040—line 6d or on Form 1040A—line 6d. For Form 1040EZ or TeleFile, **see page 2**. `3`

76-77. How much did your parents earn from working (wages, salaries, tips, etc.) in 2004? Answer this question whether or not your parents filed a tax return. This information may be on their W-2 forms, or on IRS Form 1040—lines 7 + 12 + 18; 1040A—line 7; or 1040EZ—line 1. TeleFilers should use their W-2 forms.

Father/Stepfather (76) $ `5 7 , 9 0 0`

Mother/Stepmother (77) $ `0`

Parent Worksheets (78-80) ⑳

78-80. Go to page 8 and complete the columns on the right of Worksheets A, B, and C. Enter the parents' totals in questions 78, 79 and 80, respectively. Even though your parents may have few of the Worksheet items, check each line carefully.

Worksheet A (78) $ `0`

Worksheet B (79) $ `0`

Worksheet C (80) $ `0` ㉑

81. As of today, what is your parents' total current balance of **cash, savings, and checking accounts**? $ `1 5 , 4 8 3`

82. As of today, what is the net worth of your parents' **investments**, including real estate (not your parents' home)? *Net worth* means current value minus debt. **See page 2.** $ `0` ㉒

83. As of today, what is the net worth of your parents' current **businesses and/or investment farms**? Do not include a farm that your parents live on and operate. **See page 2.** $ `,`

Now go to Step Six.

Page 5

For Help – www.studentaid.ed.gov/completefafsa

FIGURE 16-1 **SAMPLE FAFSA FORM**

Step Five: Complete this step only if you (the student) answered "Yes" to any Step Three question.

84.	Go to page 7 to determine how many people are in your (and your spouse's) household.			85.	Go to page 7 to determine how many people in question 84 will be college students, attending at least half-time between July 1, 2005, and June 30, 2006.	

(23) (24)

Step Six: Please tell us which schools may request your information, and indicate your enrollment status.

Enter the 6-digit federal school code and your housing plans. Look for the federal school codes at **www.fafsa.ed.gov**, at your college financial aid office, at your public library, or by asking your high school guidance counselor. If you cannot get the federal school code, write in the complete name, address, city and state of the college. For state aid, you may wish to list your preferred school first.

(25)

	1st FEDERAL SCHOOL CODE	OR	NAME OF COLLEGE / ADDRESS AND CITY	STATE	HOUSING PLANS	
86.		OR	STANFORD UNIVERSITY / 520 Lasuen Mall, Stanford 94305	C A	87.	on campus ● 1 / off campus ○ 2 / with parent ○ 3
88.		OR			89.	on campus ○ 1 / off campus ○ 2 / with parent ○ 3
90.		OR			91.	on campus ○ 1 / off campus ○ 2 / with parent ○ 3
92.		OR			93.	on campus ○ 1 / off campus ○ 2 / with parent ○ 3
94.		OR			95.	on campus ○ 1 / off campus ○ 2 / with parent ○ 3
96.		OR			97.	on campus ○ 1 / off campus ○ 2 / with parent ○ 3

98.	See page 7. At the start of the 2005-2006 school year, mark if you will be:	Full time ● 1	3/4 time ○ 2	Half time ○ 3	Less than half time ○ 4	Not sure ○ 5

(26)

Step Seven: Read, sign and date.

If you are the student, by signing this application you certify that you (1) will use federal and/or state student financial aid only to pay the cost of attending an institution of higher education, (2) are not in default on a federal student loan or have made satisfactory arrangements to repay it, (3) do not owe money back on a federal student grant or have made satisfactory arrangements to repay it, (4) will notify your school if you default on a federal student loan and (5) will not receive a Federal Pell Grant for more than one school for the same period of time.

If you are the parent or the student, by signing this application you agree, if asked, to provide information that will verify the accuracy of your completed form. This information may include your U.S. or state income tax forms. Also, you certify that you understand that **the Secretary of Education has the authority to verify information reported on this application with the Internal Revenue Service and other federal agencies.** If you sign any document related to the federal student aid programs electronically using a Personal Identification Number (PIN), you certify that you are the person identified by the PIN and have not disclosed that PIN to anyone else. If you purposely give false or misleading information, you may be fined $20,000, sent to prison, or both.

99. Date this form was completed.

| 0 1 | 0 6 | 2005 ○ | or | 2006 ● |

100. Student (Sign below)

Christy Jones

Parent (A parent from Step Four sign below)

If this form was filled out by someone other than you, your spouse or your parents, that person must complete this part.

Preparer's name, firm and address

_____

_____

_____

101. Preparer's Social Security Number (or 102)

___ - ___ - ___

102. Employer ID number (or 101)

___ - ___

103. Preparer's signature and date

SCHOOL USE ONLY: Federal School Code

D/O ○ 1

FAA Signature

DATA ENTRY USE ONLY: ○ P ○ * ○ L ○ E

Page 6

For Help—1-800-433-3243

FIGURE 16-1 **SAMPLE FAFSA FORM**

Worksheets
Calendar Year 2004

Do not mail these worksheets in with your application.
Keep these worksheets; your school may ask to see them.

Worksheet A
Report Annual Amounts

Student/Spouse For question 40		Parents For question 78
$	Earned income credit from IRS Form 1040—line 65a; 1040A—line 41a; 1040EZ—line 8a; or TeleFile—line L	$
$	Additional child tax credit from IRS Form 1040—line 67 or 1040A—line 42	$
$	Welfare benefits, including Temporary Assistance for Needy Families (TANF). Don't include food stamps or subsidized housing.	$
$	Social Security benefits received, for all household members as reported in question 84 (or 65 for your parents), that were not taxed (such as SSI). Report benefits paid to parents in the Parents column, and benefits paid directly to student (or spouse) in the Student/Spouse column.	$
$ —Enter in question 40.		Enter in question 78. —$

Worksheet B
Report Annual Amounts

Student/Spouse For question 41		Parents For question 79
$	Payments to tax-deferred pension and savings plans (paid directly or withheld from earnings), including, but not limited to, amounts reported on the W-2 Form in Boxes 12a through 12d, codes D, E, F, G, H and S	$
$	IRA deductions and payments to self-employed SEP, SIMPLE, and Keogh and other qualified plans from IRS Form 1040—total of lines 25 + 32 or 1040A—line 17	$
$	Child support you received for all children. Don't include foster care or adoption payments.	$
$	Tax exempt interest income from IRS Form 1040—line 8b or 1040A—line 8b	$
$	Foreign income exclusion from IRS Form 2555—line 43 or 2555EZ—line 18	$
$	Untaxed portions of IRA distributions from IRS Form 1040—lines (15a minus 15b) or 1040A—lines (11a minus 11b). Exclude rollovers. If negative, enter a zero here.	$
$	Untaxed portions of pensions from IRS Form 1040—lines (16a minus 16b) or 1040A—lines (12a minus 12b). Exclude rollovers. If negative, enter a zero here.	$
$	Credit for federal tax on special fuels from IRS Form 4136—line 10 (nonfarmers only)	$
$	Housing, food and other living allowances paid to members of the military, clergy and others (including cash payments and cash value of benefits)	$
$	Veterans' noneducation benefits such as Disability, Death Pension, or Dependency & Indemnity Compensation (DIC), and/or VA Educational Work-Study allowances	$
$	Any other untaxed income or benefits not reported elsewhere on Worksheets A and B, such as workers' compensation, untaxed portions of railroad retirement benefits, Black Lung Benefits, disability, etc. Don't include student aid, Workforce Investment Act educational benefits, or benefits from flexible spending arrangements, e.g., cafeteria plans.	$
$	Money received, or paid on your behalf (e.g., bills), not reported elsewhere on this form	XXXXXXXX
$ —Enter in question 41.		Enter in question 79. —$

Worksheet C
Report Annual Amounts

Student/Spouse For question 42		Parents For question 80
$	Education credits (Hope and Lifetime Learning tax credits) from IRS Form 1040—line 49 or 1040A—line 31	$
$	Child support you paid because of divorce or separation or as a result of a legal requirement. Don't include support for children in your (or your parents') household, as reported in question 84 (or question 65 for your parents).	$
$	Taxable earnings from need-based employment programs, such as Federal Work-Study and need-based employment portions of fellowships and assistantships	$
$	Student grant and scholarship aid reported to the IRS in your (or your parents') adjusted gross income. Includes AmeriCorps benefits (awards, living allowances and interest accrual payments), as well as grant or scholarship portions of fellowships and assistantships.	$
$ —Enter in question 42		Enter in question 80. —$

Page 8

For Help — 1-800-433-3243

THE PROFILE: CSS FINANCIAL AID FORM

Here's what you need to know:

1. The PROFILE is the form you and your parents or guardians will fill out to apply for *non-federal* financial aid (see Figures 16-2 to 16-4). It is a program run by the College Board (except here the company is called CSS). Only certain colleges require this form. Therefore, check each of your applications to see if the school wants the PRO-FILE. I have also included a list of schools that require the PROFILE on pages 229 and 230. However, this list is the most recent at the time of printing, so you can double check online at www.collegeboard.com.

   Important: Some schools have their own financial aid forms *in addition to* the FAFSA and the PROFILE. They usually have to be sent to the schools directly, so check your applications.

2. Unlike the FAFSA, the PROFILE is not free. It costs $5 to register for it and then $18 for each school you send it to. If you have to add schools later, there's a $7 processing fee, as well as the same $18 per school.

3. Unlike the FAFSA, you can now only fill out the PROFILE online. Apply online at www.collegeboard.com. Please note: many colleges and programs will ask families to submit copies of their completed income tax returns, including other financial documents. One of the most common is called the "Business/Farm Supplement." I have included a sample of this form on page 246. Please note, however, that this is only for reference, as the form changes each year. Your colleges and programs will let you know if tax return copies are required. Some colleges require that documents be sent directly to the financial aid office. Other schools participate in what is called the College Board's Institutional Documentation Service (IDOC) and want students to forward documents to a College Board address. Check with each of your schools to find out their preferences for submitting documentation.

4. Register online or by phone at least four weeks before the earliest due date specified by your schools. Then submit your PROFILE at least one week (online) or two weeks (paper) before this due date. You see, CSS is a processing agency that takes your one form, summarizes it, and sends it to all your schools. Therefore, it needs time to process all the info and then disseminate it. CSS wants the online form submitted by December 31; however, if you are applying for early decision or early action, most schools want the PROFILE earlier (say, in November), so they can give you an aid package with your admission decision. So once again, check your applications, and make a note of the due dates on your MOAC in chapter 6.

5. When you submit the PROFILE online, you will receive an online acknowledgment.

6. If you need help or have questions beyond these instructions, call the College Board or CSS at 1-305-829-9793.

Note: The PROFILE form is kind of a pain to fill out. There are more questions on the PRO-FILE than on the FAFSA, and there are so many different family situations that students and their parents often have numerous questions about them. Because the application itself is pretty long, my advice is to take it in little chunks. Many of the questions are the same as those on the FAFSA, so if you have already filled it out, you will be ahead of the game.

Because the PROFILE application is online and CSS provides a substantial step-by-step process and list of commonly asked questions, I have deviated from my practice of circling numbers on an actual application. Instead, I have included a blank CSS PROFILE Worksheet (Figure 16-0), which you can use as your own worksheet. Then, when you go to complete the actual online application, you will have all the figures in front of you. Remember, this work-sheet was the latest available at the time of publication. Consequently, all the questions should be the same, but the numbers might vary from year to year.

If you have any questions that are not answered online, you can ask your counselor or call the PROFILE people directly.

Here's what you'll need:

1. Social Security number (student, parents).

2. Driver's license (student, parents).

3. W-2 forms, if employed (student, parents).

4. Federal tax return, if you have worked (student).

5. Federal tax return (parents) (unless the student is independent — the parents no longer claim the student on their taxes and the student is making his or her own money). See www.finaid.org/calculator/dependency.phtm for independent status criteria.

6. Untaxed income records — that is, Social Security benefits, veteran's benefits, or welfare benefits (parents).

7. Bank statements (student, parents)

8. Business and investment mortgage information, business and farm statements, and other investment records (student, parents).

Note: Students and parents will both need some or all of the preceding information, including financial records or estimates. You do not need to have filed a tax return for the year in which you are filling out the PROFILE, although having the numbers will make it easier. You will, however, have to submit a tax return to the schools eventually.

More information you'll need to know before you go online:

1. When filling out the PROFILE form, round all amounts to the nearest dollar. Do not enter a comma (,) or cents (.35) in the dollar field.

2. If a question does not apply to you, enter a zero (0) instead of leaving it blank.

3. Once you have registered, save the information in the online version as you go along. You don't have to fill out the whole form at one time. You can also print a paper copy at any time.

4. Fee waivers are available for certain students to cover the costs of registration and up to two schools. If you think you are eligible, ask your counselor for the form.

CSS® Code List

The schools and scholarship programs below are all PROFILE users. Instructions distributed by their financial aid offices will describe their application requirements in detail. A school with an asterisk (*) next to its name uses PROFILE for Early Decision or Early Action applicants only.

ALABAMA
1813 Tuskegee University

ALASKA
8849 Aleutian/Pribilof Islands Association
0245 Tanana Tribal Council Scholarship

CALIFORNIA
0651 Association of Woodworking and Furnishing Suppliers
4034 California Institute of Technology
8301 Charles R. Drew University of Allied Health
4054 Claremont McKenna College
4063 College of Notre Dame
4341 Harvey Mudd College
1344 Hebrew Union College
4403 Loyola Marymount University
4581 Occidental College
0763 Otis Spunkmeyer Foundation
4620 Patten College
4619 Pitzer College
4607 Pomona College
0585 Salvation Army Student Loan Program
4851 Santa Clara University
4693 Scripps College
4392 Southern California College of Optometry
Stanford University:
4704 -All Undergraduates
0265 -Graduate School of Business
University of California, Los Angeles (UCLA) Graduate & Professional Schools:
4890 -School of Dentistry
7158 -School of Medicine
4852 University of Southern California
4952 Whittier College

COLORADO
4072 Colorado College

CONNECTICUT
3284 Connecticut College
0594 Eugene Atwood Fund
3390 Fairfield University
0277 Guilford High School Scholarship Committee
0060 Guilford Scholarship Association
3145 Jewish Home for Children Scholarship
1236 Lyme Academy of Fine Arts
7929 New Canaan H.S. Scholarship Foundation
7350 New England Health Care Employees Scholarship Program
3780 Sacred Heart University
3899 Trinity College
3959 Wesleyan University
0044 Wilton High School Scholarship Committee
3987 Yale University

DISTRICT OF COLUMBIA
2707 American Council of Teachers of Russian (ACTR)
0540 American Foreign Service Association
George Washington University:
5246 -All Undergraduates
5587 -National Law Center
Georgetown University:
5244 -Undergraduates Only
7306 -Law Center
0518 International Brotherhood of Teamsters Scholarship Foundation

FLORIDA
5327 International Fine Arts College
0176 Legacy Foundation, The
5437 Lynn University

GEORGIA
*5002 Agnes Scott College
*5110 Clark Atlanta University
0729 Clark-Holder Clinic Medical Education Foundation
5187 Emory University:
0140 -Schools of Medicine (4yr MD) & Allied Health
5417 Morris Brown College
5186 Oxford College of Emory University
5628 Spelman College

HAWAII
*4105 Chaminade University of Honolulu
0274 Kamehameha Schools

ILLINOIS
1031 Archeworks
1707 Benedictine University
1070 Bradley University
1245 Garrett-Evangelical Theological Seminary
1318 Illinois Institute of Technology
1320 Illinois Wesleyan University
0294 Joseph Blazek Foundation Scholarship Program
1392 Lake Forest College
1484 Monmouth College
Northwestern University:
1565 -Incoming Freshmen & Transfer Applicants
3593 -Continuing & Returning Undergraduates
1630 Principia College
1755 St. Joseph College of Loyola University-Chicago
0097 Seabury-Western Theological Seminary
1717 Shimer College
1832 University of Chicago, The College

INDIANA
1079 Bethel College
1073 Butler University
1166 DePauw University
1251 Goshen College
1309 Holy Cross College
0264 Indiana University – School of Music (Precollege Programs Only)
1702 Saint Mary's College
0619 Scholarship Foundation of Saint Joseph County
0063 Trinity Episcopal Church Scholarship Program
1208 University of Evansville
1841 University of Notre Dame (Undergraduates Only)
1895 Wabash College
0346 Wells Fargo Bank Scholarship Program

IOWA
6869 University of Dubuque

KANSAS
6964 Washburn University, School of Law

KENTUCKY
8839 Institute of Electronic Technology
1808 Transylvania University

LOUISIANA
6832 Tulane University
6975 Xavier University of Louisiana

MAINE
3076 Bates College
3089 Bowdoin College
3269 Bridgton Academy
3280 Colby College

MARYLAND
0038 Alpha Epsilon Phi Foundation
7363 American Association of Colleges of Osteopathic Medicine Application Service
3823 College Financial Aid Counseling
5257 Goucher College
5370 Loyola College in Maryland
5421 Mount St. Mary's College
5598 St. John's College

MASSACHUSETTS
3003 Amherst College
0613 Attleboro Scholarship Foundation
3075 Babson College (New First-Year & Transfer Students Only)
0778 Bement Educational Grants Committee
Bentley College:
3096 - All Undergraduate Students
3098 - All Graduate Students
3083 Boston College
Boston University:
3087 - All Undergraduates
Graduate Programs:
7423 - Grad. Law School
8928 - Grad. School of Dentistry
3116 - Grad. School of Medicine
8930 - Grad. School of Public Health
Brandeis University:
3092 - All Undergraduates
0046 - Graduate School of Arts & Sciences
3165 - Heller Graduate School
0520 Caroline E. Hill Scholarship Fund
3279 Clark University
3282 College of the Holy Cross
0161 Concord Carlisle Scholarship Fund
9267 Duxbury High School Scholarship Program
0042 Eliot School of Fine & Applied Arts
3367 Emerson College
0467 Francis Ouimet Caddie Scholarship Fund
3417 Gordon College
3447 Hampshire College
Harvard University:
3434 - Harvard College
3442 - Divinity School
3454 - JFK Grad. School of Government
3457 - Law School
3445 - Medical School
3441 - School of Dental Medicine
0672 Marblehead Sr. H.S. Scholarship Fund
3461 MAS Associates
3514 Massachusetts Institute of Technology
0113 Massachusetts Rehabilitation Commission
3525 Merrimack College
3529 Mount Holyoke College
3666 Nichols College
3667 Northeastern University
3689 Pine Manor College
3753 Scandinavian Seminar

3761 Simmons College
3795 Simon's Rock College of Bard
3762 Smith College:
3775 - School for Social Work
3763 Springfield College
3770 Stonehill College
3905 Town of Chelmsford Scholarship Fund (Town Residents Only)
Tufts University:
3901 - All Undergraduates
8865 - School of Dental Medicine
3936 University of Massachusetts Medical School
3957 Wellesley College
3963 Wheaton College
3965 Williams College
3969 Worcester Polytechnic Institute

MICHIGAN
1001 Adrian College
0248 Ave Maria College
1295 Hillsdale College
1365 Kalamazoo College
9950 Karla Scherer Foundation Scholarship
*1452 Marygrove College
1595 Olivet College
1672 Reformed Bible College
1753 St. Mary's College
1719 Siena Heights University

MINNESOTA
*6014 Augsburg College
6081 Carleton College
6253 Gustavus Adolphus College
6390 Macalester College
6638 Saint Olaf College
0240 Simley High School Scholarship Committee

MISSOURI
6293 Aquinas Institute of Theology
6123 Culver-Stockton College
6929 Washington University

NEW HAMPSHIRE
3351 Dartmouth College:
3355 - Thayer School of Engineering
3748 St. Anselm College

NEW JERSEY
9887 Alumax Scholarship Program
0473 Brown Brothers/Harriman & Company Scholarship Program
0088 Cabot Scholarship Program
9911 Campbell Soup Scholarship Program
0616 Charles T. King Student Loan Fund
9866 Citibank Employees Scholarship Program
2090 College of St. Elizabeth
0307 Cone Mills Scholarship Program
2193 Drew University, Undergraduates
5474 Edward K. Welles Scholarship Program
0326 Ensign-Bickford Foundation Scholarship
0238 Fortis Foundation Scholarship Program
0051 Frank and Louise Groff Foundation
0546 GTE Scholarship Program
9897 Harleysville Insurance Co. Scholarship Program
0662 Household Finance Corporation Scholarship
0460 HSBC Scholarship Program

0512 IBM Thomas J. Watson Scholarship Program
9901 ITT Industries, Inc. Scholarship Program
9991 James J. Kerrigan Scholarship Program
9957 Jim Beam Brands Foundation Scholarship
9915 Kraft Foods International Scholarship Program
9864 Kraft Foods Scholarship Program
9039 Kyocera Mita Scholarship Program
9923 Lexmark Scholarship Program
0235 Marjorie & Frank Mundy Scholarship Fund
0392 Morgan Stanley Scholarship Program
0607 Mountain Lakes Home Scholarship Association
0517 NARM Scholarship Foundation
9955 Philip Morris Scholarship Program
9954 Philip Morris USA Tobacco Farmer Partnering Program
2672 Princeton University
2703 Proctor and Gamble Fund
9967 Rayonier Employee Scholarship Program
9959 Reader's Digest Foundation Scholarship Program
0398 R.J.R. Nabisco Voc./Tech. Scholarship Program
0328 Rouse Company Scholarship Program
9820 Salomon-Roberson Scholarship Program
9982 Schwab Rosenhouse Memorial Foundation
9881 Siemens Information & Communication Networks Scholarship Program
9984 Southern Wine & Spirits Scholarship Program
9904 Starr Foundation Scholarship Program
0638 Teagle Foundation Scholarship Program
0188 Teaneck Community Scholarship Fund
9964 Textron & Div. Scholarship Program
0550 The "200" Club of Morris County Scholarship Program
9963 Thomas Labrecque Smart Start Scholarship Program
0078 William Salomon Scholarship Program

NEW MEXICO
4737 St. John's College

NEW YORK
7041 Albany Law School
2995 Albert Einstein College of Medicine
2489 Allied Health Education, NYU Medical Center
2037 Bard College
2038 Barnard College-Columbia University
0029 Buttonwood Foundation
2894 Cochran School of Nursing -St. John's Riverside Hospital
2086 Colgate University
Columbia University:
2116 -Columbia College
2148 -College of Physicians and Surgeons
2133 -School for Social Work
2101 -School of Dental and Oral Surgery
2111 -School of Engineering & Applied Science
2097 Cooper Union
2098 Cornell University:
2822 -College of Veterinary Medicine
6787 Council on International Educational Exchange
0174 Daughters of Cincinnati
2011 Dowling College
2226 Elmira College
Fordham University:
3031 -Lincoln Center Campus
2259 -Rose Hill Campus
0087 Gruss Life Monument Scholarship
2286 Hamilton College
2294 Hobart College
0206 Horace Greeley Education Fund
*2325 Ithaca College
Jewish Theological Seminary of America:
2339 -Albert A. List College
2618 -Cantor's Institute
2679 -Graduate School
2470 -Rabbinical School

0272 Joseph Tauber Scholarship Program
2850 King's College, The
Long Island University:
*2369 -Brooklyn Campus
2070 -C.W. Post Campus, Brookville
2396 Manhattan School of Music
*2511 Nazareth College of Rochester
2504 New York College of Podiatric Medicine
2561 New York Institute of Technology (All Campuses)
2669 Pratt Institute
2805 St. Lawrence University
2810 Sarah Lawrence College
2815 Skidmore College
2823 Syracuse University
2920 Union College & University
0658 United States Trust Co. of N.Y. Scholarship
2928 University of Rochester:
2224 -Eastman School of Music
2956 Vassar College
*2971 Wells College
2294 William Smith College
2990 Yeshiva University

NORTH CAROLINA
5692 Albert H. Bangert Memorial Student Loan/Scholarship Fund
0062 Brooks, Aubrey Lee Scholarship
5150 Davidson College
5156 Duke University:
5152 -School of Medicine
0289 Eastern College of Music
5183 Elon University
0093 Jagannathan Scholarship
*5003 North Carolina A&T State University
5496 North Carolina State University (New Freshmen & Transfers Only)
0290 UNC Board of Governors Dental/Medical Scholarships
5816 University of North Carolina at Chapel Hill
Wake Forest University:
5885 -Undergraduates Only
5084 -School of Medicine
7596 -School of Law

OHIO
1029 Athenaeum of Ohio
0009 C. Mitchell Morgan Scholarship Fund
Case Western Reserve University:
*1105 - All Undergraduates
1104 - School of Medicine
1124 Cleveland Institute of Music
*1134 College of Wooster
1305 Hebrew Union College
0285 Jacob H. Otto Scholarship Trust
1370 Kenyon College
1587 Oberlin College
Ohio Northern University:
*1591 -Incoming Freshmen & Transfer Applicants
1606 -All Other Applicants
1594 Ohio Wesleyan University
1597 Otterbein College

OREGON
*4387 Linfield College
4654 Reed College
*4847 University of Portland
4595 Warner Pacific College
*4954 Willamette University

PENNSYLVANIA
7011 Abraham L. Buckwalter Assistance Fund
2049 Bryn Mawr College
2050 Bucknell University
2100 Curtis Institute of Music
2186 Dickinson College
2704 Eastern Baptist Theological Seminary
2261 Franklin and Marshall College
0019 Friends of Philadelphia Scholarship Program
2275 Gettysburg College
2289 Haverford College
7188 Hughesian Free School Trust

0430 Kosak and Associates
2361 Lafayette College
2365 Lehigh University
0740 Lower Merion Township Scholarship Fund
2418 Moravian College
2424 Muhlenberg College
0798 Radnor High School Scholarship Fund
2763 Rosemont College
2812 Seton Hill College
0059 Student Aid Fund, The
2820 Susquehanna University
2821 Swarthmore College
University of Pennsylvania:
2926 -Incoming Freshmen and Transfer Applicants
2933 -Returning Undergraduates
*2929 University of Scranton
2931 Ursinus College

RHODE ISLAND
9483 Arabic Educational Foundation
3189 Brown University (New Freshmen & Transfers Only)
3095 Bryant College
3693 Providence College
3726 Rhode Island School of Design
3729 Roger Williams University (First-Time Entering Undergraduates Only)
3759 Salve Regina University (New Freshmen & Transfers Only)

SOUTH CAROLINA
5117 Columbia College
*5222 Furman University (Early Decision Only)
5540 Presbyterian College
2598 Rose Hill College
0061 Sirrine Foundation Scholarship Program
5912 Wofford College

TENNESSEE
1192 East Tennessee State University, Medical School
7549 Meharry Medical College
1730 Rhodes College
1809 Trevecca Nazarene College
Vanderbilt University:
1871 -All Undergraduates
0769 -Divinity School
1684 -School of Law

TEXAS
0401 Minnie Stevens Piper Foundation
6609 Rice University
6660 Southern Methodist University

VERMONT
*3080 Bennington College
3418 Green Mountain College
9934 Landmark College
3509 Marlboro College
3526 Middlebury College
3669 Norwich University
3757 St. Michael's College

VIRGINIA
0547 Army Emergency Relief National Headquarters
5654 Former Agents of the FBI Foundation
5291 Hampden-Sydney College
9814 Henrico County - St. Mary's Hospital School of Practical Nursing
2804 Patrick Henry College
5625 Southern Virginia College
5887 Washington and Lee University (Undergraduates Only)

WASHINGTON
0254 George T. Welch Fund, The
*4067 University of Puget Sound
4951 Whitman College

WEST VIRGINIA
5151 Davis and Elkins College
5272 George E. Stifel Scholarship Fund
5905 West Virginia Wesleyan College

WISCONSIN
1012 Alverno College
1059 Beloit College
1100 Cardinal Stritch College
0275 Great Lakes Teacher Training
7590 Milwaukee Institute of Art & Design
1490 Mount Mary College
University of Wisconsin:
1921 - Whitewater

CANADA
0935 McGill University
0949 Queen's University at Kingston
0982 University of Toronto

FRANCE
0866 American University of Paris

GERMANY
3665 International University Bremen

HONG KONG
3984 International Asian Studies Program at the Chinese University of Hong Kong

SWITZERLAND
0922 Franklin College

2005-06 PROFILE Pre-Application Worksheet

Use this worksheet to help collect your family's financial information before you begin your online PROFILE Application. You can print instructions from the Help Desk by clicking on "Application Instructions." As you complete your online application, you will find more detailed online help.

This worksheet contains the questions found in the PROFILE Registration and application (Sections A through P). In general, these are standard questions that all families must complete.

- When you complete your online application, you may find questions in Section Q that are not found on this pre-application worksheet. Once you register, you should print the Supplemental Information Worksheet to obtain these questions. These are additional questions required by one or more of the colleges or scholarship programs to which you are applying. If your application does not contain a Section Q, it means that none of the colleges and programs to which you are applying require questions beyond those collected in Sections A through P.

- Based on the student's dependency status, you may not be required to complete all of the questions in Sections A through O. When you complete your PROFILE Application, questions that are not required will not be presented to you. For example, if the student is younger than age 24, you will not be asked to complete Questions 1 and 2, or Questions 24 and 25.

Do not mail this form to the College Board. It is a Pre-Application Worksheet and cannot be processed. Any worksheets received for processing will be destroyed.

1

Pre-Application Worksheet

Registration

Student's Social Security Number: ⬜ ⬜ ⬜

Student's name: ⬜ ⬜ ⬜
Last name   *First name*   *M.I.*

Student's title   O Mr.   O Miss, Ms, or Mrs.

Student's email address: ⬜

Student's date of birth: ⬜ ⬜ ⬜
Month   *Day*   *Year*

Student's postal address location

O Domestic (U.S., Puerto Rico, U.S. Territories)   O Canada   O Other international

Student's permanent mailing address:
(domestic addresses)

Number, street, and apartment number

⬜ ⬜ ⬜
City   *State*   *Zip code*

Student's home telephone number: ⬜ ⬜ ⬜
Area code

What will be the student's year in school during 2005-2006?

O 1st year (never previously attended college)   O 5th year or more undergraduate
O 1st year (previously attended college)   O First-year graduate/professional (beyond a bachelor's degree)
O 2nd year   O Second-year graduate/professional
O 3rd year   O Third-year graduate/professional
O 4th year   O Fourth-year graduate/professional

What will be the student's financial aid status during 2005-2006?

O First-time applicant, entering student (or transfer student)   O First-time applicant, continuing student
O Renewal applicant, continuing student

What is the student's current marital status?

O unmarried (single, divorced, widowed)   O married/remarried   O separated

What is the student's citizenship status?

O U.S. citizen
O Eligible non-citizen
O Neither of the above

If you answered "Neither" in the question above, what the student's country of citizenship? ⬜

If you answered "Neither" in the question above, what is the student's Visa classification?
O F1   O F2   O J1   O J2   O G1   O G2   O G3   O G4   O Other

Is the student a veteran of the U.S. Armed Forces?   O Yes   O No

Are both of the student's parents deceased, or is the student or was the student (until age 18) a ward/dependent of the court?
O Yes   O No

Does the student have legal dependents (other than a spouse)?   O Yes   O No

Are the student's biological or adoptive parents separated or divorced, or were they never married? (Answer "no" if the student's biological or adoptive parents are living together, regardless of their current marital status.)   O Yes   O No

If you answered "yes" above, with which of the student's biological or adoptive parents did the student live with more during the past 12 months?   O Father   O Mother   O Neither parent

If you answered "neither parent" above, which parent provided more support during the past 12 months?   O mother   O father

Do the student's parents own all or part of a business, corporation, partnership, or farm, or is either parent self-employed?
O Yes   O No

Where will the student live while enrolled in college?
O On campus   O Off campus   O With parents   O With relatives

2

Section A - Student's Information
(Dependent students skip Questions 1 and 2.)

1. How many people are in the student's (and spouse's) household? <u>Always include the student (and spouse)</u>. List their names and give information about them in Section M. [ ]

2. Of the number in 1, how many will be college students enrolled at least half-time between July 1, 2005 and June 30, 2006? Include the student. [ ]

3. What is the student's state of legal residence? [ ]

4. Where is the computer that the family is using to complete the PROFILE Application?

- O Home
- O Father's work
- O Mother's work
- O High School
- O College

- O Library
- O Community Center
- O Friend or relative's home
- O Other

Section B - Student's 2004 Income & Benefits

Questions 5-14 ask for information about the student's (and spouse's) income and benefits. If married, include spouse's information in Sections B, C, D, E, and F.

5. The following 2004 U.S. income tax return figures are: (Fill in only one oval.)

- O estimated. Will file IRS Form 1040EZ, 1040A, or Telefile. Go to 6.
- O estimated. Will file IRS Form 1040. Go to 6.
- O from a completed IRS Form 1040EZ, 1040A, or Telefile. Go to 6.
- O from a completed IRS Form 1040. Go to 6.
- O a tax return will not be filed. Skip to 10.

6. 2004 total number of exemptions (2004 IRS Form 1040, line 6d or 1040A, line 6d or 1040EZ or Telefile) [ ]

7. 2004 adjusted gross income (2004 IRS Form 1040, line 36 or 1040A, line 21 or 1040EZ, line 4 or Telefile, line I) $ [ ]

8. a 2004 U.S. income tax paid (2004 IRS Form 1040, line 56 or 1040A, line 36 or 1040EZ, line 10 or Telefile, line K) $ [ ]

b 2004 Education Credits - Hope and Lifetime Learning (2004 IRS Form 1040, line 48 or 1040A, line 31) $ [ ]

9. 2004 itemized deductions (IRS Schedule A, line 28. Fill in "0" if deductions were not itemized.) $ [ ]

10. 2004 income earned from work by student $ [ ]

11. 2004 income earned from work by student's spouse $ [ ]

12. 2004 dividend and interest income (2004 IRS Form 1040, lines 8a and 9a or 1040A, lines 8a and 9a or 1040EZ, line 2 or Telefile, line C) $ [ ]

13. 2004 untaxed income and benefits (Give total amount for year.)

a Social security benefits (untaxed portion only - see help) $ [ ]

b Welfare benefits, including TANF $ [ ]

c Child support received for all children $ [ ]

d Earned Income Credit (2004 IRS Form 1040, line 65 or 1040A, line 41 or 1040EZ, line 8 or Telefile, line L) $ [ ]

e Other - write in the total from the worksheet at the end of this document. $ [ ]

14. 2004 earnings from Federal Work-Study or other need-based work programs plus any grant, fellowship, scholarship, and assistantship aid reported to the IRS in your adjusted gross income. Include AmeriCorps benefits. $ [ ]

3

Section C - Student's Assets

Questions 15-22 ask for information about the student's (and spouse's) assets. Include trust accounts in Section D.

15. Cash, savings, and checking accounts (as of today) $

16. Total value of IRA, Keogh, 401k, 403b, etc. accounts as of December 31, 2004 $

17. Investments (Including Uniform Gifts to Minors)

   a What are these worth today? $

   b What is owed them? $

18. Home

   a What is it worth today? (Renters write in "0") $

   b What is owed on it? $

   c Year purchased

   d Purchase price $

19. Other real estate

   a What is it worth today? $

   b What is owed on it? $

20. Business and farm

   a What is it worth today? $

   b What is owed on it? $

21. If a farm is included in 20, is the student living on the farm? O Yes O No

Section D - Student's Trust Information

22. a Total value of all trust(s) $

   b Is any income or part of the principal currently available? O Yes O No

   c Who established the trust(s)? O Student's parents O Other

Section E - Student's 2004 Expenses
(Dependent students skip Questions 23 and 24.)

23. 2004 child support paid because of divorce or separation $

24. 2004 medical and dental expenses not covered by insurance $

Section F - Student's Expected Summer/School-Year Resources for 2005-2006

25. Student's veterans benefits (July 1, 2005 - June 30, 2006)

   Amount per month $

   Number of months

(Section continues on next page.)

4

THE ULTIMATE COLLEGE ACCEPTANCE SYSTEM

<u>**Section F - Student's Expected Summer/School-Year Resources for 2005-2006 - continued**</u>

26. Student's (and spouse's) resources (Don't enter monthly amounts.)

Student's wages, salaries, tips, etc.

a Summer 2005 (3 months) $ _____

b School year 2005-2006 (9 months) $ _____

Spouse's wages, salaries, tips, etc.

c Summer 2005 (3 months) $ _____

d School year 2005-2006 (9 months) $ _____

Other taxable income

e Summer 2005 (3 months) $ _____

f School year 2005-2006 (9 months) $ _____

Untaxed income and benefits

g Summer 2005 (3 months) $ _____

h School year 2005-2006 (9 months) $ _____

i Grants, scholarships, fellowships, etc. from sources other than the colleges or universities
to which the student is applying (List sources in Section P.) $ _____

j Tuition benefits from the parents' and/or the student's or spouse's employer $ _____

k Amount the student's parent(s) think they will be able to pay for 2005-2006 college expenses $ _____

l Amounts expected from prepaid tuition plan withdrawals, other relatives, spouse's parents, and all $ _____
other sources (List sources and amounts in Section P.)

<u>**Section G - Parents' Household Information**</u>

27. How many people are in your parents' household? <u>Always include the student and parents.</u> List their names and give
information about them in Section M. _____

28. Of the number in 27, how many will be college students enrolled at least half-time between July 1, 2005 and June 30, 2006?
Do not include parents. Include the student. _____

29. How many parents will be in college at least half-time in 2005-2006? O Neither Parent O One Parent O Both Parents

30. What is the current marital status of your parents? O Never married O Separated O Widowed
(Fill in only one oval.) O Married/Remarried O Divorced

31. What is your parents' state of legal residence? _____

32. What is your parents' preferred email address? _____

5

FINANCIAL AID   235

Section H - Parents' Expenses

33. Child support paid because of divorce or separation

   a 2004 $ _____
   b Expected 2005 $ _____

34. Repayment of parents' educational loans

   a 2004 $ _____
   b Expected 2005 $ _____

35. Medical and dental expenses not covered by insurance

   a 2004 $ _____
   b Expected 2005 $ _____

36. Total elementary, junior high, and high school tuition paid for dependent children

   Amount paid (Don't include tuition paid for the student.)

   a 2004 $ _____
   b Expected 2005 $ _____

   For how many dependent children? (Don't include the student.)

   c 2004   _____
   d Expected 2005   _____

Section I - Parents' Assets

If parents own all or part of a business or farm, enter its name and the percent of ownership in Section P.

37. Cash, savings, and checking accounts (as of today) $ _____

38. a Total value of parents' assets held in the names of the student's brothers and sisters who are under age 19 and not college students $ _____

   b Total value of assets held in Section 529 **prepaid tuition** plans for the student's brothers and sisters (Do not include assets in Section 529 **savings** plans.) $ _____

   c Total value of assets held in Section 529 **prepaid tuition** plans for the student (Do not include assets in Section 529 **savings** plans.) $ _____

39. Investments

   a What are they worth today? $ _____
   b What is owed on them? $ _____

40. Home

   a What is it worth today? (Renters fill in "0" and skip to 40e.) $ _____
   b What is owed on it? $ _____
   c Year purchased   _____
   d Purchase price $ _____
   e Monthly home mortgage or rental payment (If none, explain in Section P.) $ _____

41. Business

   a What is it worth today? $ _____
   b What is owed on it? $ _____

42. Farm

   a What is it worth today? $ _____
   b What is owed on it? $ _____
   c Does family live on the farm?   O Yes   O No

43. Other real estate

   a What is it worth today? $ _____
   b What is owed on it? $ _____
   c Year purchased   _____
   d Purchase price $ _____

6

Section J - Parents' 2003 Income & Benefits

44. 2003 adjusted gross income (2003 IRS Form 1040, line 34 or 1040A, line 21 or 1040EZ, line 4 or Telefile, line I) $ [ ]

45. 2003 U.S. income tax paid (2003 IRS Form 1040, line 54 or, 1040A, line 36 or 1040EZ, line 10 or Telefile, line K) $ [ ]

46. 2003 itemized deductions (2003 IRS Form 1040, Schedule A, line 28. Enter "0" if deductions were not itemized.) $ [ ]

47. 2003 untaxed income and benefits (Write in the total from the worksheet at the end of this document.) $ [ ]

Section K - Parents' 2004 Income & Benefits

48. The following 2004 U.S. income tax return figures are: (Fill in only one oval.)

     O estimated. Will file IRS Form 1040EZ, 1040A, or Telefile. Go to 49.

     O estimated. Will file IRS Form 1040. Go to 49.

     O from a completed IRS Form 1040EZ, 1040A, or Telefile. Go to 49.

     O from a completed IRS Form 1040. Go to 49.

     O a tax return will not be filed. Skip to 53.

49. 2004 total number of exemptions (IRS Form 1040, line 6d or 1040A, line 6d or 1040EZ or Telefile) [ ]

50.a Wages, salaries, tips (2004 IRS Form 1040, line 7 or 1040A, line 7 or 1040EZ, line 1) $ [ ]

   b Interest income (2004 IRS Form 1040, line 8a or 1040A, line 8a or 1040EZ, line 2 or Telefile, line C) $ [ ]

   c Dividend income (2004 IRS Form 1040, line 9a or 1040A, line 9a) $ [ ]

   d Net income (or loss) from business, farm, rents, royalties, partnerships, estates, trusts, etc. (2004 IRS Form 1040, lines 12, 17, and 18) To enter a loss, use a minus (-) sign. $ [ ]

   e Other taxable income such as alimony received, capital gains (or losses), pensions, annuities, etc. (2004 IRS Form 1040, lines 10, 11, 13, 14, 15b, 16b, 19, 20b and 21 or 1040A, lines 10, 11b, 12b, 13, and 14b or 1040EZ, line 3 or Telefile, line D) $ [ ]

   f Adjustments to income (2004 IRS Form 1040, line 35 or 1040A, line 20) $ [ ]

   g 2004 adjusted gross income (2004 IRS Form 1040, line 36 or 1040A, line 21 or 1040EZ, line 4 or Telefile line I). This entry is the sum of 50a to 50e, minus 50f. $ [ ]

51.a 2004 U.S. income tax paid (2004 IRS Form 1040, line 56 or 1040A, line 36 or 1040EZ, line 10 or Telefile, line K) $ [ ]

   b 2004 Education Credits - Hope and Lifetime Learning (2004 IRS Form 1040, line 48 or 1040A, line 31) $ [ ]

52. 2004 itemized deductions (2004 IRS Schedule A, line 28. Fill in "0" if deductions were not itemized.) $ [ ]

53. 2004 income earned from work by father/stepfather $ [ ]

54. 2004 income earned from work by mother/stepmother $ [ ]

(Section continues on next page.)

7

Section K - Parents' 2004 Income & Benefits (continued)

55. 2004 untaxed income and benefits (Give total amount for the year. Do not give monthly amounts.)

  a Social security benefits received for all family members except the student (untaxed portion only see help) $ ___

  b Social security benefits received for the student (See help.) $ ___

  c Welfare benefits, including TANF $ ___

  d Child support received for all children $ ___

  e Deductible IRA and/or SEP, SIMPLE, or Keogh payments (2004 IRS Form 1040, lines 25 and 32 or form 1040A, line 17) $ ___

  f Payments to tax-deferred pension and savings plans $ ___

  g Tuition and fees deduction (2004 IRS Form 1040, line 27 or 1040A, line 19) $ ___

  h Amounts withheld from wages for dependent care and medical spending accounts $ ___

  i Earned Income Credit (2004 IRS Form 1040, line 65 or 1040A, line 41 or 1040EZ, line 8 or Telefile, line L) $ ___

  j Housing, food, and other living allowances received by military, clergy, and others $ ___

  k Tax-exempt interest income (2004 IRS Form 1040, line 8b or 1040A, line 8b) $ ___

  l Foreign income exclusion (2004 IRS Form 2555, line 43 or Form 2555EZ, line 18) $ ___

  m Other - write in the total from the worksheet in the instructions at the end of this document. $ ___

Section L - Parents' 2005 Expected Income & Benefits

If the expected total income and benefits will differ from the 2004 total income by $3,000 or more, explain in Section P.

56. 2005 income earned from work by father/stepfather $ ___

57. 2005 income earned from work by mother/stepmother $ ___

58. 2005 other taxable income $ ___

59. 2005 untaxed income and benefits (See 55a-m.) $ ___

Section M - Family Member Listing

*Give information for all family members entered in question 1 or 28. Only six family members are shown here but you will be able to enter up to seven family members in addition to the student on our website. If there are more than seven, list first those who will be in school or college at least half-time. List the others in Section P. **Failure to complete all information could reduce your aid eligibility**.*

Question 60.

Student - Family Member 1

Full name of family member ___   Claimed by parents as tax exemption in 2004?   O Yes   O No

2004-2005 school year

Name of school or college ___   Year in school ___

Scholarships and grants $ ___   Parents' contribution $ ___

(Section continues on next page.)

8

Section M - Family Member Listing (continued)

Family Member 2

Full name of family member [   ] Claimed by parents
as tax exemption in 2004? O Yes   O No

Relationship to student: O Student's parent O Student's stepparent O Student's brother or sister
Age: [   ] O Student's husband or wife O Student's son or daughter O Student's grandparent
O Student's stepbrother/stepsister O Other (explain in Section P)

<u>2004-2005 school year</u>
Name of school or college [   ] Year in school [   ]
Scholarships and grants $ [   ] Parents' contribution $ [   ]
<u>2005-2006 school year</u>
Attend college at least one term O Full-time O Half-time O Will not attend
College or university name [   ]
Type: O 2-year public college O 2-year private college O 4-year public college/university
O 4-year private college/university O graduate/professional school O proprietary school

Family Member 3

Full name of family member [   ] Claimed by parents
as tax exemption in 2004? O Yes   O No

Relationship to student: O Student's parent O Student's stepparent O Student's brother or sister
Age: [   ] O Student's husband or wife O Student's son or daughter O Student's grandparent
O Student's stepbrother/stepsister O Other (explain in Section P)

<u>2004-2005 school year</u>
Name of school or college [   ] Year in school [   ]
Scholarships and grants $ [   ] Parents' contribution $ [   ]
<u>2005-2006 school year</u>
Attend college at least one term O Full-time O Half-time O Will not attend
College or university name [   ]
Type: O 2-year public college O 2-year private college O 4-year public college/university
O 4-year private college/university O graduate/professional school O proprietary school

Family Member 4

Full name of family member [   ] Claimed by parents
as tax exemption in 2004? O Yes   O No

Relationship to student: O Student's parent O Student's stepparent O Student's brother or sister
Age: [   ] O Student's husband or wife O Student's son or daughter O Student's grandparent
O Student's stepbrother/stepsister O Other (explain in Section P)

<u>2004-2005 school year</u>
Name of school or college [   ] Year in school [   ]
Scholarships and grants $ [   ] Parents' contribution $ [   ]
<u>2005-2006 school year</u>
Attend college at least one term O Full-time O Half-time O Will not attend
College or university name [   ]
Type: O 2-year public college O 2-year private college O 4-year public college/university
O 4-year private college/university O graduate/professional school O proprietary school

(Section continues on next page.)

9

Section M - Family Member Listing (continued)

Family Member 5

Full name of family member [_____] Claimed by parents
as tax exemption in 2004? O Yes O No

Relationship to student: O Student's parent   O Student's stepparent   O Student's brother or sister

Age: [____]   O Student's husband or wife   O Student's son or daughter   O Student's grandparent

O Student's stepbrother/stepsister   O Other (explain in Section P)

2004-2005 school year

Name of school or college [_____]   Year in school [_____]

Scholarships and grants $[_____]   Parents' contribution $[_____]

2005-2006 school year

Attend college at least one term   O Full-time   O Half-time   O Will not attend

College or university name [_____]

Type: O 2-year public college   O 2-year private college   O 4-year public college/university

O 4-year private college/university   O graduate/professional school   O proprietary school

Family Member 6

Full name of family member [_____] Claimed by parents
as tax exemption in 2004? O Yes O No

Relationship to student: O Student's parent   O Student's stepparent   O Student's brother or sister

Age: [____]   O Student's husband or wife   O Student's son or daughter   O Student's grandparent

O Student's stepbrother/stepsister   O Other (explain in Section P)

2004-2005 school year

Name of school or college [_____]   Year in school [_____]

Scholarships and grants $[_____]   Parents' contribution $[_____]

2005-2006 school year

Attend college at least one term   O Full-time   O Half-time   O Will not attend

College or university name [_____]

Type: O 2-year public college   O 2-year private college   O 4-year public college/university

O 4-year private college/university   O graduate/professional school   O proprietary school

Section N - Parents' Information

(to be answered by the parent(s) completing this form)

61. a Select one: O Father   O Mother   O Stepfather   O Stepmother   O Father deceased (skip 62b - j)

O Mother deceased (skip 62b - j)   O Legal guardian   O Other (Explain in Section P.)

   b Name [_____]

   c Date of birth (MMDDYYYY) [_____]

   d Select if: O Self-employed   O Unemployed

   e If unemployed, enter date unemployment began [_____]

   f Occupation [_____]

   g Employer [_____]

   h Number of years employed by employer listed above [_____]

   i Preferred daytime telephone [_____]

   j Retirement plans (Check all that apply.)

     O Social security   O Civil service/state   O Military

     O Union/employer   O IRA/Keogh/tax-deferred   O Other

(Section continues on next page.)

10

Section N - Parents' Information (continued)

62. a Select one: O Father   O Mother   O Stepfather   O Stepmother   O Father deceased (skip 62b - j)

O Mother deceased (skip 62b - j)   O Legal guardian   O Other (Explain in Section P.)

b Name [_____]

c Date of birth (MMDDYYYY) [_____]

d Select if: O Self-employed   O Unemployed

e If unemployed, enter date unemployment began [_____]

f Occupation [_____]

g Employer [_____]

h Number of years employed by employer listed above [_____]

i Preferred daytime telephone [_____]

j Retirement plans (Check all that apply.)

O Social security   O Civil service/state   O Military

O Union/employer   O IRA/Keogh/tax-deferred   O Other

Parent Loan Information

The questions that follow are intended to provide the student's family with options for financing the parents' share of the student's college costs. Many families choose to borrow through the Federal Parent Loan for Undergraduate Students (PLUS) Program to supplement the financial aid offer. This program, as well as most private loan programs, requires a check of parent credit worthiness to qualify.

Families that answer the questions on this page will:

- get information about their eligibility to borrow through the PLUS program.
- learn what their monthly payment responsibilities would be, should they decide to borrow (a valid email address is required to receive financing guidance).
- learn about loan programs sponsored by the College Board.

By answering Questions **B-G** below, you are authorizing the College Board (or its agent), to use the information you provide below and the student's full name and Social Security Number to evaluate the parents' credit record and report the results of the credit evaluation to the parent whose information is provided below. A positive credit rating will mean that the parent is pre-approved to borrow a PLUS Loan from most lenders, including the College Board's PLUS Loan program, should additional financial assistance be necessary. (Most other lenders use the same criteria in approving families' applications for PLUS Loans.) The College Board will not share this information with the student, the student's colleges, or anyone else. Reporting of credit worthiness results will begin in February 2004 to ensure that your credit results remain valid when you are ready to apply for a PLUS loan. (The results are valid for only 180 days.)

You may skip the questions below if you are not interested in learning about your eligibility for the Federal PLUS program.

A. Does the parent want to be considered for an educational loan to cover college costs?   O Yes   O No

If you answered "Yes," complete Questions **B-G**.

B. Parent's name: [_____] [_____] [____]

         Last name   *First name*   *M.I.*

C. Parent's home address: [_____]

         Number, street, and apartment number

[_____] [____] [_____]

         City   *State*   *Zip code*

D. Telephone number: [____] [____] [_____]

         Area code

E. Parent's social security number: [____] [____] [_____]

F. Parent's date of birth: [_____] [____] [_____]

         Month   *Day*   *Year*

G. Parent's email address: [_____]

11

Section O - Information About Noncustodial Parent

(to be answered by the parent who completes this form if the student's biological or adoptive parents are divorced, separated, or were never married to each other)

63. **a** Noncustodial parent's name:

    b Home address-street

    c Home address-city, state, zip

    d Occupation/Employer

    e Year of separation

    f Year of divorce

    g According to court order, when will support for the student end? (MM/YYYY)

    h Who last claimed the student as a tax exemption?

    i Year last claimed

    j How much does the noncustodial parent plan to contribute to the student's education for the 2004-2005 school year? (Do not include this amount in 27g.)

    k Is there an agreement specifying this contribution for the student's education?   O Yes   O No

Section P - Explanations/Special Circumstances

Use this space to explain any unusual expenses such as high medical or dental expenses, educational and other debts, child care, elder care, or special circumstances. Also give information for any outside scholarships you have been awarded. If more space is needed, use sheets of paper and send them directly to your schools and programs. When online, please limit your responses to no more than 27 lines of information.

WORKSHEET

12

PROFILE Online 2004-2005 Worksheets

Question 13e

Complete the worksheet below and calculate the total at the end of the questions. Enter the total in question 13e. **Don't include:** any income reported elsewhere on the PROFILE Application, money from student financial aid, food stamps, "rollover" pensions and "rollover" IRA distributions, Workforce Investments Act educational benefits, or gifts and support, other than money, received from friends or relatives.

Deductible IRA and/or SEP, SIMPLE, or Keogh payments from IRS Form 1040, total of lines 25 and 32 or 1040A, line 17	$
Tax exempt interest income from IRS Form 1040, line 8b or 1040A, line 8b	+
Payments to tax-deferred pension and savings plans (paid directly or withheld from earnings), including but not limited to, amounts reported on the W-2 Form in Boxes 12a-12d, codes D, E, F, G, H, and S. Include untaxed payments to 401(k) and 403(b) plans.	+
Additional child tax credit from IRS Form 1040, line 67 or 1040A, line 42	+
Workers' Compensation	+
Veterans noneducational benefits such as Death Pension, Disability, etc.	+
Housing, food, and other living allowances paid to members of the military, clergy, and others (including cash payments and cash value of benefits)	+
Cash received or any money paid on the student's behalf, not reported elsewhere on this form	+
VA educational work-study allowances	+
Any other untaxed income and benefits	+
TOTAL =	$

Question 17

Complete the worksheet below and calculate the total at the end of the questions. Enter the total in question 17.

Uniform Gifts to Minors (or similar accounts)	$
Stocks, stock options (if less than $0, enter $0), bonds, savings bonds, & mutual funds	+
Money market funds	+
Certificates of deposit	+
Non-qualified (non-retirement) annuities	+
Commodities	+
Precious and strategic metals	+
Installment & land sale contracts (including seller-financed mortgages)	+
All other investments	+
TOTAL =	$

13

Question 39

Complete the worksheet below and calculate the total at the end of the questions. Enter the total in question 39.

Trust funds	$
Stocks, stock options (if less than $0, report $0), bonds, savings bonds, & mutual funds	+
Money market funds	+
Certificates of deposit	+
Coverdell savings accounts	+
Section 529 college savings plans	+
Non-qualified (non-retirement) annuities	+
Commodities	+
Precious & strategic metals	+
Installment & land sale contracts (including seller-financed mortgages)	+
All other investments	+
TOTAL =	$

Question 55m

Complete the worksheet below and calculate the total at the end of the questions. Enter the total in question 55m. **Don't include: any income reported elsewhere on the PROFILE Application, money from student financial aid, Workforce Investments Act educational benefits, gifts and support, other than money, received from friends or relatives, or veterans educational benefits.**

Untaxed portions of IRA distributions (excluding "rollovers") from IRS Form 1040, lines 15a minus 15b or 1040A, lines 15a minus 15b or 1040A lines 11a minus 11b	$
Untaxed portions of pensions (excluding "rollovers") from IRS form 1040 lines 16a minus 16b or 1040A lines 12a minus 12b	+
Additional child tax credit from IRS Form 1040, line 67 or 1040A, line 42	+
Veterans noneducational benefits such as Disability, Death Pension, Dependency & Indemnity Compensation	+
Workers' Compensation	+
Cash received or any money paid on your behalf (Don't include child support.)	+
Black Lung Benefits, Refugee Assistance	+
Credit for federal tax on special fuels	+
Untaxed portions of Railroad Retirement benefits	+
Any other untaxed income and benefits	+
TOTAL =	$

14

Question 47

*Complete the worksheet below and calculate the total at the end of the questions. Enter the total in question 47. Give total amount for the year. Do not give monthly amounts. **Don't include** any income reported elsewhere on the PROFILE Application; money from student financial aid; Workforce Investment Act educational benefits; gifts and support, other than money, received from friends and relatives; or veterans educational benefits.*

Social security benefits received for all family members except the student (untaxed portion only)	$
Social security benefits received for the student	+
Welfare benefits, including TANF	+
Child support received for all children	+
Deductible IRA and/or SEP, SIMPLE, or Keogh payments from 2003 IRS Form 1040, lines 24 and 30 or Form 1040A, line 17	+
Payments to tax-deferred pension and savings plans	+
Tuition and fees deduction from 2003 IRS Form 1040, line 26 or 1040A, line 19	+
Amounts withheld from wages for dependent care and medical spending accounts	+
Earned Income Credit from 2003 IRS Form 1040, line 63 or 1040A, line 41 or 1040EZ, line 8 or Telefile, line L	+
Housing, food, and other living allowances received by military, clergy, and others	+
Tax-exempt interest income from 2003 IRS Form 1040, line 8b or 1040A, line 8b	+
Foreign income exclusion from 2003 IRS Form 2555, line 43 or Form 2555EZ, line 18	+
Untaxed portions of IRA distributions, excluding "rollovers," from 2003 IRS Form 1040, lines 15a minus 15b or 1040A lines 11a minus 11b	+
Untaxed portions of pensions, excluding "rollovers," from 2003 IRS Form 1040, lines 16a minus 16b or 1040A lines 12a minus 12b	+
Additional child tax credit from 2003 IRS Form 1040, line 65 or 1040A, line 42	+
Veterans non-educational benefits such as Disability, Death Pension, or Dependency & Indemnity Compensation	+
Workers' Compensation	+
Cash received or any money paid on your behalf (Don't include child support.)	+
Black Lung Benefits, Refugee Assistance	+
Credit for federal tax on special fuels	+
Untaxed portions of Railroad Retirement benefits	+
All other untaxed income and benefits	+
TOTAL =	$

15

Return this form directly to the college(s) that requested it.

Business/Farm Supplement
School Year 2005-06

INSTRUCTIONS FOR COMPLETING THE BUSINESS/FARM SUPPLEMENT

- If you have more than one business or farm, or a business and a farm, complete a supplement for each of them. **Return this form directly to the college, not to the College Board.**
- When completing this supplement, refer to both your 2003 and 2004 IRS tax returns—specifically, Form 1040, Schedules C, D, and F, as applicable. If an incorporated business is involved, refer to Form 1120 as well. If a partnership is involved, also refer to Form 1065 and/or Schedule K1. **For any year for which tax forms have not been completed, estimate as accurately as possible.** The financial aid administrator may later ask you to provide copies of your tax returns, including your corporate and partnership tax return(s).
- If you are the owner or part owner of a partnership or a corporation: (1) enter your percentage of ownership (question 6); (2) enter total income, expense deductions, and profit for the entire business entity (questions 11–15); and (3) enter your share of net profit (question 16).
- **IMPORTANT:** If a business is a major source of family support but no salaries are reported and business net profit is under $10,000, explain on an attached sheet how basic family expenses are met.

- Don't submit balance sheets, profit and loss statements, cash flow statements, or tax returns in place of the Business/Farm Supplement, unless specifically requested by your college.
- If your home is part of the business or farm, enter its value and the amount of its mortgage on the CSS/Financial Aid PROFILE® Application. Don't include your home value on the Business/Farm Supplement.
- If farm income is reported on an accrual basis, the required information can be found on IRS Form 1040, Schedule F, Part III. In this case disregard questions 11a through 11c below and begin your entries with Gross Income in question 12.
- If you have gains or losses from the sale or exchange of livestock and/or farm machinery, report the full amount of such gains or losses in question 16 below. Don't include in this question gains or losses arising from the sale or exchange of other property, as reported on your IRS Form 1040, Schedule D.
- If a financial question does not apply to you, write 0. Do not leave questions blank unless the instructions tell you to do so.

STUDENT'S INFORMATION

STUDENT'S NAME					DATE OF BIRTH		
	LAST NAME	FIRST NAME	MID. INIT.	SOCIAL SECURITY NO.	MONTH	DAY	YEAR

PARENTS' BUSINESS/FARM INFORMATION

1. NAME OF BUSINESS/FARM

2. DATE BUSINESS COMMENCED OR FARM PURCHASED   MONTH   DAY   YEAR

3. LOCATION OF BUSINESS/FARM
STREET ADDRESS   CITY/TOWNSHIP   COUNTY   STATE   ZIP CODE

4. TYPE OF BUSINESS/FARM ☐ Sole proprietor ☐ Corporation ☐ Partnership   Indicate type _____

5. GIVE NAME(S) OF OWNERS AND PARTNERS, THEIR RELATIONSHIP TO THE PARENT(S), AND THEIR PERCENTAGE OF OWNERSHIP.

6. YOUR PERCENTAGE OF OWNERSHIP _____ %

7. NUMBER OF EMPLOYEES _____

8. DESCRIBE PRINCIPAL PRODUCT OR SERVICE.

9. RESIDENCE AND MORTGAGE INFORMATION

Monthly mortgage payment on the business or farm $_____

Farm owners: Do you live on the farm?   ☐ Yes ☐ No

Business owners:

Is the business a part of your home?   ☐ Yes ☐ No

If yes, what percentage of home is claimed for business use? _____ %

10. TOTAL ACRES OWNED (FARM OWNERS ONLY)

	Market value per acre	No. of acres owned	No. rented to others
Tillable land			
Nontillable land			
Woodlands and waste			
Agricultural reserve			
TOTAL			

BUSINESS OWNERS ONLY
INCOME AND EXPENSES

	2003 (Jan. 1–Dec. 31)	2004 (Jan. 1–Dec. 31)	Estimated 2005 (Jan. 1–Dec. 31)
11. BUSINESS INCOME			
a. Gross receipts or sales less returns and allowances	$_____	$_____	
b. Cost of goods sold and/or operations (Don't include salaries paid to yourself, your dependents, or others, or any item listed below.)	_____	_____	
c. Gross profit (Line 11a minus 11b.)	_____	_____	
d. Other business income	_____	_____	
12. TOTAL INCOME (Add 11c and 11d.)	_____	_____	
13. BUSINESS DEDUCTIONS (Don't include any amount entered in 11b above.)			
a. Depreciation	_____	_____	
b. Interest expense	_____	_____	
c. Rent on business property	_____	_____	
d. Parents' W-2 wages from this business	_____	_____	
e. Salaries and wages paid to family members other than yourself employed in the business			
Name and Relationship	Salary		
_____	_____		
_____	_____		
_____	_____		
f. All other salaries and wages	_____	_____	
g. Other business expenses (Itemize on a separate sheet any single item over $1,000.)	_____	_____	
14. TOTAL DEDUCTIONS (Add 13a–13g.)	_____	_____	Estimated 2005
15. NET PROFIT (OR LOSS) (Line 12 minus line 14.)			$_____
16. YOUR SHARE OF LINE 15 (Multiply line 15 by your percentage of ownership, question 6.)	$_____	$_____	$_____

FARM OWNERS ONLY
INCOME AND EXPENSES

The IRS line references are for 2003. For 2004 use the corresponding lines from 2004 IRS forms.

	2003 (Jan. 1–Dec. 31)	2004 (Jan. 1–Dec. 31)	Estimated 2005 (Jan. 1–Dec. 31)
11. FARM INCOME			
a. Profit (or loss) on sales of livestock and other items purchased for resale (from Form 1040, Schedule F, line 3)	$_____	$_____	
b. Sales of livestock and produce raised (from Schedule F, line 4)	_____	_____	
c. Other farm income (from Schedule F, lines 5b, 6b, 7a, 7c, 8b, 8d, 9, 10)	_____	_____	
12. GROSS INCOME (Add 11a–11c.) (from Schedule F, line 11)	_____	_____	
13. FARM EXPENSES			
a. Farm deductions less depreciation (from Schedule F, lines 12–15 and lines 17–34)	_____	_____	
b. Depreciation (from Schedule F, line 16)	_____	_____	
14. TOTAL EXPENSES (Add 13a and 13b.) (from Schedule F, line 35)	_____	_____	
15. NET FARM PROFIT (OR LOSS) (Line 12 minus line 14.) (from Schedule F, line 36)	_____	_____	
16. FARM-RELATED CAPITAL GAINS (OR LOSSES) from sale or exchange of livestock and farm machinery (from Form 1040, Schedule D)	_____	_____	
17. NET PROFIT (OR LOSS) (Add lines 15 and 16.)	_____	_____	Estimated 2005 $_____
18. YOUR SHARE OF LINE 17 (Multiply line 17 by your percentage of ownership, question 6.)	$_____	$_____	$_____

— 1 —

BUSINESS/FARM ASSETS

The figures you report in column C should reflect the fair market value of the business or farm (a reasonable estimate of what each asset is worth and could be sold for). Filers of IRS Form 1120, 1120S, or 1065 should refer to Schedule L to complete columns A and B. **If you don't file any of these IRS forms, you may leave columns A and B blank.**

1. CURRENT ASSETS		Column A		Column B	Column C
		Book Value at Beginning of Tax Year 2004		Book Value at End of Tax Year 2004	Fair Market Value at End of Tax Year 2004
a. Cash and short-term investments					
b. Receivables (total)					
c. Allowance for bad debts		( )		( )	( )
d. Inventories					
e. Other current assets not included above (Do not include loans to partners or shareholders.)					
f. Total current assets (Add a, b, d, and e, then subtract c.)					

2. FIXED ASSETS		Accumulated Depreciation	Book Value at Beginning of Tax Year 2004	Accumulated Depreciation	Book Value at End of Tax Year 2004	Fair Market Value at End of Tax Year 2004
a. Land						
b. Buildings (purchase price)						
c. Accumulated depreciation on buildings						
d. Machinery and equipment (purchase price)						
e. Accumulated depreciation on machinery						
f. Other fixed assets						
g. Total fixed assets (Add a, b, d, and f.)						
h. Total depreciation (Add c and e.)						

3. ALL OTHER ASSETS			Book Value at Beginning of Tax Year 2004		Book Value at End of Tax Year 2004	Fair Market Value at End of Tax Year 2004
a. Total loans to partners or shareholders listed in 5 on side 1						
Itemize by partner or shareholder	Name:					
	Name:					
	Name:					
	Name:					
b. Loans to others than partners or shareholders						
c. All other assets						
d. Total other assets (Add a–c.)						

4. TOTAL ASSETS		Book Value at Beginning of Tax Year 2004		Book Value at End of Tax Year 2004	Fair Market Value at End of Tax Year 2004
a. Add 1f, 2g, and 3d					
b. Your share of total assets (Multiply line 4a by your percentage of ownership.)					

BUSINESS/FARM LIABILITIES

	Beginning of Tax Year 2004	End of Tax Year 2004
5. LIABILITIES		
a. Accounts payable	$_____	$_____
b. Other current debts	_____	_____
c. Total current debts (Add 5a and 5b.)	_____	_____
6. LONG-TERM LIABILITIES (Don't include any amount listed above.)		
a. Mortgages on land and buildings (Don't include home mortgages.)	_____	_____
b. Debts secured by equipment	_____	_____
c. Loans from partner(s) or shareholder(s) Itemize by shareholder:		
Name: _____	_____	_____
Name: _____	_____	_____
Name: _____	_____	_____
Name: _____	_____	_____
d. Other debts	_____	_____
e. Total long-term debts (Add 6a–6d.)	_____	_____
7. TOTAL LIABILITIES (Add 5c and 6e.)	_____	_____
8. YOUR SHARE OF TOTAL LIABILITIES (Multiply line 7 by your percentage of ownership.)	$_____	$_____

REMARKS

Use this space to explain any special circumstances. If more space is required, attach a letter to this form.

SIGNATURES

RETURN THIS FORM TO THE COLLEGE(S) THAT REQUESTED IT.

FATHER'S OR STEPFATHER'S SIGNATURE _____ DATE _____

MOTHER'S OR STEPMOTHER'S SIGNATURE _____ DATE _____

THE ART OF FREE MONEY: SCHOLARSHIPS

The first thing you should do is determine how a school allocates outside scholarships in your financial aid package. As mentioned, some schools use part of your outside scholarship money to reduce *their* grant portion in your aid package, rather than reduce *your* contribution. Therefore, you are not benefiting 100 percent from your scholarships. Also, most outside scholarships require additional applications and extra essays, so if you decide to go after scholarships, you should start looking into them immediately.

Below are some resources you can use to find scholarships. Fastweb.com, in particular, helps you to search for scholarships by allowing you to enter your personal info and having a database match you with potential scholarships.

Here are some resources you can use:

1. Make a list of potential connections. Many local clubs and national businesses offer money for students like you. Find out if your parents or grandparents are involved in any companies, branches of the military, unions, or clubs—for example, the Rotary Club, Kiwanis, Optimists, American Legion, Jaycees, and Masons. You can also go to your city's chamber of commerce for the names of social organizations or civic clubs that may give scholarships.

2. Ask your counselor if there are local scholarships available for students at your school. Also ask if he or she can recommend any scholarship programs that match your profile.

3. Check with the colleges to which you are applying to see if they offer campus scholarships. The University of California system, for example, lists campus scholarships in the back of its application booklet.

4. Other resources

Books

>   *How to Go to College Almost for Free* by Ben Kaplan

>   *The Scholarship Book* by Daniel J. Cassidy

Internet Scholarship Searches

>   FinAid: www.finaid.org

>   FastWeb: www.fastweb.com

>   Mach 25: www.collegenet.com/mach25

>   U.S. Department of Education: www.ed.gov

- Minority Scholarship Organizations

Hallie Q. Brown Scholarship Fund, National Association of Colored Women's Clubs

McDonald's Hispanic American Commitment to Education Resources (HACER)

United Negro College Fund (www.uncf.org)

U.S. Department of the Interior, Bureau of Indian Affairs, Higher Education Grant Program (www.doi.giv/bureau-Indian-affairs. html or www.oiep.bia.edu)

Organization of Chinese Americans

Xerox Technical Minority Scholarship Program

Beware of companies offering to find you scholarships for a fee. While a few of these companies are legit, there are also many scams out there. For the most part, you should be able to dig up your own scholarships. If you do want to use an outside source, investigate its background first.

CHAPTER SEVENTEEN
THIN AND THICK ENVELOPES

ACCEPTING A SCHOOL: THERE GOES THE MONEY

You get home for your daily rush to the mailbox, and there are several envelopes waiting for you. Some are big thick envelopes; some are small and thin.

Oh . . . My . . . God.

First, a thin envelope or a regular-sized envelope does not mean rejection. Some schools don't send their acceptance letters in big thick envelopes, while others do send fat envelopes with the words "You got in!" printed all over the front.

Each school has its own date to notify students of admissions status. So don't freak, if all your friends get their letters, but you don't get yours. Or if you get rejection letters first. It often takes a few days to a few weeks for applicants to hear from every school, and because of Murphy's Law, you'll probably wait until the very last letter to hear from your top choice.

Hopefully, you applied to six to twelve schools, making sure they were balanced between reaches, likelies, and safeties. As a result, you should be pretty confident you will get into at least a couple of schools. *The key is to keep things in perspective.* If you don't get admitted to a few schools, this does *not* say anything about you as a person; nor does it mean you are not qualified to go those schools. By now, you should know how crazy the admissions process is.

I believe you will go where you are supposed to go. In a recent survey, around 90 percent of all freshmen couldn't imagine attending another school after their first year. Trust me, if you have made a good list, you should have a great time no matter where you end up.

Now, there are several things you might discover in those thick or thin envelopes:

- You got accepted.

- You got denied. In this case, you can appeal if you have some good reasons—see page 253.

- You got in Early Decision I or II, in which case you are done with college applications by December (or by January or February for ED II).

- You got in Early Action. In this case, you might choose to see where else you get in before making a final decision.

- You got deferred from Early Decision or Early Action—that is, you were put back into the regular pool of students and will find out in April whether you have been accepted.

- You got wait-listed. In this case, the school needs to find out how many of the students it accepted will actually go. Then, if it has spaces left, it will go to the wait list. This can be frustrating because you have to pick a school to attend and then you may have to change it if you are admitted from the wait list someplace else. This in fact happened to me. I enrolled at Pomona and sent in a deposit by May 1, while I was on the wait list at Stanford. When I later got into Stanford, I still had to wait for its financial aid package to see if I could afford to go. I then cancelled Pomona, lost my deposit, and headed to Palo Alto.

- You got accepted to start in the spring term of a school's academic year.

The bottom line is you are not quite done yet. Here are some steps you might want to take, along with some things you have to do to make sure you get a space:

1. If you were wait-listed, decide whether you want to stay on the wait list. There is usually a card with the wait-list letter that you will have to send in stating your preference. (If there is no card, call or send the school a letter stating your preference.) Also, follow the guidelines on page 253 to help your chances. Realize, however, that you will most likely have to pick another school and send in the deposit and your commitment (see no. 5). A school may notify you about a change in your wait-list status anytime between May and September, so be ready to lose the deposit and to change your plans if you get in and decide to go. Remember, though, that most students do *not* get in off the wait list. But, hey, it happens. It happened to me.

2. If you were rejected, decide if you are going to appeal. Again, check out page 253.

3. If you got in Early Decision and you received an aid package that will allow you to attend (see no. 6), all you have to do is send in your final confirmation (usually included with the acceptance letter) and your deposit.

4. If you got in Early Action, decide if you want to accept now and be done with college applications, or if you want to apply to other schools and wait until April to make your decision. If you accept early, you need to send in your acceptance and a deposit.

5. If you got in, send in your commitment to attend along with the deposit (usually around $100 to $500) by May 1. (Note: The deposit must be *received* by May 1, not *postmarked* by May 1. Don't forget this—it would be a shame to lose your space because of one little mistake.) The acceptance letter will tell you how to respond and usually includes a card for you to send in.

6. If the financial aid package that is not enough to allow you to attend, contact the financial aid office and appeal, as discussed on page 211. *Note*: Not "winning" an ap-

peal is one of the only reasons a student can get out of an Early-Decision commitment. If you do not receive enough aid upon appeal, you can ask to be released from Early Decision and then apply to other schools (if ED I) or accept another school (if ED II).

7. If you don't know which college you want to attend, it's time to visit your final choices. Many schools plan weekends when prospective freshmen come to check out the campus, and they can often stay in a dorm. These events are a lot of fun, and offer various activities to try to woo you into attending the school. If you cannot afford to go to this weekend event, tell the school. It will not want to lose you at this point and will often make arrangements for you to attend.

8. If you were accepted for the spring term, decide if the school is worth waiting for. Remember, you won't start school with the other new freshmen, but will come in months after the others have gotten set up. However, colleges usually go out of their way to make you feel welcome, and you'll be going to a place you really want to attend. You also might not graduate with your class unless you make up the first part of the year, perhaps by spending the fall taking classes locally that may be transferable. Or you might use the time to work or travel before you start school in the spring.

What if you you don't want to go to any of the schools you get into?

Well, no one says you have to go to college right after high school. It's the first time in your life when no one makes you go to school. Whether you want to take a year off or you got rejected by every school (this shouldn't happen if you follow this program), your life is far from over. In fact, there are many options for students who want more time.

1. Defer to spring. If you can't take any more schoolwork or you want to travel or just take a break, you can request a deferral to start college in the spring instead of fall. Most schools will allow you to do this as long as you send in your deposit to hold your space. *You should also send a letter stating why you want to defer and why you still want to attend the school.*

2. Defer a year. Schools like to know what you are going to do with a year off. If you have an internship or are going to work, it will help you get the deferral.

3. Take a year off to travel or work. Let's say you were rejected by a certain school, do not want to attend a college you did get into, or just need some time off because of a personal situation. If you are rejected or don't want to attend, you take off a year. You can simply not go to school for a year or more and then reapply in a future year. Many students who have taken time off have had great experiences, saved up money by working, and gained a bit more maturity before they reapplied. If you want to take off a year to improve your chance of being admitted to the college of your choice, ask your counselor for suggestions of how to do this. If, for example, you want to be a lawyer, an internship in a law firm would show your commitment. If you then volunteered at a legal defense fund or on a political campaign, you would be setting your-

self up for a stronger marketing attack in future years. Remember, however, that schools will still look at your GPA and SAT scores from high school.

Many people will tell you that if you take time off you might never reapply to college. This is your decision, and I can argue either way on this. Do you need college to be successful? Absolutely not. Is college for everyone? Nope. Does it help prepare you for the "real world"? A lot of times, no. But does it give you an environment in which to grow and learn? Yup. Do employers like to see a college degree? Absolutely.

Is college a lot of fun and a place where you will meet many of your greatest friends? I think so. Remember, there are a lot of different types of schools (art, music, computer, etc.) that may suit you if you're not into academics. Take it from someone who has not done what everyone else thinks he should do. Trust your heart, but also look at the big picture of what you want for your life. Successful people don't always spend every moment doing what they want. However, they do have goals that make the hard work worthwhile.

4. Take a postgraduate year. In a postgraduate year, you spend an extra year, usually at a private school, taking classes and giving yourself a chance to mature, increase your GPA and scores, and improve in athletics if that's your thing. Then you reapply to college. You are not repeating a grade, but simply taking an extra year of high school to focus and to improve your profile.

5. Attend a local community or state college to save money and then transfer. A lot of students who want to go to a selective school think going to a local one is beneath them. You may be able to improve your chances of transferring by rocking classes and you can also save yourself some money. On the other hand, certain really selective schools only have a certain number of spaces for transfer students, so ask the schools what your chances would be, what they are looking for, what colleges they take the most transfer students from, and how to improve your profile.

JOE BANANAS AND HIS BUNCH: ADMISSIONS WITH AP-PEALS

What should you do if you get wait-listed or rejected?

I once had a student, Lloyd, who went to a pretty tough private school in California. He had a 2.8 GPA, 1520 on the SAT, and ranged 510 from 620 on the SAT II subject tests. Not bad, not great, and not eligible for the University of California system.

Lloyd decided on a list of eight schools and wrote a pretty good essay on the challenges of his learning disability. Lloyd's school counselor told him he would never get into a college like USC or his other reaches. But Lloyd decided to apply to all the schools on his list anyway, including Berkeley where, based on his numbers, he would almost automatically get rejected. Lloyd was rejected by six schools, except his two safeties. He is now attending USC.

What? Now I could tell you that Lloyd went to community college and transferred to USC after a couple of years. There is nothing wrong with this path, and many very successful students have taken this route. But this is not Lloyd's story.

For the majority of his desired schools, Lloyd fell either outside or at the bottom end of the main criteria for acceptance. He could have picked different, really good schools, which definitely would have admitted him. But he wanted to stay near California, and so his list was weighted a bit toward the unrealistic. Although Lloyd should have examined his restrictions, really researched more schools, and spent time using CSI to make sure he got into a good school he liked, his story must be told.

Although what happened to Lloyd will not happen for everyone, it does show that determination and persistence can produce results that most people wouldn't even consider possible. Lloyd contacted the UC Berkeley Office of Student Disabilities (OSD). He filled out its supplemental application. Then, through discussions with the OSD and with LD students at Berkeley, he found out a few things. If the OSD thought his supplemental application was really good, they wouldn't just notify the admissions department that he had a learning disability; they would actually advocate on his behalf and put in a good word in favor of accepting him. Lloyd never would have found this out by simply requesting an application online and filling it out.

After the initial letters of acceptance were sent out, Lloyd was notified by admissions that they were still evaluating all his information. Unfortunately, he didn't get into Berkeley, but neither was he automatically rejected for not meeting minimum qualifications.

What about USC? Well, Lloyd was flat-out rejected by USC. No wait list, no nothing. Lloyd was pretty upset when he got rejected by six of his eight schools. Did he stop though? Nope. His first choice by far was USC. He believed in his heart that if the school gave him a chance, he would prove he could make it there. You see, Lloyd was driven. His grades weren't that strong the first two and a half years of high school. But learning disability or not, he put in the time to keep raising his grades. He ended up getting mostly Bs, but he had to give up his extracurriculars, including soccer, to have the time necessary to study. Therefore, after all this hard work, he wasn't going to give up because of a little rejection.

Lloyd wrote a letter to the director of admissions explaining his desire, his hard work, and his accomplishment of getting two As the fall semester of his senior year. He got extra recommendations from people who could speak to his character. He asked his counselor to call USC and put in a good word on his behalf (despite discouraging him to apply, the counselor was how really pulling for him). Lloyd went to the admissions office several times to set up a face-to-face interview with the director. It was not easy, but Lloyd eventually got to meet with the director. **Because Lloyd was honest, sincere, and didn't walk in trying to show how great he was, the director cut him a deal.** If Lloyd was willing to do the following, the director would guarantee his admission to USC for the second semester:

1. Continue improving his grades during his last semester of senior year.

2. Take two summer classes at the local community college and get at least Bs.

3. Take one semester of courses from the same school and continue to get Bs.

The result? Lloyd will soon be graduating from USC. And he has done great!
Would you be willing to do all this? I could tell you stories of students getting in off the

wait list or even overturning an initial rejection. But I could also tell you of many more who appealed and still got rejected. The good news is that most of these students went to other schools and now can't imagine going anywhere else.

Remember, *whether or not you appeal a nonadmittance, you can still get into a school you will really enjoy and where you will get a great education.* So if you do get rejected or wait-listed, it is not the end yet. If you're determined and willing to put in the effort to improve, it is possible that you can defy the odds and make your dream a reality.

HOW TO APPEAL

If you want to appeal, here is a summary of what you should do:

1. *Take stock of your true chances.* Does your profile match those of last year's incoming class? If not, do you have a special circumstance or a flag (see page 41) that would increase your chances? For example, if you want to go to Princeton, but your GPA is 3.0 and you have an 1650 on the SAT, this does not mean you aren't intelligent or don't deserve to get in, only that you are probably not what Princeton is looking for. Unless you have an exceptional circumstance, you probably shouldn't bother appealing.

    If, however, you are wait-listed at a good, but less selective school, you improve your grades and SATs, and you do something like win a statewide award in a science fair in the time since you applied, you should have a shot at getting in off the wait list. This, of course, depends on whether the school has to use the wait list to fill the class. Let the school know that you want to stay on the wait list for admission consideration.

2. *Write the admissions office a letter* informing them that their school is your first choice (if it is), and stating why you want to attend and what you can bring to the school. You do not have win a science fair, but the school needs some reason to change its mind about you other than you really, really want to go.

3. *Get additional recommendations* from people who know you well and can speak to your drive, your passion in a certain activity, or something you didn't tell the school the first time around. *Recommendations must show the admissions people who you are*, and not just say, "Danny is a good student." (See page 198.)

4. *Ask your counselor* to call the admissions office on your behalf. Don't just say, "Hey, I want you to call Vanderbilt and tell them to let me in, damn it!" Explain why you think you should be admitted and tell your counselor what you're willing to do for it. Hopefully, he or she is already on your side. If not, see if you can contact the local interviewer or the school's representative for your area. Tell him or her of your intention, and ask what you can do to make your case. He or she might discourage you—but you still should ask.

5. *Contact the admissions office*, and keep it posted about new developments in your life. Yes, your parents could do this, but schools aren't admitting your parents, they're admitting you—so *you* have to be the one to stand up for yourself. Calling and de-

manding to know why a school screwed up is not a good idea. But sending letters, additional grades, test scores, and accomplishments is a good way to get its attention. Don't stop with one letter. Write the school with new information, and then call to follow up. Try to talk to the highest person you can. Be ready to make your case. If you can, try to go to the school and meet face-to-face with an admissions officer. Ask if there are options like Lloyd was given—spring or even summer acceptance. You must be passionate and show that you are determined and will do whatever it takes. Remember, the worst thing the school can say is no, and it has already done that, right?

Again, you're going to be fine no matter what happens. I know this is hard to hear when you're in high school, *but it's only college.* **If you demand success in life, you will get success no matter where you go to school.**

Figures 17-1 and 17-2 show sample appeal letters. These letters are also included on the Resource CD.

FIGURE 17-1 **WAIT-LIST APPEAL LETTER**

Jessie James
1234 Zippy Road
Los Angeles, CA 90049
January 28, 2006

Richard Shaw
Dean of Admissions
Stanford University
520 Lasuen Mall Old Union 232
Stanford, California 94305-3005

Dear Dean Shaw,

My name is Jessie James. My purpose in writing this letter is to reaffirm my desire to attend Stanford University, as it is my first choice, and to update you on recent developments that have taken place since I applied.

I recently met a Stanford graduate from the class of 1994. He was very enthusiastic about the school, and after hearing about my interests, he recommended I look into the Human Biology major. This program is exactly what I am looking for as an undergraduate. Biology is the subject I am most passionate about, and my ultimate goal is to go to medical school and become a pediatrician. The human biology major would enable me to fulfill the premed requirements without limiting me to the confines of a basic biology major. Through this program, I would be able to combine my interest in biology with my interest in human development, psychology, and art.

The amazing research opportunities are yet another reason why Stanford is my first choice. I have recently begun conducting advanced research at USC that seeks to examine the inheritance of biological and social risk factors for antisocial behavior. I am currently developing a new observational test for nine-year-old twins, which uses physical manipulatives to elicit aggressive behavior. I am including a brief summary of my work for your review. At Stanford, I hope to continue my research in this general field. I am particularly interested in the research of Dr. Allan Reiss that explores behavioral neurogenics, a topic I have not been able to investigate due to the limitations of my current laboratory.

I am not only interested in Stanford because of its academic and research opportunities. I am passionate about art, especially photography. This year, I am the Visual Arts Representative on the student body council. It is my job to organize and promote the art exhibits we have in our gallery. I am currently organizing an invitational art show, which features the work of high school students from over twenty schools around Los Angeles. I have also submitted a portfolio to the regional Scholastic Art Contest, and I will be photographing children with developmental disabilities at a local physical therapy clinic in the upcoming months. Two weeks ago, I had the unique opportunity to videotape a cesarean section from the surgeon's vantage point, and I am in the process of editing this piece. The Cantor Center for the Visual Arts is an incredible resource that I would definitely take advantage of at Stanford. I am impressed by its permanent collection of photography, which includes work by two of my favorite photographers, Berenice Abbott and Ansel Adams.

As I mentioned in my application, my work at the National Conference for Community and Justice has inspired me to organize a series of open-forum discussions on social issues. This semester, I am working with the other members of the Student Diversity Organization on additional discussions about homophobia and religious tolerance. At Stanford, I plan on joining Amnesty International and Kids with Dreams in order to continue my involvement in social justice and community service.

Thank you for taking the time to review my additional information. I look forward to making a strong and lasting contribution to Stanford if accepted off the wait list.

Sincerely,

Jessie James

FIGURE 17-2 REJECTION APPEAL LETTER

William Hitchcock

9999 Zephyr Way

Beverly Hills, CA 90210

March 24, 2006

University of Arizona

PO Box 210040

Tucson, AZ 85721

Dear Director:

My name is William Hitchcock, and I am a prospective applicant to the University of Arizona. Although I have been initially rejected, I wanted to write you to update you with some information and to let you know my future goals and hopefully a little more about my character. Although I am sure you receive many letters similar to this one, I believe that the passion with which I write will make mine not just words on a page, but a sincere portrait of who I am and why I want to attend the University of Arizona.

In my application essay, I spoke of the learning challenges I have faced in striving to achieve the goals I have set for myself. I am not naive enough to think that I have been alone in my striving. I also know that there are others who have gone through more difficult hardships. I believe, however, in my ability to persist and succeed, and I do not accept the word "no" when I have a personal mission.

Although I have applied through the disability program, I have never used my learning differences as a crutch, and I simply see the benefits of the disability center as a means to get more out of my education. Therefore, even though I did not initially get accepted to the University of Arizona, I absolutely know three things:

1. The University of Arizona is my first choice of schools.

2. The intensity of my work habits is far above that of many other students based on the effort I have had to put forth to achieve my grades. Consequently, my desire for a college education and the desire to make the most of it are unsurpassed.

3. If it is true that universities want students who are self-motivated and who believe in and support the university, then the University of Arizona deserves me as a student as much as I deserve the opportunity to make you proud of a decision to admit me.

In short, I am requesting admission into your school. From the location, to the diversity, to the available resources, Arizona fits me like a glove. Please give me the chance to prove that I am a perfect fit as well. If you need any additional information or documentation, please contact me. I also want to let you know that my third-quarter grades are the highest I have ever earned. They are as follows: humanities, A-; math, B; history of Japan, B; English, B-; and art history, B. Although I have no intention of being an annoyance, I am determined to go to Arizona and would feel honored to someday call myself an alumnus. I appreciate your time and consideration.

Sincerely,

William Hitchcock

HOUSING AND OTHER GOOD TIMES

Once you get accepted to a school, you will still have a bunch of paperwork to fill out. Here are some choices you will most likely have to make:

1. Housing. Your school may require you to live on campus or may offer it as an option. I suggest you live on campus for at least a year. It's fun, you get to meet a lot of other students who will support you, and you can find out from older students the dirt on which classes to take.

   Depending on the school, you will have to indicate your preference for the following:

   - All-frosh or four-class? Do you want to live in a dorm that houses only freshmen or that has all four classes mixed? There are benefits to both. All-frosh tends to be more fun and lively, as everybody there is a brand-new student and ready for action. Four-class gives you access to older students, who can help you out but who also tend to be more serious because their wild and crazy days are over. These dorms will still have other freshmen though, so they offer the best of both worlds. I myself lived in an all-freshman dorm and wouldn't have had it any other way.

   - Dorm rooms or suites? A dorm room is typically one room that two students share. Suites are like small apartments. They often consist of two rooms, each with two students in it, and a small shared living room area. Suites are often nicer in terms of accommodations—some even have a kitchen. However, you have to put up with living in close quarters with three other people instead of one, and suites sometimes aren't as social as, say, a traditional dorm.

2. Your first classes. Sometimes a school wants your preferences for the mandatory classes you will take as a freshman. For the most part, you will usually get to school a week early for freshman orientation and have time to choose your classes. However, if you have to pick a fall class in the summer, mail any appropriate forms in right away. Read through the course descriptions, and if you can, talk to someone who attends the school to get the "real story." What the descriptions say and what the classes really are can be two different things.

3. You'll receive other information, including a course book (which is a book that details all the available classes offered), and information about your roommate. Although at some schools, you don't get to meet your roommate until the first day, you might be able to contact your roomie before you go off to school. This way you can get to know one another and figure out who is bringing the coffeemaker.

CHAPTER EIGHTEEN
WRAPPING UP

FINAL CHECKLISTS AND OTHER IMPORTANT STUFF

Are you tired of my writing and my dumb jokes? Don't you feel like you deserve some big old award just for getting through this book? I agree. So now, there are no more checklists, no reviews, no reminders.

You're done!
Congratulations!
I'm really proud of you—you made it!

If I can help you in anyway, please get in touch. I have included my contact information on page 267. By the way, I live for success stories, so if *The Ultimate College Acceptance System* has helped you or if you want to simply brag about what school you got into, email me, and I may use your story or name in future editions of this book.

I have included a summary of things you can do to succeed in college on the next few pages. Good luck!

FRISBEE 101: HOW TO SUCCEED IN COLLEGE

Here's the very last list of things you can do to succeed and have a really good time in college. This list is the ultimate insider view and contains things you probably won't hear from conventional sources, so go to it and have a *great* time!

1. Go out of your way to meet as many people as possible—other students in your dorm, professors, the president of the school, your teaching assistants (TAs), and others. This may not be easy for some of you, but it can benefit you in a lot of ways. It's also the one thing I didn't do nearly enough of. Not only can meeting with profs and TAs save you tons of work, but these individuals are also great contacts to make for recommendations for grad school, future jobs, and possible mentorships. Odds are that you will also keep many of the friends you meet during college. I'm not suggesting you meet people simply to schmooze about future jobs. But I am suggesting that there are so many cool people with different backgrounds that you will often learn more from them than you will from class.

2. Take classes that really interest you. Challenge yourself to take ancient Mesopotamian basket weaving if it seems interesting, even if you may never use it. The truth is that unless you want to be a doctor, lawyer, or something specific, you'll forget about many of the classes you take once you graduate. So since *you* get to choose your classes, go for it.

3. Talk to students who have already taken the classes that interest you. What a course description says about a class is not always accurate. So find out who the good profs are, how to get a good grade, which section is best, which TA is best, and more from those who have already been there.

4. Come up with a plan of attack for each class. College is just another game, like high school. It just has some different rules. So figure out how to best approach a class after you have spent a couple of weeks listening to the professor and talking to other students. You'll know a lot after your first test as well. Here are some specifics that you should think about:

   • Many classes, especially English, political science, psychology, sociology, and other "nonmath or science" classes often require way more reading than you can possibly manage. Therefore, determine what you have to do to pass. Of course, if you're interested in the material, by all means read it. But remember, you have to do work for your other classes as well. Some classes will require that you simply go to class and listen. Some teachers base their test questions solely on their lectures. Others base their questions on the reading assignments. If this is the case, go to class, but understand that the reading is your priority. Most students will tell you that even though missing class is easy to do, attending class can really help you, especially if you establish a relationship with the professor.

   • For science and math classes, the work is more cut and dry. You will typically have more assignments than in nonscience classes, and you will have to complete them all in order to do well. However, realize that intro math and science classes, especially during the first few weeks, can be very tough. These classes are called "weeder" classes and are designed to weed out those who can't cut it. Physics and chemistry are notorious for this. So hang in there; use study groups; get help from TAs, profs, or a tutor; and stick around for a while before you decide to bail.

5. Use past tests on file. Many professors put their past tests on file at someplace like the library. By all means, get these bad boys and study from them. By analyzing where the questions came from, you should be able to determine where the questions on your tests will come from. Many students just think they should go to class, read all the material, take the tests, and hope for the best. But smart students analyze how to get the most important information quickly, use their resources, and get better grades with less work. You should talk to older students about how to do this as well.

6. Use note-taking services. Some classes have note takers whose job is to take great notes and then make them available for students for a small fee. Most of the time these notes rock, but even so, don't decide to stop going to class entirely. The best way to use these notes is as a supplement to your own. There's something about taking your own notes that helps you to understand it better and to remember it many weeks later when you take your finals.

7. Be on the lookout for easier classes. Let's say you have to take some killer classes, but still need some more units for a full load. Almost every school has what are sometimes referred to as "Mickey Mouse" classes (although different schools call them different things). Ask other students about these courses. They are basically really cool and are easy to do well in or require little work. Take, for example, a course called "The Art of Conversation." This was a course where groups of students were matched up to talk about different subjects. They wrote a few summaries and bam!—they each got an A and 3 units.

8. Take advantage of—and beware of—pass/no credit (P/NC) and credit/no credit (C/NC). You can take these classes to get the units, but you have to get only a C or better to get the credit or to pass. These classes typically are not in your major field and sometimes fall into the elective category.

   You can take academic classes this way too. P/NC is a good way to take a subject you really want to learn about, when you do not want the stress of having to work for a grade. Be careful, however, not to choose this option for a class that your major requires you to take for a grade. Remember, P/NC is an *option,* so other students will often be taking the class for a grade while you take it as P/NC. It would be awful if you had to repeat a class because you were supposed to take it for a grade.

9. Pay attention and take advantage of time limits to "drop a class." Most schools will give you a few weeks to attend a class to see how it goes—and a deadline for dropping it without having it go on your transcripts. Thus you can enroll in more classes than you can actually handle and then choose to keep the best ones and drop the others. (This is easier to do in private schools where classes are sometimes easier to get into.) A very few schools have a 24-hour drop policy, and you can take a class up until 24 hours before the final and still drop it. This is great if your grade is lousy and you don't want to risk bombing the final.

10. Be sure you keep track of the courses you need to take for graduation. Schools often change their requirements from year to year, so you have to keep a record of what courses you have taken and what courses you need to take to stay on track. Do not trust an adviser or anyone else. I have met too many students, especially at larger schools, who found out during their last semester that they hadn't fulfilled all the requirements to graduate. They then had to stick around for another term, even though they did everything their academic adviser told them to do.

11. Take advantage of study groups. Because there is so much work to do in college, many students join study groups that divide up the work or where everyone helps test each other. These groups can be a lot of fun and very helpful, but be sure you have a group that can get things done and not just fool around. If you can find people who are better than you are in a subject, this is great because you will learn from them. On the flip side, if you are the strong student, you can also benefit by teaching other people. Take advice from a teacher: sometimes the best way to learn is to show it to someone else. Even if you like to study alone, try a study group or two, especially for a science class, as you can review problems or get help memorizing information.

12. Don't be too serious. Your college years are one of the only times when you will have free rein to behave like a fool and generally get away with it. In high school you had your parents; in life after college graduation, you have to work and generally be responsible. So have fun—but don't plan your whole year around spring break.

    However, do try things that you may not think you are interested in. Be spontaneous. Jump in a fountain. Go to Vegas on a whim. Play Frisbee golf at night. Paint your face for a football game. Go to Denny's at 4 a.m. Don't do this all the time, and always use good judgment—I've heard jail is not much fun.

    Let me say that again. Use good judgment.

    Some students are so excited about their freedom, especially in freshman year, that they get hurt, get into trouble, or have to stick around for an extra year because they fail all their classes. Have some restraint, please. Remember, you will be exposed to a lot more craziness than you might expect. Make up your mind what your priorities are, but allow yourself to have fun. This concludes my lecture for today, thank you.

    By the way, Frisbee golf is where a group goes around campus and plays golf with a Frisbee. Something like a statue a half-mile across campus may be the "hole." You have to see how many throws it takes you to hit the target. This may sound really dorky, but if your school has a "course," give it a shot.)

13. Don't worry if you don't immediately know what to major in. Unless you are in a specific program like engineering, or have a specific goal like going to med school, you've got time to choose a major. You'll usually have until the end of sophomore year to declare, because you'll spend most of your first two years getting the general education (GEs) or distribution requirements (DRs) out of the way. Remember, you can also change majors. I did this. I changed from political science to human biology. Be careful though. You don't want to wait too long or change too many times because each major has its own requirements to keep up with. One guy I know kept changing majors and took seven years to graduate.

    As soon as you have an idea of what you'd like to major in, talk to your adviser and plan out your remaining school years, especially if you want to study abroad, "stop out" for a term, or graduate early. Unless you have a specific goal that requires a specific major, you can major in anything and still get a job after school. For example, you don't have to be a prelaw major to go to law school or even a biology major to go to med school. You do, however, have to take the required courses for something like med school and the appropriate classes for what you'd like to do after graduation. For example, if you want to get a job in computer animation, classes like English will not be as helpful as, say, computer science and symbolic systems.

14. Take advantage of the school's resources. There are often so many resources available to you as a student that you can't possibly take advantage of them all. Remember, even though you typically have more work to do, you will have much more free time in which to do it. It may take you a year to figure this out, but believe me, you can spend a lot of time sleeping, eating, *and* participating in really cool programs.

Here are some things I want to tell you about now, so you don't have to wait until you are a junior to learn about them:

- Study-abroad programs. Study-abroad programs are offered either through your school or by outside agencies that allow you to go to other places in the world, take classes, and get credit toward graduation. These amazing opportunities are usually taken during a student's junior year. Make sure, however, if you choose a program not offered by your school, that your units can be transferred. There should be an office on campus that has information about all these programs. Discuss study-abroad plans with your adviser to make sure you can graduate on time and still take the classes required for your major.

- Cooperative programs with other U.S. colleges. Many schools are part of a consortium where you can go to other colleges around the country, take some classes, have them apply to your graduation. Again, ask around to find out what office has info on these programs.

- Public service opportunities. Most schools have programs that allow students to volunteer or to give back to the community. These opportunities can range from a weekend working with Native Americans in New Mexico to internships with the World Wildlife Fund. Investigating these opportunities during your first year will help you to plan your four years.

- Start your own company. Many college students take the time and the resources available to them and make it all work for them. In fact, many successful companies have been started while their founders were in college. Remember, you and your fellow students have access to computers, professors, and alumni that you can use to test out new ideas. If you have an idea, go to the alumni center and see about meeting with business leaders in the area you are interested in. You may be able to secure mentors, money, and resources to make your dream a reality.

- Internships. Another great thing about college is that you do not have to support yourself and a family (although you may have to work to afford school). But once you graduate and start making decent money, it's hard to go back and work for peanuts.

So take advantage of your college years to intern, especially during the summers. Sometimes these jobs pay and sometimes they don't, but you can get your foot in the door in a field you might like to pursue after graduation. You may also be setting yourself up for future employment at the place you interned. In any case, you can intern at different places to get an idea of what you want to do after college.

A friend of mine knew he wanted to be a cameraman in Hollywood. Every summer, he worked on different sets learning how to set up the wiring and the lights, and basically everything about production. He had to do a lot of grunt work, but he was learning the trade at the same time. He met a steadicam (a type of camera that a person wears and walks around with) operator who mentored him. My friend saved his earnings from the summer job and from a few jobs he had during school, and when he graduated, he bought his own steadicam. Now not too many twenty-two-year-olds possessed his experience, let alone his own camera. He has consistently worked, made good dough, and has worked on big movies such as *American Beauty*.

- Special programs. Many schools offer special programs such as marine biology labs, summer writing programs, and theater programs. If you are interested in something particular, you probably learned about these programs when you researched your schools. Even if you didn't, ask your adviser what's available, and don't rely on what's in the course book. The more you ask around, the more you will find available to you.

- Stopping out. "Stopping out" refers to the opportunity to leave school for a period of time and still be able to come back, resume your classes, and graduate. For example, I had enough AP credit to be able to take off a quarter during my junior year. I needed a break from studying, so I decided to ride my bike across the United States. So, I didn't go to school in the spring, took my little trip, worked in the summer, and resumed college in the fall with guaranteed housing and a plan to graduate on time. The more planning you do, the better off you'll be. Many students, however, stop out for a variety of reasons, and some never come back. Just be sure to you look at the big picture and discuss your options with your adviser or someone else before you plan to stop out.

There are about a thousand other things I could tell you about college, but hey, much of the fun is just figuring it out as you go. I hopefully have left you with the knowledge that college gives you a great chance to do a lot of things, as long as you give it some thought and planning. Don't think you have to know everything your first year. But don't wait until graduation to say, "Damn, I wish I had done———!" Go for it now.

Okay, that's it. I hope this book has helped. Again, let me know how it's going. Good luck.

CHAPTER NINETEEN
THE FINAL RESOURCE

As I have mentioned, I would love to hear from you. I am also available to answer questions, edit essays and resumes, and give workshops around the country.

Here's my contact info.

Danny Ruderman
www.youcangetin.com
269 S. Beverly Drive—139
Beverly Hills, CA 90212
(866) YOU-CAN-GET-IN (866-968-2264)
danny@youcangetin.com

NOTES

NOTES

ABOUT THE AUTHOR

DANNY RUDERMAN graduated with honors from Stanford University and holds a B.A. in human biology with an emphasis in education. In 1995, he was named a Merit Teacher for his work at Campbell Hall School in Los Angeles. Ruderman has worked as an education therapist for K&M Associates and as a standardized test instructor for Ivy West. Ruderman is a member of one of the industry's leading professional associations, the Western Association of College Admission Counselors. As an independent college counselor, he gives parent and student workshops around the country, in addition to working with individual students in Los Angeles. He can be reached at www.youcangetin.com.

RECOMMENDED RESOURCES

BOOKS

The Insider's Guide to the Colleges by Yale Daily News (St. Martins Press)

The Fiske Guide to Colleges by Edward B. Fiske (Sourcebooks)

The College Board College Handbook by College Board (College Board)

The K&W Guide to Colleges for the Learning Disabled by Marybeth Kravets and Imy F. Wax (Princeton Review)

Guide to Performing Art Programs by Carole J. Everett and Muriel Topaz (Princeton Review)

The Official SAT Study Guide by College Board (College Board)

Up Your Score: The Underground Guide to the SAT by Larry Berger, Michael Colton, Mariete Mistry, et al. (Workman Publishing Co.)

The Real ACT Prep Guide by ACT staff (Peterson's guides)

How to Go to College Almost for Free by Ben Kaplan (Collins)

Avco 100 Colleges Where Average Students Can Excel by Joe Anne Adler (MacMillan Publishing Company)

ONLINE

www.youcangetin.com—Danny's personal website

www.collegeboard.com—For all things college, including SAT registration, PROFILE financial aid form, and college searches

www.artschools.org—A searchable directory of art schools around the world

www.act.org—The place to go to register for the ACT

www.commonapp.org—The only site to complete and/or download The Common Application

www.fafsa.ed.gov—The site to visit to start filling out the Free Application for Federal Student Aid

www.finaid.org—Possibly the best overall site to learn about financial aid.

www.fastweb.com—Another good financial aid resource site with a searchable scholarship database

Additional Web resources are included on the Resource CD.